Sensitive to Light
The Rainbow Story

Martin Popoff

WYMER
PUBLISHING
Bedford, England

First published in Canada, 2019
Wymer Publishing
Bedford, England www.wymerpublishing.co.uk
Tel: 01234 326691
Wymer Publishing is a trading name of Wymer (UK) Ltd

ISBN: 978-1-912782- 40-6

Printed and bound by
CMP, Dorset, England

A catalogue record for this book is available from the British Library.

Typesetting, layout and design by Eduardo Rodriguez.

Table of Contents

Introduction

The magnificent Rainbow need no introduction, but this book certainly does, or at least an explanation. So, first off, thanks again for reading anything I do, be it just this book or many more.

Now, what you now hold in your hands is a massive overhaul, update and expansion over and above a book I did 14 years ago, called *Rainbow: English Castle Magic.* When my old books go out of print I tend to do this, but this one was particularly satisfying as that first Rainbow book was one of my very first band biographies, and thus ripe for re-writing, new analysis, new interview footage, new pictures, new everything.

That out of the way, let's get back to business. As I wrote (more or less—again, I'm overhaulin') in the original tome, Rainbow was something else. And after you read this book, I take pains to think you'll see why. The inflow and outflow of personnel to this band… it was staggering, one Ritchie Blackmore being the constant, and constantly evolving himself, with some of hard rock's greatest vocalists plying their trade along the way. It is a surprisingly tiny batch of records the band ever got up to making, but the adherence to quality was always high, this perhaps driven by Blackmore's classical sensibilities, manifesting themselves in an attitude that heavy metal could be smart, technical, classy, if only people would… listen.

As with sundry of my other books, the idea for *Sensitive to Light* was born of a Ye Olde Metal essay on a single album, this time on *Bent Out of Shape.* I was hell-bent, next, after another interesting chat with the always articulate, funny and candid Joe Lynn Turner, on tackling *Straight Between the Eyes.* I also had high hopes of tracking down the esteemed Graham Bonnet and dealing with my favourite Rainbow album of all time, *Down to Earth,* as well as, given Ronnie's always intelligent and forthcoming remarks on his songs, *Rising.* Something longer on *Rising* became even more of a possibility after a bloody hilarious chat with the one-of-a-kind Tony Carey. Doogie White, Roger Glover, Bob Daisley, Jimmy Bain and Bobby Rondinelli also added insight to the tale, and I thank them for being cool guys. One cool girl, Candice Night, helped out as well.

So yes, as more and more interviews with Rainbow dudes piled up, I came to the realization that stringing together Ye Olde Metal essays on all of the Rainbow records would not be an impossible task. Thus, I commenced to do so, and here you have it. As well—long story—but a few months after the original book, I did indeed promise Blackmore's Night manager Carole Stevens that I would figure out a way to make use of the historical stuff I talked about with both Ritchie and Candice, given that, as I wrote the original book, the cover story I did for Goldmine, two or three months after interviewing my favourite minstrel duo, had not yet run. It eventually did and everybody was happy. In any event post-chat, and more inspirational chats with both Candice and Ritchie after the original print date, 2005, herein lies the fulfilment of my promise to Carole—Ritchie having answered my geeky fan-boy questions about the old days had not been in vain. I dedicated the original book to Carole, Ritchie and Candice, and now, of course, we must also include the fallen Ronnie James Dio and Jimmy Bain.

So yes, pull up a chair, and let's look at Rainbow, or more accurately, their black 'n' round recorded proofs of hard rock greatness in the grand scheme of things. We've got fully four eras to report on—simply put, named for the men at the mic: Dio, Bonnet, Turner and White. So strap on a Strat, it's going to be a bumpy ride, Ritchie shuffling the deck fully and often, the records constantly challenging the fans to like it or lump it.

As with my other books of this nature, the idea here was to talk mainly about the records, and very much retaining the actual words spoken by the creators—pauses, shifts in thought, fragments of ideas, nuances left intact. I mean, consider this something that leans toward an oral history, dodgy memories and the inaccuracies spun included (Joe's always good for a right yarn... God love him).

I've also included some info about the tours and in general, the act of playing live. After all, for the guys in the band, this area constitutes way more of their lives in Rainbow than the brief spans of time it took to craft the albums. But yes, given that for us fans, the record is what leaves the biggest impression, I focus mostly on the creative process, addressing both music and lyrics. This is what I figure is important about the whole ball of wax, and really, as I say, this is what we all, as fans, get to interact with, enjoy, study, revisit time and time again (you likely won't be seeing Rainbow live again any time soon).

Also, you'll note shortly that we dive right in. The thing is, I've written four books on Deep Purple and I really try not to overlap content with my other books. As well, the first two of those are even older than my original Rainbow book, so they are ripe for a massive expansion as well. But yes, just a warning: this is about Rainbow straight up. In fact, I also did a Dio book, shortly after the original Rainbow, and so we steer clear of that narrative as well.

So that's what you get... not a lot of personal stuff, just a record by record, song by song look at Rainbow's roller coaster of a catalogue. Hope ya dig it. And whether you do or don't, feel free to shoot me an email or Facebook me and let me know either way.

Martin Popoff

martinp@inforamp.net

Martinpopoff.com

Chapter 1

"Might Just Take Your Life"

"I realized that I was in kind of a pseudo-soul band."

"I wanted to do a song called 'Black Sheep of the Family,' by a group called Quatermass, that a friend of mine was in."

Those words from Ritchie Blackmore, Deep Purple's increasingly disgruntled man in black, pretty much mark the beginning of classic hard rock storm-enders Rainbow. But really, the crux-ed crucible of Rainbow's origins go back to raging feuds with Deep Purple vocalist Ian Gillan, who, in turn, left the band, only to be replaced by one David Coverdale, and the man who turned out to be David's bluesy soul brother, Glenn Hughes.

And that was it. *Burn* rocked and *Stormbringer* didn't and Ritchie started thinking solo album.

"I took 'Black Sheep of the Family' to the band, Purple," explains Blackmore, "and I said, 'What about playing this song? It would really fit into our repertoire; it's a great song.' And that was met with a lot of reluctance along the lines of, 'Well, if we don't write something, we're not going to play it,' which I thought was incredibly narrow-minded. 'But yeah, it's such a great song!' 'Well, yeah, it is. But it's not one of ours.' And I kept thinking that's not right. So we were on tour with Elf, and I went to the studio, and Ronnie (James Dio) said that he would sing it. He heard the tune and he said, 'Yeah, I'd sing that, sure, okay.' So I did it with him and that's the first song I did away from Purple. And we got along so well; we did it very quickly, and we had the guy from ELO playing with us, actually, as well, the cellist, Hughie McDowell, and it went so quickly. It was so refreshing working with Ronnie;

he was so up and excited and positive, that it was very refreshing. So after that, I suddenly realized that this might be the way to go."

McDowell was present because both Electric Light Orchestra and Elf (what, no ELP?) were on tour with Rainbow at the time, the conspirators getting together in Tampa, Florida on December 12, 1974 (and for his efforts, Ronnie was to be paid a one-time fee in the amount of £1000). Sure, there was "Black Sheep of the Family," but the real magic would be found in a hastily composed number called "Sixteenth Century Greensleeves," this track being the true birth of the Rainbow sound as it existed at least through to the end of the Dio era.

"We were getting very stale as Purple in about '75," continues Blackmore. "Things were getting... everything was a business meeting. It was a lot of briefcases and men in suits walking about with lots of money. And it didn't have much to do with music anymore, and everybody was becoming very isolated in Purple. Even Jon (Lord), for instance, would kind of be very independent, and I would only ever see him on stage. Drugs started coming into the band, not from my angle, but from a couple of the others. And then they wanted to become more of a soul band, getting into this pseudo-soul stuff. Which, I've never been into soul music, you know, the Motown stuff. It's never done anything for me. I can respect that it's good music, and in those days nearly everybody loved it. I was the only one where it didn't do anything for me at all. And they were going that way."

"And I thought, this is no longer rock 'n' roll. This was after *Burn*. It was *Stormbringer* where it came to a head where I realized that I was in kind of a pseudo-soul band. And that's when I thought, I want to be with a group of musicians playing rock 'n' roll, you know, symphonic rock. And that's why I got Elf involved. And obviously I kept Ronnie. We realized that when we started to go on the road and were rehearsing, that the rest of the band didn't measure up, his band. So gradually, one by one, we had to fire them and get other people who were better. Not that they were better; they were just different musicians for the style that we wanted."

The Ronnie of which Ritchie speaks is of course Ronald James Padavona, otherwise known as Ronnie James Dio, born in Portsmouth, New Hampshire on July 10th, 1942, since passed on from stomach cancer May 16th, 2010, in hospital in Houston, Texas. His home turf growing up, however, was upstate New York, and he spent most of his illustrious career working out of Los Angeles, from a sort of miniature castle, no less. After a career as a child star crooner, Ronnie transitioning into psychedelic rock with The Electric Elves. This band morphed into Elf, who produced three records of hard honky-tonk rock 'n' roll, becoming tour mates of Purple and soon after, friends with the guys.

Elf, in fact, were more or less discovered by Roger Glover, who went on to produce for them. Roger had already collared Ronnie to play a part on his multi-singer/multi-instrumentalist *Butterfly Ball* project, Ronnie providing that record's highlight track "Love Is All." But when it came to bringing the record to the stage, Ronnie couldn't be a part of it.

Says Roger, "When I first did the *Butterfly Ball* at the Albert Hall in 1975, Ronnie didn't come, and that posed quite a problem for me at the time. And the reason he didn't come the first time is because of the various politics that we're going on. He had just joined Rainbow. In fact there was kind of a division between him and I at the time."

"I didn't do the live show," affirms Ronnie. "At that time we'd just put Rainbow together, Ritchie and I, and he felt it was not something that I should do, that we should be concentrating on the Rainbow thing and not be sidetracked by that. It was his band, and he was another one of my heroes, so I figured he knew what he was doing. In retrospect I'm quite glad I didn't do the show."

Ronnie adds his twist to the tale of that first Rainbow session. "This was a time, again, as I say, Ritchie wanted to do a single for himself. He had always loved that song. He asked me if I would sing a song with him on his single thing and I said 'What song?' And he said, 'I'm sure you don't know it. It's called "Black Sheep of the Family."' And I said, 'Oh, Quatermass song. Yeah, I like that song.' 'You know that song?!' 'Well yeah, love that song.' So right away that confirmed Ritchie's feeling that I was on the same thinking plane that he was."

Ronnie provides a quick history of his somewhat murky past, which actually includes recordings dating back to 1957! "I'm from a small town in upstate New York called Cortland. I moved to LA about 20 years ago; I wanted to get out of the cold weather, as everybody does, I'm sure! My wife is my manager. We don't have any children (although Ronnie had one previous, a boy, Danny). I've spent my whole life doing this, I think. Maybe that's why it's not so interesting. I started playing the trumpet when I was five years old, which was great training for me as a singer. It taught me the correct way to do it because I've not taken singing lessons from anyone. I went to the University of Buffalo; I was a pharmacy major. After I finished my university education I did what I always wanted to do, which was to become a musician. From that time that I decided to be a musician it was a matter of traveling all the time and loving every minute of it. And then to be lucky enough to form a band with Ritchie and then to be in Sabbath after that, and to have the great success with Dio that we did after that. Most of it's been working; it's been a pretty normal life other than the musical part of it."

As Ronnie explained to Dmitry Epstein in 2005, "Those who influenced me were Deep Purple, Led Zeppelin, mainly English bands of that era, but especially Purple and Zeppelin. That's what made me want to do this more and more and more, because the first band I was in back then, Elf, were much more a kind of honky-tonk rock 'n' roll band, but I always wanted to be able to play heavier music. I loved their musicianship—I thought they were the best musicians on Earth!—those were the people I really cared about when I was into this kind of music."

Explaining the shift in singing style needed as he would transition from Elf to Rainbow, Ronnie explains that, "when it becomes more metal kind of music, when it becomes more 'blacky,' where the songs lead themselves along, there's not a lot of spaces, not a lot of holes for soul. In Elf we had a lot of space. We had the piano player (Mickey Lee Soule) that was featured really in the band, and that made for a lot of open holes for me to sing that way. But it was the music itself, really. I mean, the music was a lot more bluesy, perhaps—I think this is the word for it—bluesy and soulful, so I could do it that way."

"Once you start writing songs like 'Man on the Silver Mountain,' a little more 'blacky' songs, there's not that much space to be that soulful. But that was okay with me. I know I can sing soulfully, but I just liked the strength and power of the music that didn't have a lot of spaces. It's never really been my attitude, really, to want to be in a 'ballad' band of any kind, or a soft band; that's not something that ever made me happy. That's why eventually I became what I have become: from Elf and the soulful times to what it is now. It's what I've always wanted to do. I take a chance and sing a few little soft things here and there in some of the songs that we do, but they usually lead to the big heavy sounds. That's kind of to make you think, 'Oh, this is gonna be a soft song!' and then bang!—you get hit with it."

Concerning "Love Is All," his song for Roger, and its similarity to "Carolina Country Ball," Ronnie clarifies that, "I didn't write that song; it was written by Roger Glover and Eddie Hardin. You know, maybe it is a little bit (laughs). You must remember that Roger Glover was a producer for our band, for Elf, for three albums, and maybe that had a bit to do with it. It was a little bit like that but more like a Beatles song than anything else, more like 'All You Need Is Love' than 'Carolina County Ball.' But we liked the Beatles in Elf as well, and Roger liked the music that we made a lot. But I didn't deserve credit for that; they wrote that song."

Ronnie is philosophical about what led him from Elf to Rainbow, and eventually to Black Sabbath and Dio. "I think you should take everything that comes your way as it's been happy and enjoy it, while things that would happen that seem to be really terrible and make you angry are better left unsaid. There are two roads to take, the low road and the high road. And I've always felt with people I've worked with, if it ended badly it didn't matter, because all the good things that happened, whether it's musically or the good times we had together as people, are more important than to shout it to the rest of the world. You have to remember that if you're strong enough, you can just carry on, on your own anyway. It doesn't matter what anyone else has done to you: just put that away and be poised to be carrying on.

So I have no reason to say anything bad about anybody. They've all been such an important part of my life that it's something I just keep in my heart."

"It's from my parents," continues Ronnie, explaining his legendary groundedness. "They always told me, 'Don't think that you're better than anyone else, that you're so special just because you can do one thing well.' I mean, I can sing well but I can't repair my car, so that doesn't make me better than the man who can repair my car, which doesn't make him better than me because he can't sing. So my parents told me, 'It's your way to make, and along the way you're going to have problems, but it's always better to smile with the problems and to carry on and just go on with your life.' It all comes from them."

His Italian heritage also helped. "Yes, when you live in this country, in America, you're surely born here, but not a lot of people who lived here 40 of 50 years ago… they all came from immigrants. And because of that, most of the people in this country have taken their ethnic attitude and bonded together. They created Italian neighbourhoods everywhere. There are Greek neighbourhoods everywhere, there are German areas everywhere, there are English areas everywhere in this country. And I think it's a very important thing that people have continued to remember their heritage. I grew up with my grandmother and grandfather who were immigrants from Italy, and so I had a great chance to look into that and be proud of where I came from and proud of where they came from. But the world has changed quite a bit in the last 30 or 40 years, because more people are being born in this country and consider it not really that important to worry about where their grandparents came from. But not for me; for me it's always been very important that Italians want to sing and that they laugh aloud, because it's made me what I am."

Deep Purple bassist Glenn Hughes charts the beginning of the end for Ritchie as part of the Anglo institution known and loved as Deep Purple.

"Yes, I distinctly remember him doing a solo; I think it was on 'Holy Man.' And I asked him… you didn't really suggest too much to him. But I did ask him, as I had written the track, if he wouldn't mind playing a bottleneck, and he looked at me and rather than take a bottleneck up, he picked a screwdriver up and played it, almost in defiance. And the funny side is, he played it wonderfully. I mean, he didn't react mean to me. He looked me like, 'Hmm, okay.' But as I've said in the years since, Blackmore didn't like the way the band was going and the way the interaction was. The thing is, when you get two guys in a band like Coverdale and Hughes, we changed the spin on things dramatically. And the thing is, with Ritchie Blackmore, bless him, I have nothing but good things to say about Ritchie, but Ritchie had a problem with singers: Ian Gillan, Ronnie Dio, Joe Lynn Turner... he just has a problem with the colour they bring to the band or whatever, the ego; whatever you want to call it."

"Ritchie just became the... he wasn't mean, he wasn't angry, as he can be. He just sort of disappeared into the woodwork a little bit. It all happened in a matter of... on the last American tour. He told us, even before we did the European tour, that he was leaving. It was all in a matter of three months that he was gone. I would say halfway through the record, or even before we started, he was looking to leave anyway. I think he had gone as far as he wanted to go in Deep Purple. You know, I think the format of Gillan and Glover and all that stuff was a great metal band, whatever you want to call it. And when David and I came in, the band started to become more, and I'm going to say, soulful. Because we grew up in the north of England; we grew up listening to American R&B. Rather than try replacing Gillan and Glover with two look- and sound-alikes, they replaced them with two totally different commodities, and it showed very strongly on *Stormbringer*, what it was all about. And I like change in music. I don't want to make *Burn II*. Led Zeppelin did a really good job in their careers of making different records every time out. So that's how I feel about *Stormbringer*—it's a different record."

Concerning whether Ritchie was civil with everybody through this tense time, Hughes figures, "Blackmore isolates, as we all do. But Blackmore isolated and didn't communicate with anyone. Ever. Never. That's Ritchie Blackmore. Ritchie, midway through the *Stormbringer* tour, realized that the end was nigh for him, because the power was being taken from him, in the music.

Because it was all being written by all of us guys. And he just didn't understand and like what he called shoeshine music."

Turning his attention to Mr. Ronnie James Dio, Glenn says that, "Oh, God, yes. Elf were fantastic, absolutely fantastic. Ronnie was part of the family. Elf was opening up for us all the time. Ronnie Dio has had a well-deserved career. Ronnie Dio is a tremendously gifted metal performer, entertainer, whatever you want to call him. He's got a great voice and he's a super guy, really good, good person and I've got the greatest admiration for Ronnie; I love him to pieces." Ritchie, of course, concurred, at least with respect to his talent: "Ronnie, obviously, being a great trumpeter, he's a trumpeter, he knows music inside out. So he knows where to improvise and where to go with his notes; he has a very strong voice and his pitching was always perfect."

I asked Glenn if, indeed, he ever saw or heard Ritchie plotting to work with Ronnie one day. "Yeah, you know, I mean, Blackmore never really mingled with anybody in Purple. He never really came out with that family of Purples. On tour Ritchie was totally separated from all of us. He never really spoke to us at all. He continues to be the same way, he does, Ritchie. But he did mention a couple of times in passing that he thought Ronnie was a great, great singer, blah blah blah. So when he formed Rainbow, it wasn't really a surprise."

"We had done three Elf albums with Roger Glover, who is the bass player from Purple," explains Ronnie, picking up the story. "After we did the first album with him, Roger took it back to the Purple guys and we signed a contract with Purple Records that was a company owned by the band. We became their opening act in Europe. The guys liked it. I don't know why they did, but they did! We did about eight world tours with Deep Purple. You get the tendency to rub elbows with someone eventually. Ritchie was hard to rub shoulders with. It took a long time for Ritchie and I to get to know each other. I think we did two tours with him before he even said hello to me! That was okay. I understood where he was at. We were the opening act and I wasn't looking to stick my nose up Ritchie's behind and get something out of it that I did not deserve. Eventually, Ritchie came up to me and he said, 'You're a great singer' and he walked out and that was the end of it. From then on, he would say hello and we would start to talk a little bit. He then invited me to work on his first solo single that he was going to do but it turned out to be the first Rainbow album."

On the subject of the rift with Roger over the situation, Ronnie explains that "Roger was not in the band anymore. He was there when Ian was the singer. Then David Coverdale and Glenn Hughes came in. We did about four more tours with them after that. One day Ritchie came to me and said, 'I'm leaving Purple and I would like to know if you would put a band together with me.' I said, 'If you want to take the guys in my band, then no problem.' Roger was hurt because Roger, my keyboard player Mickey Soule and I were going to put a band together (a southern-tinged concept provisionally named Footloose). Then I got the offer from Ritchie and I went to talk to Roger. I said, 'All I can tell you is thank you so much for what you have done for me and I would have loved to play with you but this is an opportunity that I just absolutely can't say no to.' Plus, I was bringing the rest of the guys from the band with me. At least I was honest with him and he understood. But he was very hurt by it. All these years later, Roger is one of my best friends. He is the greatest person on earth. It hurt him but he understood. These things do happen in life."

Chapter 2

Ritchie Blackmore's Rainbow

"He liked Bach and I liked Bach."

And so we have it, in August of 1975, an album called *Ritchie Blackmore's Rainbow* (named for the infamous Rainbow Bar & Grill in LA) was born, beginning a long string of records (seven studio, one double live) over what is actually quite brief a spell as a band—eight years—until an oddball album in the '90s would emerge. But the debut, *Ritchie Blackmore's Rainbow*, surprised a lot of people at the time, being not, in fact, the blazing metalfest many expected from the man who complained Deep Purple were becoming too much of a funky blues band for his axe-wielding liking.

As Ritchie explained to Steve Rosen back in 1975, after doing "Black Sheep of the Family" as a single, "We were all thinking the same thing at the same time: 'When are we going to make an LP then?' So we said, 'Okay.' I had about six weeks off from Deep Purple before we started touring, so I said, 'Let's get together now.' We rushed about and rehearsed in two weeks, and we put the LP down in a month. And it all came together and it's come out. I'm being modest in saying it's kind of brilliant. It came out very well."

"After I did the LP and during making the LP, I was thinking about Purple and thinking it was so refreshing to be able to work with new musicians and to have a rapport that I didn't have with Deep Purple. It was just professionalism with Deep Purple rather than a rapport. Our drummer (Ian Paice) would be good enough to back anything, but not really to put any of his ideas forward, to make a song. It was, 'Whatever's there I'm gonna play and play very well.' With this particular setup, everybody listened to everybody else and would listen to ideas, whereas Purple—myself included—got very blasé about other people's ideas. It was a case of, 'Well, let's just shove down, you know, more or less anything.' And it's a bit about money to a degree. It was getting to that stage where I was dreading to go into the studio."

"We finished the LP," continues Blackmore, referring now to the Rainbow record, "and I was really crazy about it. Then we had a tour with Deep Purple and after that first gig I realized I had been spoiled. During the making of this LP, I enjoyed it so much that now Deep Purple was becoming a hardship because everybody was egotistical, including myself. So about halfway through the tour, I knew that we hardly spoke to each other. Not because everybody hated each other, but just because we had known each other so bloody long. It was really getting very hard to put together an LP. Nobody really had that many ideas. And what ideas were going around, I didn't particularly like. Most of the band was going towards funk and shoeshine music and I wanted to get back to rock. I had been very into classical the last few years, medieval music, very light music really."

"Two tracks on *Stormbringer* were so hard to put together just because certain people in the band wanted to play funk. It was a real hardship to get across to them, 'Let's just put a melody down. We're not gonna have the kind of brilliant solos from anybody.' You know, kind of, what's the word? Virtuoso kind of parts, no organ solos, just a good song. But it was always the old story of, 'There must be an organ solo, a guitar solo, drum beat must be pretty good and this and that,' which detracted from a good song. One song I'm thinking of in particular, 'Soldier of Fortune,' I really had to twist a couple of the band's arms to kind of get the song down, which is one of my favourites. But because it's so laid-back and it's very melodic and there's not a lot of funk there, it was getting to the point where I thought, you know, we're moving apart."

"So, anyway, I got about halfway through the tour and I decided to tell the band (Deep Purple). I said, 'Look, I don't want to go into the studio.' And they took it well. They had a holiday and got another guitarist. They tried someone else out. And I hope it worked for them because they didn't know whether to break up or whether to carry on. And they decided to carry on, but they won't be on the road 'til January, February (1976). They'll be in the studio in, I think, it's next month with Tommy Bolin. He's very good, one of my favourite American guitarists."

As for the new band, Ritchie explained that, "It's not Elf as a lot of people know Elf. It's really Rainbow. It's another band because the music we're making is so different. The people wouldn't even know it was Elf. There's a few members of Elf involved. That's why the press always keep saying Elf. But Elf aren't really involved. It's a new band completely with different members and the whole bit. But it's not my band. It's a band that I got together with Ronnie.'"

"I put my name to the first LP as being Ritchie Blackmore's Rainbow to get people to know that I've left Deep Purple," continues Ritchie, on the messy titling of the project. "More to kind of say, 'If you like that kind of music, this is where I'm at.' I hope to drop that later because I couldn't handle the responsibility of doing all the interviews and all that bullshit, which I'm doing now, that goes with having your own group. Plus, I don't want to have my own group. This group, they're so good. You know, I'm part of the group. It's not me and the group, no way. I don't want to have that scene at all. And that's why at first it's gonna be called that. But within six months people will be coming to see the other people in the band. That's how good they are. I'm very pleased with the whole thing. The LP worked out really well."

"But it's definitely a new band, same as like Purple was," stresses Ritchie. "It's not me and the band. To start, I don't consider myself that good to front the band and I don't want to front the band. I'll only do my flash business on stage, which I like doing. But I just don't like being known as a leader of the band. I'd like to be a pusher, obviously, of the band. Nobody can be a leader of a band if they're really truthful. And if you're someone like Rory Gallagher, well Rory's good, but everybody else is his side band, kind of playing to back him up. This is not that kind of band. With Rainbow, they're all stars in their own right, especially the singer. He'll prove himself, you know. But at first, it's gonna be slanted my way because of being with Purple. But it's good in a way because people will take a listen to what else we've got to offer, whereas maybe if we were a completely unknown band, they wouldn't take the time."

Personnel for the *Ritchie Blackmore's Rainbow* album was Ritchie and most of Elf, soon to be discarded and departed parties being Mickey Lee Soule on keyboards (he was the least enthusiastic about the concept to begin with, and in fact wasn't fired, but quit the band), Gary Driscoll on drums and Craig Gruber on bass. Our man Ronnie Dio—reconfigured to Ronnie James Dio for numerological purposes—would command the mic with classic rock aplomb for miles, but even he would not make it to the end of the Rainbow.

"We were opening up for Deep Purple for three years as Elf," begins Gruber, reiterating but also filling in a few gaps with respect to how the very first Rainbow lineup came to be—I conducted this interview with Craig in 2010; Gruber has since passed away, succumbing to prostate cancer on May 15th, 2015, at the age of 63. "We were signed to Purple Records and we became very good friends with Deep Purple and they kept us under their wing for three straight years. So in other words there was a lot of interaction with Deep Purple and their way of writing and their kind of medieval Sir Lancelot influence, if you will, lyrically and image-wise. If you look at Purple's album jackets, and the way they set their tours up, it all had continuity; there was a thread that held it together. So being with them so many years in a row influenced us."

"And if you listen to Elf, we were primarily a good time rock 'n' roll piano kind of funky blues rock band, and Ronnie hadn't really come full circle yet as far as his direction. It was an excellent band. We did very, very well worldwide, and our fans nowadays are even stronger than they ever were. In fact, Ronnie and I and Mickie Lee were planning on doing another Elf album this fall, a reunion of Elf, which is pretty cool."

"But anyway, when Purple was coming to a final end at the end of 1974, we had done the *Burn* tour with them, and that was after Glenn Hughes and David Coverdale joined the band in 1973. Ritchie was unhappy with the direction unfortunately, but they were great, an incredible band live. And Glenn Hughes is a great bassist and vocalist, but he's very soul-filled. His favourite band in the whole world is Rufus and Chaka Khan, you know what I mean? You can hear that in his vocal lines. And David Coverdale is very bluesy, very soulful. And they took over Roger Glover's and Ian Gillan's positions in the band."

"In other words, Purple took on a more bluesy, funky kind of R&B feel, which Ritchie was totally against. There were other songs that Ritchie wanted to record and they refused to record them. And then the *Stormbringer* album came out a year-and-a-half later and we went and did that tour with them too. Midway through the tour Ritchie and Ronnie started to get really very, very close, and they started to write backstage between concerts, and Ritchie started isolating himself from Deep Purple and hanging out with us guys. So we were actually writing in Ritchie's dressing room a couple of days a week backstage. That consequently gives you a direction where those lyrics came from. It was that transition. At the end of Deep Purple, when we actually started to form Ritchie Blackmore's Rainbow—that's what that transition became."

"David and Glenn wouldn't record, specifically, 'Black Sheep of the Family,' any of the rock stuff Ritchie had," continues Craig. "Because they were more soul players, beautiful players, wonderful guys, those guys. But near the middle of the tour, Ronnie and I and all of us… Ritchie never let any of the guys in his dressing room, even the guys in Purple, which is sad. But all of a sudden Ritchie and Ronnie are very chummy, and Ritchie's dressing room door was open and we could walk in and he would say, 'Sit down' and he was very friendly—holy shit! I guess he was looking for some friends or something, because he's so lonely anyway."

"But he was very, very nice to us, and he started saying we should possibly get together at the end of this tour and have a blow. We thought he was kidding. Play with Ritchie Blackmore? Give me a break. And he said to Ronnie, 'We should go and play some dates!' And we're going huh?! Because we didn't know Purple were going to break up. But it actually came up in conversation backstage in Ritchie's dressing room, and then there were whispers and whispers, with Ronnie going back and forth with Bruce Payne, the management. And then you're at the end of that tour, and Ronnie came to us and said, 'Ritchie is thinking about leaving Deep Purple and doing a solo project and he may be interested in using us on it.'"

But there was a problem. Elf, of course, had a guitarist, and it was unlikely that he was going to be included in Ritchie's new band.

"Yes, well, Steve Edwards was very distraught because he loved Elf," says Craig. "I had rescued Steve from a small bar band. He had a lot of talent, and this was Steve's only main thing that he has ever done—Elf, that is—that was actually recording and touring, especially on that level. You know, we were playing 20,000-seaters every night with Purple. So he was very distraught. And Ronnie put it to him gently and said, 'Listen, this is probably not going to become a band, Steve, okay? Ritchie is... we're going to do an album, we'll put you on retainer—which they did—and you'll be okay money-wise. And when we finish the album and do any dates, if we ever do any... Elf is not ending.' I mean, Ronnie had no intention of letting go of Elf at that particular time. But the album came out, it went to #30 with a bullet, and #7 in England, and the rest was history."

Indeed the record came out, called *Ritchie Blackmore's Rainbow*, resplendent in gatefold sleeve, featuring on the front, a shining castle shaped like a guitar, rainbow up above, approaching path leading through the fortress up to the sky.

Comments Gruber, "The medieval motif, if you will, it was Deep Purple and castles, and the rainbow is obviously Ritchie Blackmore's Rainbow, and with the amount of purple, if you look at the band Deep Purple, that's obviously their kind of colour scheme, so it was a natural transition—it felt right."

Very much so—one could see this cover as part of a narrative with the *Stormbringer* jacket art. That one too has weather and some purple, plus the hint of a rainbow.

"In the beginning there was no castle involved," continues Craig. "We didn't really have that in our mind. And then we contacted this graphic artist, David Willardson, when we were recording the album in West Germany. He was a graphic artist and photographer, and he got involved with Deep Purple and us, there, and actually came into Musicland Studios with us and listened to what we were doing. I saw Ritchie and him having a chat at the hotel. I didn't even get to see any of the artwork, but when it came out it was iconic, and that's the word I like to use. It's iconic— something that creates a very powerful image in your mind. In fact, I have a ten-inch tattoo of that on my right shoulder from the top of my shoulder to my elbow. On the cover it's got a Fender Stratocaster coming out of the middle of the castle because that's what Ritchie played. But I play my own brand of basses. I own Infinite Metal Werkz, so I had the guitar taken out of the centre of the castle and I had my bass put in the centre of it, to commemorate the multimillion selling album. That album changed everybody's lives in the band."

Within the gatefold, the label had to perform a bit of sleight of hand. Because the band had never performed live, the live shots presented were of Ritchie playing with Deep Purple and of Elf, of course, without Ritchie. There was however one studio shot of all of them together, Ritchie at the point of the spear wearing his iconic pilgrim's hat, which, alternately, amusingly enough, was called a Witchfinder General's hat in an NME piece at the time.

Ritchie Blackmore's Rainbow was recorded under the auspices of legendary producer Martin Birch (Deep Purple, and later Whitesnake, Black Sabbath, Blue Öyster Cult and Iron Maiden), over a three-week period, February 20th through to March 14th of 1975, at Munich's Musicland Studios. The production credit goes to Birch, Blackmore and Dio, which reflects Ronnie's importance in the band—under circumstances such as these, typically someone like Martin would insist upon and get sole credit, while conversely a marquee name like Ritchie would not even consider his new lead singer worthy of credit. This, on the other hand, represents a generosity, and backs up Ritchie's words that he didn't want to be the leader of the band.

An interesting fact is that Ritchie still had three weeks of Deep Purple tour obligations to fulfil after the album had been completed, Ritchie quitting after the final date in Paris, April 7th, 1976. Elf did a bit of time-travel themselves, having their completed *Trying to Burn the Sun* record released a few months after the issue of the Rainbow slab. Ritchie did not want his album to come out under the Purple Records imprint, so management created Oyster Records, which wound up as a boutique label under Polydor after a buyout of EMI.

"Yeah, changing people's beers," answers Craig, asked if any of Ritchie's famous practical jokes had been played during the sessions. "You know, if you were drinking a certain beer... but nothing major. He never did anything really, really mean. He would switch people's drinks around. He was a trickster, he really was, but he had Colin Hart (from the road crew) do all the mean stuff. Colin would do some weird stuff under Ritchie's auspices, if you will, or supervision. But there was never any major explosions or fights. There wasn't too much going on. I think he pulled all he wanted to pull on Purple, those poor guys, Jesus. We went into Musicland Studios and just turned stuff up, had some drinks and just started to blast. There was no weird stuff."

Two oddball cover versions would make the *Ritchie Blackmore's Rainbow* album—issued August 4th, 1975—but the rest of the record would be written by (or at least credited to) Ritchie and Ronnie alone, the two discovering themselves of like mind when it came to blanketing words and music under a plush, crushed velvet cloak of gothic, royal… purple.

"The only writers were Ritchie and I," affirms Ronnie. "No one else wrote anything in the band. So it was our creation. It was what we wanted that band to be and the band really just played what we wanted them to play. There is no honky-tonk piano on that album because that's not the kind of band we were. So that immediately took the flavour of what Elf was away. So the keyboard player would then have to play B3 or Clavinet or something that was more of a supporting instrument rather than being a lead instrument like it was in Elf."

As it worked out, opening track on the debut album "Man on the Silver Mountain" was about as far away from Elf as you could get. In fact, it's pretty much, after all these years, Rainbow's "Smoke on the Water," both tracks supported by big, dumb, sluggish riffs, which somehow prove irresistible to coursing male blood. As well, the track instantly establishes Ronnie as a medieval, wizardly, dragons, rainbows and fire kind of lyricist. The break section (and Ritchie's trills therein), the solemn melodic tradition, the track's two alternating sets of Neanderthal riffs… all of this combines to create a certifiable epic that sounds more like a centuries-old fortification than a new solo track from Ritchie Blackmore.

"I just thought the songs were brilliant on that album," recalls Ronnie fondly. "I really, really liked the songs on that album. I thought 'Man on the Silver Mountain,' which of course, became a fixture for the band, and has become a fixture for me as well, was a great song and a very important song—a real good transition from 'Smoke on the Water' to Rainbow, I thought. And the guys I played with in Elf were on that album as well. But it's not that. I thought they played extremely well, but it wasn't a matter of that, more than it was the songs. I just think the songs were so good and so naturally done that we didn't have to worry about success, if you know what I mean. You don't really have to worry about success when you've attained it. This was a matter of, 'Well, this is going to be fun; this is going to be enjoyable,' especially for Ritchie. I can do what I want to do myself and play with people I want to play with and these are the songs I like. So I think it was good for everybody all the way around, and it just worked out so well. And Martin Birch did such a great job of the production. I just think all around it was a happy time, a really happy time. So I'll always like that album."

"For 'Man on the Silver Mountain' I wanted to write something that had more of a mythical story quality to it," continues Ronnie. "And for some strange reason, the man on the silver mountain came to me, probably just from the rhythm of the song and what I was getting for a melody. And that translated itself into this all-powerful wizard-like figure who is the man on the silver mountain, who is continually asked to come down from his place and help us solve our problems and my problems etc. So he was a God figure, I guess."

Taking a crack at the lyric in conversation with Jon Tiven from Circus, Blackmore said, "It's supposedly about some guy on top of a mountain who's like a Jesus Christ—it's kind of religious in a way. My interpretation is that some guy goes on top of a silver mountain, finds the silver and realizes that he can't get down again. It's vaguely a classical progression with about 25 chords in it, but you don't realize it because they're all relative, and it resolves after about 30 bars. It's one of my favourite numbers, very much like a Purple thing: what we call the 'Bagshot Bullet' guitar playing, Bagshot being where I come from. We recorded the album in a hotel, and it was really loud... I had one of the speakers down in a cellar to get echo on one side, and this was reverberating throughout the whole hotel so everybody was complaining."

Asked by Dmitry Epstein about his predilection for writing from a first person point of view, as demonstrated by this song, Ronnie takes a long pause to reflect, venturing, "I think I always sing from the first person point of view because, again, I always consider myself to be more of a storyteller than a songwriter. I have the greatest sources of subjects in the world: that's the people who live on this planet, who are always the best things to write about because they're very predictable and also very unpredictable."

"And if you write about a subject that people know about—and everybody know about the people because we see each other all the time—that's very important. What I do is I try to write those songs about real subjects but I put them in a different place. I put them in a fantasy place, perhaps, or I put them back thousands of years because that makes you have to use your imagination. You have to think about what a dragon looks like because none of us has even seen one; we've only seen pictures that people drew up in their minds. It's very important for people to use their imagination. But again, I'm telling the same story, probably, that everyone else has told; I'm just saying it in a different way, maybe in a way that, perhaps, is a little bit more interesting and imaginative."

There's usually both darkness and anger laced into Ronnie's fanciful tales, but then again, that's heavy metal. "There's darkness in everyone," figures Ronnie. "There's pain in many people. There's goodness in everyone. We have choices to make, and our choices are: 'Am I going to be at that dark side or am I going to be at the good side?' That's up to each person to make that determination. I'm worried about things that are inside of me and inside of everybody else too, 'cause I'm not just writing the songs from the first person's aspect: there's a message inside of every song. It's meant to be said to the people I'm singing a song for. So there are songs that I have written a little bit more in the first person than others, but mainly I write songs so that people can make judgements as to what I'm saying—and perhaps have a better time of it, so to speak."

"I get angry as much as anyone else does," continues Dio. "I get angry when I see injustice. I get angry when I see people suffer. Of course, I am very sad when I see people suffer but I'm very angry too, because this suffering shouldn't be. We waste so much in this world on pleasure things and don't really seem to care about the people, and especially children—that's the worst kind of suffering and that makes me very, very angry. Government makes me angry because of the bad choices that it makes, not just about this government here in this country, but governments everywhere. I'm angry about those things just like any other person should be. Of course, I'm angry sometimes about the music if it's not right: I get angry because I need to have it right. So there are many things that can make me angry. But I'm not an angry person all the time. I'd like life to be good and I like to share the good things with other people."

With "Man on the Silver Mountain," buttressed by four or five other songs across the record, Ronnie and Ritchie have built an album that can validly and substantially be argued as the first "power metal" album, that is, heavy metal with strong, traditional classical overtones and historical and/or fantasy themes. Other records that fit this narrative would be Rush's *Caress of Steel*, issued a month later, but also a couple of Uriah Heep albums, *Demons and Wizards* and *The Magician's Birthday* issued a few years earlier. Excepting the Rush, the Heeps win on being earlier, but the Rainbow wins with its more direct link to heavy metal—oddly, not by being particularly heavy in and of itself, but by the band becoming much heavier on the next two albums, each of which build even more intensely the case for Rainbow as the originators of power metal.

Gruber paints the picture of even deeper ties for this track with 1972's "Smoke on the Water," stating that "when we worked that up in Munich at Musicland Studios, we were playing around with 'Smoke on the Water.' Truthfully, the drummer and I were playing that (sings it), that kind of feel, and Ritchie was literally playing 'Smoke on the Water,' that riff, and he said, 'That's a great feel—remember that feel. In fact track that right now.' So Martin

Birch, our engineer/producer just said, 'Okay, go guys. I don't know what key it's in.' 'It's in the key of G; it's Ronnie's key,' blah blah blah. We tracked about 15, 20 minutes of it and I forgot about it."

"I came down a couple days later to the studio. At the Musicland Studios there's a hotel and recording studio. The Rolling Stones actually built that studio, Musicland, at the Arabella house in Munich, Germany, and it was brand-new. So we lived at the hotel and you just took an elevator to the bottom floor and there's Musicland Studios. And so Ritchie got up, went downstairs one morning really early, and we came in around 11 AM, Ronnie and I, the keyboard player and the drummer, and the track was playing. We walked into the control room and Ritchie was working out the riff (sings the 'Man on the Silver Mountain' riff), and we all looked at each other and went, 'Oh-oh, here we go.' Ronnie put his left arm out and the hair was standing up on his arm and he said, 'Craig, this is it, mate.' That's how that song came together."

"We did the drums on that one in three edits," says Ritchie, "because we had a good friend of ours playing drums, Gary Driscoll, and he was a very funny drummer. We would be recording and he would often just stop. And we would say, 'Why did you stop?' And he would go, 'Well, I thought someone told me to stop through the headphones.' And we'd go, 'Well no, nobody told you to stop.' So we would carry on playing. The next time… he was one of these drummers who moved around a lot and his headphones would start to come off as he was playing, and it was hilarious to watch him trying to keep his headphones on his head and balanced, when he was playing the drums. Of course he failed every time, because halfway through the song, his headphones would come off and crash onto the cymbals and we'd have to stop again. So it was really hilarious how we got through that song."

"Yeah, yeah, Chops," laughs Craig. "That was his nickname. Chops always wore headphones, because he played very, very hard and very, very loud, and Chops, he wasn't the greatest technician. He was a very technical drummer, but sometimes he would get behind the beat. Yeah, great feel and I loved him and we all did, we all still do, but sometimes he'd turn the beat around. He would do a fill, but come in on the second beat of the next four-count instead of beat number one, so he would twist the beat around sometimes.

So we suggested, 'Listen, take everything out of the mix; we'll just put you in—your drum kit—and you can monitor yourself.' And we would be bashing along recording, actually. I'm doing a take with him and he would nod his head and rock while he was doing it, and they would slowly loosen up and literally—they did—they would fall off and come down around his neck. And then the cord—back then they weren't wireless—it would get wrapped around his arm and shit. It was comical. I mean, Ritchie knew that Gary was very, very much a sweetheart of a person and would never do anything to interrupt a recording sessions or waste time, so Ritchie took that with ease, which was very nice. He didn't scold him or call him any names or throw a drum stick at him. He was very cool about it."

Driscoll had been with Ronnie since the Ronnie Dio and the Prophets days, joining in June of 1965. He was found murdered in the house of an acquaintance in Ithaca NY, June 1987—the case has never been solved.

"I was actually in New York when that happened," recalls Gruber, who in the early '80s formed a band with Gary called Bible Black, known mostly for being the launching ground of Joey Belladonna into Anthrax. "It was about a week before my birthday. And I know that he was hanging around some very strange people. Gary was a very nice person, was not a druggie like everybody thinks. He liked to drink, but he was not heavily into drugs or anything. But he was a very friendly guy, very, very nice. But he befriended these strange people. Gary always hung out with eccentric-type people. I don't know where he met them."

"But to try and answer what happened, what I heard from his family was he was house-watching, like watching this house while the owners had left for a weekend. And they happened to be high-end drug dealers, cocaine, that kind of stuff. I think that was the drug; I'm not sure but that's what I heard. And some people, some foreigners, I think they were Colombians, they were dark-skinned, dark-haired guys, from what the police report said and from what the witnesses supposedly saw in the area that evening… anyway, I don't know how many there were, but they entered the home and they were looking for the owners of the home while Gary was watching the home for a couple of days, just house-sitting in the home. And he had no information to give them. He didn't know or Gary would've told them. Before someone actually kills you, Gary would've told them. But he had no idea where they were. And they beat him and killed him."

"Man on the Silver Mountain" would be floated as a single two months after the full record's issue, backed with album track "Snake Charmer." The song would fail to chart on either side of the Atlantic, but would become a perennial Rainbow staple, indeed becoming part of the Dio band canon as well.

"Self Portrait" is next and, in fact, this is a criminally under-rated, forgotten Rainbow track. Its good qualities are many: its dark melody and its mystical lyric adhere nicely to the philosophical thrust of the album, and its arrangement is both proggy and heavy, the perfect balance to satisfy Ritchie's thirst for "symphonic rock." Amusingly, it also finds Rainbow catching the fusion fever afflicting Purple members in late '70s, as can be heard on records by Paice Ashton Lord and The Ian Gillan Band, as well as solo material from David Coverdale, Glenn Hughes, Roger Glover and Jon Lord, much of it weird and non-rock down various rabbit holes—not a Purple-y album among them.

Ritchie liked this one so much that he revived it for use in Blackmore's Night, with his wife Candice, recording a version for the *Under a Violet Moon* album. He's described the 6/8 time signature song as a cross between the Jimi Hendrix Experience classic "Manic Depression" and Bach's cloying and over-played "Jesu, Joy of Man's Desiring"—I hear the former but not the latter.

Ronnie opines over the fortunate meeting of minds between himself and the Man in Black that could create vaguely Renaissance music like this track. "I think maybe classical music. He liked Bach and I liked Bach. I liked Beethoven. He didn't like him as much as Bach, but we really liked most of the same classical themes. I think that was reflected in the writing as well. That is one of the reasons we were able to come together. We thought the same way musically. We thought in big, melodic, orchestral terms. That was our point of contact. And in terms of stories about our interest in the occult, well, they are all true. They are very, very true. I don't bother to dabble in that anymore because we had some rather scary experiences. I've given it up. Once you invite the devil into your house he doesn't go away! We did all those things and they were sometimes scary and sometimes they were really interesting. But we weren't demonic. We weren't trying to converse with the devil or anything. As soon as the devil popped up we all got away pretty fast!"

Next up was Quatermass' "Black Sheep of the Family" and, ironically, this unassuming and modest track would fit happily on any given Elf record. In fact, it's more than a little funky, its thumping, halting rhythm creating a pulse that wouldn't have been out of place on *Stormbringer*. To my mind, it doesn't fit the landscape of Rainbow much at all, even less, given that it's a cover, albeit an obscure one. Really, it's quite baffling: "Black Sheep of the Family" sounds like a song Coverdale or Hughes would write for inclusion on *Stormbringer*, and then Ritchie would hate it and quit the band. And also, if you are going to pick a song, of the tens of thousands out there, to break up an institution like Deep Purple and impregnate then conceive a new band, how on earth does one pick a short, angular, funky pop song?

Nothing about "Black Sheep of the Family" makes sense, other than the fact that it came from a respected dark prog band which… again, that doesn't make sense either. But go listen to the Quatermass version, and it's indeed presented with the sort of ominous Atomic Rooster/ELP arrangement one would expect from Quatermass. Whether Ritchie knows it or not, his version was hijacked by Elf and played elfin, or played like Glenn's *Play Me Out* band or David Coverdale's *Northwinds* band. Again, nothing makes sense here.

But there it is, with Craig confirming the known narrative: "That's one of the songs that Ritchie brought into Deep Purple, and they refused, absolutely flatly refused. They laughed at him, and you don't laugh at Ritchie Blackmore and give him a hard time, because you're not there much longer. So they refused to play that Quatermass 'Black Sheep of the Family' song. But he says, 'I've got a song, I really want to use it, I really want to put it on an album.' So I listened to it, we listened to it, we all had a tape made of it, we say wow and it fit right in. It was a perfect song for Ronnie. It was really a transition song from Elf; it was a perfect bridge at that time."

And therein is a shred of sense made: indeed it was a transition song. But then again, no one asked for a transition song. And there's only one other transition song on the album and that's "If You Don't Like Rock 'n' Roll" and nobody thinks that one was a good idea.

Also underscoring the point that a *Rising*-type cover would have fit the stated thought process better, Ritchie back in 1975 framed this record as more or less a follow-up to his two favourite Purple albums, *In Rock* and *Machine Head*, even calling it his third record. He didn't want keyboard solos and not even a ton of guitar solos. He didn't want virtuoso players as he wanted to feature guitar and vocals more than anything. Noted Ritchie, in Circus, "I'm quite pleased with my guitar playing. I got very excited by Ronnie's voice. Not that I'm ripping up and down the fingerboard all the time, but I'm playing well, getting off on his singing and vice-versa. I'd usually put down some chords and ask which ones Ronnie'd prefer, he'd pick one set and we'd take it from there. He'd always write the lyrics. Sometimes I'd give him a vague melody but most of the time the melodies came from him. He's got an uncanny knack for writing melodies over nonsense."

Essentially this was to be a hard rock band, which is why post-release, any prideful talk was about "Sixteenth Century Greensleeves" and "Man on the Silver Mountain" and maybe a bit of praise for "Catch the Rainbow." And if we were to pare that down, really only "Man on the Silver Mountain" exists at any sort of appreciable recognition level within the rock zeitgeist decades later. And amusingly, even though Ritchie sort of had in mind what he wanted, he sure didn't get it. The drumming is quite busy on the record, often with a jazz-fusion vibe, as is Gruber's highly inventive bass playing.

Speaking of "Catch the Rainbow," this melancholy Hendrix-style blues ballad closes side one of the original vinyl, its dark Mellotron-enhanced tone finding Ronnie singing clean, high and confident. Somewhat surprisingly, this song would endure in the set list well into the Joe Lynn Turner years, taking on a life of its own, doubling in size and more, extended soloing becoming the order of the day.

Ritchie relates a tale concerning this quiet, morose song. "'Catch the Rainbow,' we did it, and I suddenly realized in the studio that we hadn't really finished it. And there was a hook that Ronnie sang, just by luck or coincidence. He was ad-libbing at the end, and when I heard it, I suddenly realized that we hadn't made the most of it. And I said to him, you know, you should have done that each time—that would've been the big hook. And he agreed. So we said to the management, 'Let's go back into the studio and just put that little part in.' It was three notes. 'Catch the rainbow,' just repeated."

"Then we found out that we had to leave the country and record it somewhere, because we were on a tax plan that meant that I couldn't record anything in America. It had to be done in another country, otherwise I would have to pay tax on that record. So we had to go to Jamaica and put on three notes, in the studio. Now that studio was dreadful. I don't know the name of it, but it was an awful studio. We managed to get the three notes on but I'm glad we weren't putting anything else on because this studio in Jamaica was just an awful place. And our engineer that came with us said that it was very difficult for him to work the equipment, to line things up. We had to go out of the country, just for three notes. The part where he goes 'Da, catch the rainbow.' It repeats itself."

"'Catch the Rainbow,' all those things, Ritchie and I wrote, with the exception of 'Sixteenth Century Greensleeves,' here in California," explains Ronnie. "I was still living back East. Ritchie was living here, actually in Oxnard, California. So I went out and stayed with Ritchie for about a month and we wrote together and put those things together and got the band and we played them together. Most of those things, as I say, were just written with Ritchie and I. When we did the second album, we did a lot of the writing together as a band, and we would jam and play. Ritchie would have an idea, I would have an idea, Cozy would have an idea, somebody else would have an idea, and then I would take the thing away and just write it melodically and lyrically. So those were done in a different kind of situation. The first album was written pretty much by the time we went in to do it."

"But yes, 'Catch the Rainbow' is one of my all-time favourite songs that I've ever been involved with. I love that song; I loved it when we wrote it, I love it to this day, I think it's a great song. Again, a story. A story of love, but not a love ballad, so to speak. My favourite Rainbow album is the first one. Not the second, third or fourth, whatever it is. It's always been the first one. Look at the songs... God, 'Man on the Silver Mountain,' 'Catch the Rainbow.' I mean sure, there were some great songs on *Rising*—'Stargazer' and whatnot, and 'Tarot Woman' I guess—but I just preferred the first album. I thought it had a lot of cohesiveness to it."

As Ritchie told Jon Tiven back in '75, tongue firmly in cheek, "It's about ships of wonder and chains made of steel—from Sheffield—and our vocalist who wanted to be blessed at the time. That's why we had a vicar in on the sessions—we had this vicar walking around blessing everybody. That's why you'll hear Ronnie singing I want to be blessed all the time. I think he actually did get blessed at one point. The vicar played bass on one of our sessions as well."

Recalls Craig, "We were listening to Jimi Hendrix, '1983 (A Merman I Should Turn to Be)' (sings it), and it sounds like 'Catch the Rainbow.' Ritchie was working on that and he said, 'Craig, here's the sequence.' It's got about 25 chords in it. Ritchie has a lot of chords. He's not one of those guys who plays things in three chords. But he says, 'Here's the rhythm track; I want you to listen to this.' I like 'Little Wing' a lot—I love that song and I love the Hendrix thing. And Ritchie's a big Hendrix fan—who isn't? So he played that riff, and, 'Wow, that's strong,' and we laid the beat down and it felt so good and Ronnie dropped in with some lyrics and it became 'Catch the Rainbow.'"

"Snake Charmer" perks the record back up, this one also being a bit of a dark horse deep album track like "Self Portrait." Again it's more than a little funky, Ritchie confusing those who expected the record to comprise five "Highways Star"s, two "Smooth Dancer"s and perhaps a "Lady Double Dealer" or two. Sure Ronnie is in character, his melodies even sounding swami, but Ritchie is caught red-handed with wah-wah.

Says Ronnie, "We wrote that in the studio, in Germany. That song is about Ritchie. That's what Ritchie is—he's a snake charmer. That was purely about him. If you listen to the lyrics, you'll see it relates to him." Indeed, Ronnie paints an edgy, slightly cruel, quite detailed and admirably poetic picture of a deceptive, uncaring, but charismatic man, Dio twice referring to rootlessness, implying that this fuels the central character's already considerable supply of callousness.

"That was Ritchie's idea," adds Craig. "That's one of my favourite songs, great bass line on that. Ritchie got this tune and I went off on it. But I get, without exaggerating, 15 to 20 emails a month—that's not much but…--just on that song for complimenting me on the bass line. The bass part is unbelievable. But the song was Ritchie's, absolutely, completely a Ritchie song, and he came in with the actual title. Him and Ronnie were hashing around the actual title 'Snake Charmer.' 'What about a song about a snake charmer?' Because that was right in the same line as 'Temple of the King,' that other song, and we were chatting up ideas for titles and the title usually became the chorus for the verse, you know what I mean? So we were blowing around different ideas for titles and out came 'Snake Charmer.'"

As Ritchie told Jon Tiven, "Ian Broad, my best friend, thought up the title. Ronnie wrote a whole bunch of things around the title, and several parts had been written years ago. A lot of people might think it's the weakest track on the LP, but I liked it. With the guitar/voice thing it's really strong, and the three guitars sound fine together. It was a hard one to mix, as there's so much going on."

"The Temple of the King" follows, and we're back in ballad land, this one sounding ornately and mysteriously courtesan, Ronnie full on with his magicianly imagery, as the track builds in thespian manner. Ritchie had said in interviews that the musical track had been inspired by Jimi Hendrix's laid-back and introspective classic, the aforementioned "Little Wing."

Comments Ritchie, "The first one was probably my favourite of the albums because I was just getting to know Ronnie, and we did almost medieval-influenced stuff, like

'Temple of the King,' quieter stuff, which I had never approached before with Purple. Everything before with Purple was loud and upfront. And we would do these things around the house, and just record it on a two-track Revox, just to see how they sounded. I had never done it that way before. We had always been in the studio right from the word go."

Adds Ronnie, "'Temple of the King' was a riff that Ritchie had heard on television, on a yoga program, and he came to me and said, 'Check this out,' and he played it for me on an acoustic guitar—nice, beautiful. And he changed it around a little bit so it wouldn't look like he stole the thing. And he said, 'I'd like you to write something to this.' He always did that to me. 'Can you write something around this?' 'Of course I can. I can write something around anything.' Okay. So we wrote 'Temple of the King,' and again, I wanted it to be a story. And it was set in an eastern kind of situation, once again, with my own ideas of what it must have been like to live in a society that dealt with big black bells ringing, magic all around, strange, eerie things happening. So that little riff he played in the beginning really set it up for me, to write the song. And it was cool; it felt like a really good feeling song to sing."

The name of the yoga show Ronnie refers to was Yoga for Health, and indeed, Ritchie seems to have had a secondary track written with an even closer resemblance to the show's theme music, Blackmore naming the song, aptly enough, "Yoga for Health."

"That was a cool song," says Craig. "Ritchie backstage always carried around a $50 Fender acoustic guitar. It didn't even have a case; he just carried it under his arm. He even had it on the plane, because back then there wasn't a lot of security, so he could go through security with it. He was always noodling on it, doing this medieval-type dissonant chord sequence. And 'Temple of the King,' those were his scales he just played with all the time. And the same thing, he says, 'I've got a riff, guys. You're good at coming up with stuff—just play along with me right now.' And then Ronnie came in, 'One day in the year of the fox.' Ronnie was a master of mimicking the melody. When he heard a melody that the guitar was playing, he would write a melody lyrically in moments, in minutes, around what he was hearing. Ronnie was a genius; he really was. And his music forever will influence people in the future."

Craig affirms Ritchie's love for English folk music and the British folk boom of the mid to late '60s, a time when Blackmore was an unheralded session man. This song essentially fits that mould, and indeed in interviews at the time, he'd name-check Jethro Tull in particular.

"You're absolutely correct with that, Martin. Those English folk songs… if you listen to Blackmore's Night, right now that literally is the crux of Ritchie, along with the blues. But Ritchie has gone back to that completely now with Blackmore's Night. He has really gone down that corridor, if you will, and pulled those melodies out. Those are old English melodies and Irish jig melodies, and really, those melodies are hundreds and hundreds of years old; they really are."

And this was steeped in a great appreciation for classical music. "Extreme. Backstage in his tune-up room, he had Brahms playing. He loves Brahms, he had those scales, medieval scales, and he loved pianists. He was always listening to Brahms and you would hear those influences in his music; he was very deep into that. Although there are a lot of complicated melodies, chord patterns if you will, Ritchie doesn't play a lot of chords—even live. I call them counter-melody parts. He would play a counter-melody part, which is a song within a song, that really supported the vocal line. It's a very interesting way of playing guitar."

"The Temple of the King" features two different classical guitar parts, a background electric guitar track and brief Mellotron flourishes. There's also a clean electric guitar solo evocative of something George Harrison might do. At the vocal end, Ronnie harmonizes with himself. Ritchie cracked at the time that the band wouldn't be playing it live, as it would probably put everybody to sleep. It was however revived for use in the Blackmore's Night era, where it fits just fine.

What comes next on *Ritchie Blackmore's Rainbow*, but a full-on honky-tonk Elf celebration called "If You Don't Like Rock 'n' Roll." Essentially a happy-go-lucky boogie with barrelhouse piano included… again, one comes away perplexed at the fragmented nature of the first Rainbow record (and yes, I'm aware that Ronnie lauded its abundant "cohesiveness!").

"I think it's only because that's what came out of me, via the backing track itself," says Ronnie, when asked if this song was designed to lighten up the album a bit. "I just think that Ritchie's writing style, for some reason, sometimes shoved me towards those kinds of songs, like 'Do You Close Your Eyes' or 'If You Don't Like Rock 'n' Roll.' As far as the title goes, probably at that point in time we were taking some flak for being a rock 'n' roll band and it probably pissed me off. So that was my way of saying, 'If you don't like rock 'n' roll, you know, shove it.'"

Contradicting Ronnie's recollection, Craig says, "That was a song we had with Elf. We'd co-written it—Ronnie and I and Mickey Lee; we had written it to go on the last Elf album called *Trying to Burn the Sun*, and that was pretty much together. The riff was there, the verses were there, but it wasn't 100% together, but it was an easy song to put together. We were needing another song or two for the Rainbow album, and we were pressed for time and we all talked to Ritchie and said, 'Hey, listen, we've been touring with Purple for three years, you know our material, we would like to put a rock song on. Because there's no up-tempo rock 'n' roll song on the Rainbow album.' So he hemmed and hawed, and Ronnie said, 'Craig, do you remember the song you and I played a lot, and we didn't have a title for it? The rock 'n' roll tune, the up-tempo one.' So Gary, the drummer, and Ronnie and I blasted it out and Ritchie picked it up really fast and we knocked it out in three hours or something."

"We did it as a tongue-in-cheek thing about rock 'n' roll," noted Ritchie at the time. "We wanted an out-and-out rock 'n' roll thing, so I thought this one up and figured we could get it done in about half an hour and rip it down because it was so simple. You would not believe the hassles we went through to get it right— because it was so simple, nobody could play it. It became one gigantic headache, and in the end it took us two days to get it perfect."

"Sixteenth Century Greensleeves" refocuses the record however, this one (nearly) book-ending the mid-record conundrums along with "Man on the Silver Mountain," both being grand, blustery, stone-carved medieval metal monoliths that would enter the annals of classic rock royalty through endless live renditions over the ensuing years from both the Rainbow and Dio bands.

"Well, anything that Dio did, he had a melodic voice," Ritchie told me. "So definitely, 'Sixteenth Century Greensleeves' was my way of… at the time, it was a heavy rock song, and we still do it on stage (with Blackmore's Night). But it does have a really great lilt to the melody. It can be interpreted in a way, on a lute. You could hear it on a lute. It's a very light melody, but we just put heavy chords to it and of course, when I was in Rainbow... I think when I first got Rainbow together with Ronnie Dio, it was another step in the direction I ended up now, from kind of dramatic classical rock with Deep Purple. Then I got into the Renaissance themes. And that was a step closer, when I got with Dio. And now, of course, with Blackmore's Night, it's another step."

Blackmore was a bit more cavalier describing the song back in 1975, telling Jon Tiven, "My favourite rock track on the album is 'Sixteenth Century Greensleeves.' It was written by Robin Hood of Sherwood Forest. I went to the door one night and there was an arrow in the door holding a piece of paper, and it had this song written on it. There was a note attached reading, 'Please record this song or I'll shoot you.' My favourite all-time song is the old tune 'Greensleeves,' and in England I used to live just a little ways from Windsor Castle. I was always up there just looking at the place. We wanted to record a song about castles and crossbows, and I was pleased that we were able to keep that hard rock thing within a classical mode. This is what our music is all about, really, Henry the VIII and all his friends."

Adds Ronnie, "We did 'Black Sheep of the Family' as just a session, but when we needed another song, that's when we wrote 'Sixteenth Century Greensleeves.' That was on the road, in Minneapolis, when Ritchie called me over to his hotel and asked me if I could write something, and I wrote it that night and we recorded it the next day. And that became 'Sixteenth Century Greensleeves,' which then led Ritchie to the conviction that he didn't want to be in Purple anymore, that he wanted to do something with us. It's again, a story; I like to write stories. They're hard to write, because you don't have a lot of time to flesh everything out, in a song. But if you're good enough, you can, I guess. But the song came about because Ritchie wanted to do something, and play 'Greensleeves' before it, in a live setting. Before we had written the song, he loved 'Greensleeves.'"

Ronnie is referring to what is an English folk song with origins back to 1580. The finished hard rock song does not borrow at all from the original's instantly recognizable melody.

Qualifies Ritchie, "We didn't want to call it 'Greensleeves,' otherwise people would think it was the old 'Greensleeves,' which was written by Henry the VIII. It's been often put down as an anonymous, but it has been traced back that he wrote it. He was a very accomplished musician."

"We had no title at all," remembers Ronnie. "It happened to be one of those kind of songs that had to tell a story, me being a lyricist, and in that particular case the melody-writer of the songs. We finished it off and I tell a particular story about a medieval concept of a lady who was taken away by the black knight and so on and so forth. We had no title and at the very end of it we said, 'Fantastic song but what do we call it?' 'Oh God, I don't know.' And Ritchie said, 'Can we put "Greensleeves" in it somewhere?' And I said, 'That's already been done; someone already wrote that song once.' And he said, 'What about "Sixteenth Century Greensleeves?"' Great idea. So at one point in the song—I don't know how many people know this—but you hear way in the distance, only one time, a little line being shouted by me saying '16th century greensleeves' and so from that we took the title."

"But that music led me right away to that medieval period," figures Dio. "And the perspective I put it in was, there was a horrible man who had done horrible things to his subjects, and the last thing he did was he went ahead and kidnapped a young maiden from the village that everyone loved and was very young and very pure, and locked her up in a tower. And the people finally revolt and they get their pitchforks out and they go after him and they get him. And they do it before it happens to someone else. So it's the age-old story, a revolt against tyranny, but I just put it into those kinds of passages that in my mind... you know, torches and pitchforks and scythes and things like that, attacking the bulwark of the evil prince's place. That's what I thought (laughs)."

Evidently the guys thought Ronnie's classic proto-power metal lyric was good enough to feature on the back cover of the album, with none of the rest of the record's lyrics being presented anywhere within the packaging.

"It's funny, Martin," reflects Craig, "because if you listen to the last Elf album, which is called *Trying to Burn the Sun*, there's a song on there called 'Wonderworld,' and the lyrics are kind of leaning towards where Rainbow was going at the time, and we didn't even know we were going to become Rainbow. In fact, we wrote a song on tour with Deep Purple called 'Sixteenth Century Greensleeves,' and we recorded it on the road, in America, in a $500 studio, and it ended up being the first cut for Ritchie's solo album, which is all Rainbow was going to be intently in the very beginning. So yeah, we wrote that song backstage on the Deep Purple *Stormbringer* tour, and that song, 'Sixteenth Century Greensleeves,' literally defined the direction of the band."

Craig makes a couple of good points there. "Wonderworld" indeed reads like a set of rough notes for images found across Rainbow's first three albums, but also across Ronnie's work on his two Black Sabbath albums in the '80s and then the Dio band material. Also, he reinforces this idea that, really, of anything on this record, it is only this track and "Man on the Silver Mountain" that could have held their own on *Rising* or *Long Live Rock 'n' Roll*. Interesting as well that Uriah Heep had a record called *Wonderworld* released just a year earlier.

Craig has nothing but praise for Ronnie as a lyricist, confirming that no one else from the band contributed in that department. "No, we did not, Ronnie mastered that. And he just had an absolute knack for lyrical content and melody. We totally left that to him, and he's an absolute genius of a person, the sweetest person you'll ever meet in your life, a gentleman all the way through. Ronnie absolutely mastered the direction as far as lyrics goes, as well as vocal melodies."

Pushed for where his own stamp can be heard, Gruber relents with, "I don't take much credit for things, obviously—I'm a pretty humble guy—but when it comes to rhythm, the rhythm section of the band, I'm a very big Free fan, you know, the original band Free with Paul Rodgers, prior to Bad Company. And if you listen to that kind of push that they had, that natural kind of a push feel, it's a groove. If you listen to 'Fire and Water,' any of those early Free songs, I just encompass them. Plus I grew up listening to Motown. So I'm kind of a pushing, funk, R&B bass player with metal overtones to it. In fact, Ronnie called me Metal Motown— that was his nickname for me, which was cool. But me and the drummer, Gary Driscoll, we really formed that push feel, that deep kind of 'Catch the Rainbow,' 'Man on the Silver Mountain,' 'Sixteenth Century Greensleeves' feel. So I'm going to take a little bit of credit for the actual direction of the rhythm section of that band. But that's where it came from, Martin, was the influence of the band Free."

Again, a perceptive point, the type that can be sensed best from the inside. What Craig is describing contributes to the fusion effect felt throughout the record, also felt within the PAL band, both The Ian Gillan Band and the very early "Gillan" band material, as well as Judas Priest's *Sin After Sin*, due to the presence of teenage powerhouse Simon Phillips on the drums. This would be wiped away, along with the entire rhythm section, once we get to *Rising*.

Craig reiterates that what we get with this record is, logically, a combination of Deep Purple and Elf, and even an Elf already influenced by Deep Purple.

"Yeah, it was. I mean, it was a natural transition, again, coming from Deep Purple, the influence we had touring with them for those three years straight. You play 150 to 170 nights a year, that's just going to get drummed into your head. And the image of Purple and how they carried themselves offstage, they were superstars. They had their own 707 jet plane which we shared with them called The Starship, and man, when we landed, it was like the president's landing or something. The power of that band was just amazing."

"But lyrically speaking, you know, Ritchie has always embodied that 'Greensleeves' kind of influence, with the 'crossbows in the firelight' and stuff (laughs). Ritchie is a very, very interesting individual, and extremely adept and very well read, and so was Ronnie. Ronnie, I mean, I would see him reading medieval books and truthfully, I swear, that's where those images come from. You just can't conjure those things up in your mind.

It's got to come from some type of background, from history, and Ronnie was a reader of that material. And I know that he knew that that was Ritchie's thing too. Ritchie was unhappy with the direction of Deep Purple. Purple is essentially a blues band; it really is. If you listen to the chord changes, it's really a metal blues band. But Dave Coverdale, who is a beautiful guy, and Glenn Hughes also, they weren't lending themselves to that vein of music, and that's really why Purple ended. Ritchie had every intention of going on in that medieval field of lyrics and melody, and they absolutely refused to play it."

In his roundabout way, Craig is saying that the type of very European and essentially historical-type melodies that he wanted to apply to hard rock required a certain type of similarly medieval or Renaissance or fantasy lyrical matter up top. He's also implying that not only were the new guys in Purple not going to stand for "Kashmir"- or Black Sabbath-styled heavy metal at the musical end, but they weren't going to write about mystical pursuits either. In fact, David Coverdale had told me once that the song "Stormbringer," which robustly checked off both boxes, was a bone thrown to Ritchie to placate him.

Closing the record is a funky, overhauled rendition of the Yardbirds' "Still I'm Sad," which of course, evokes images of Purple classic "You Fool No One" from *Burn*, more so given that bits of the former had shown up in live renditions of the latter. Ritchie bends his neck around this one from the word go, while Gary Driscoll accompanies the boss with an endless barrage of cowbell.

"Yes," laughs Craig, "Ritchie definitely loved the early Yardbirds and the British electric blues with John Mayall. He loved John Mayall and the Bluesbreakers and Alexis Korner and was influenced by them greatly. He never said too much about Jimmy Page, other than great guitar player, obviously. Maybe they were like adversaries. But how could you not think Jimmy Page was great?" And he loved Jeff Beck as well as Paul Samwell-Smith. We were actually going to put a vocal line on there, come up with a vocal line. Ronnie kind of hummed along with it, but eventually Ritchie just said, 'Listen, this is so strong, this melody is so strong; I think if we put this kind of a beat to it, a kind of Deep Purple-ish beat underneath it… let's see if it's strong enough to support itself.' And it was. And it was a real nice change-up for the album too, I think."

And that was it. The first Rainbow album, in composite, blew no one away, and in fact, was oddly small-ish, even quite cheery at times, definitely disjointed, no surprise given that Ritchie had affirmed that it was no more than a collection of ideas he had had dating back as far as three years earlier. And despite the funky confusion of the album and the same feeling mirrored in Rainbow's newly minted fans, *Ritchie Blackmore's Rainbow* was an instant (but modest) hit, rising to #11 in the UK charts and #30 in America.

Touring for the record was not extensive, spanning only two months all over North America. The first Rainbow gig took place in Montreal on November 10th, 1975, the band drawing 1500 curious onlookers, a mere one-tenth capacity at the Forum, granted here converted into downsized "concert bowl" configuration. This took place after four East Coast US dates needed to be rescheduled, the band delaying the start of the tour simply because they weren't ready, either musically or with respect to the stage gear.

In fact, notable to the most perceptive in the crowd that night in Montreal, three of five members of the band were brand-new. Keyboardist Mickey Lee Soule was gone, replaced by Tony Carey. Drummer Gary Driscoll was gone, replaced by Cozy Powell. As well, an unknown Scottish bassist by the name of Jimmy Bain—veteran of Street Noise and Harlot, not to mention an odd spell hanging out in Vancouver, BC—had replaced sort of third in command Craig Gruber, who had never gotten over the near complete swallowing up of his group Elf.

The newly invigorated Rainbow Mk II played mostly theatres, supported by the likes of Argent and UFO, who would feature prominently in future Rainbow touring history. The tour was less than a month long, and outside the first show in Canada, the band only played the States, with some shows cancelled due to low ticket sales. Often the band was referred to as Blackmore's Rainbow, sometimes as Ritchie Blackmore's Rainbow, sometimes as Rainbow. Occasionally there'd be pictures of the old band, but then again Cozy would sometimes get mentioned in billing notices, as would Ronnie.

"You know, I don't remember us ever cancelling any shows," opines Dio, when asked about Ritchie's reputation for blowing off gigs, or at least parts of them. "I mean, if we cancelled, it wouldn't be for the reason that Ritchie didn't want to do the show, or didn't feel good or whatever. I never experienced that. As far as encores go, Ritchie had his own platform that he dealt with. If he didn't feel that the audience didn't deserve one, then he wouldn't do one. If he felt that something happened that day that really pissed him off, he perhaps just wouldn't do one. He was his own person and he was the leader of the band, so whatever he did, he did."

"Sure, there were times he didn't do encores, but what are you going to do? 'Hey Ritchie, you asshole.' You know, we got to that point a couple times, and he would just say, 'Yeah, I know' (laughs). 'You know who I am.' 'You're the most unprofessional person we've ever known.' 'Yeah, I know.' What's your response to that?! Okay. You either want to play with him or you don't. But it was his decision to make; it was Ritchie's band. He had his own good reasons for not doing that and I would never go back to him and say, 'I'm pissed-off because you wouldn't do the encore.' It's your band, man. Without you, this never would've taken off like this."

"You know, you learn things along the way," continues Ronnie. "I mean, I would not do an encore if the audience didn't deserve it—of course I wouldn't. What the hell? Why bother? And there have been nights where I haven't. That's because you feel that you're at your best, and you'd done the best you could, and there was just no response at all. That's not the audience's fault. They didn't like you, I guess. But you know yourself whether you deserve the response or whether they deserve one. It's mainly when an audience sits on their hands throughout the entire show, until the last song, and then go, 'We want more! We want more!' No you don't. You didn't want more when we started and you're sure as hell not going to get more now."

Further adding to the shows' occasional bad vibrations was Ritchie's guitar-smashing. "He got to the point where he started breaking them up every night. Expensive proposition, but they weren't top-of-the-line guitars anyway. So he had to spend some money to do it, but it was the effect, and Ritchie was a great showman. He knew what worked for himself and it was something people started to expect from him. And I think that after a while he stopped doing it because they did expect it from him!"

"I mean, they expected him to be dressed all in black—that's why he wore white shoes. They expected him to have a black guitar and that's why he played a white one. Everyone was playing Gibsons; well, Ritchie played a Fender. He just wanted to be his own person. And he was. And a very spectacular one as well. But yeah, he stopped doing it. I think we did it on the first two tours. I think he smashed them up pretty much, and then after that he kind of wound down and he just couldn't deal with it anymore (laughs). I mean, that's a pretty physical thing he had to do every night, spinning the thing around, swinging it around his head. Plus the fact that a couple people got hurt. So it just made sense not to do it anymore."

Besides Ritchie's essentially moody dramatics, Rainbow had another firecracker up their collective sleeves, and that was the massive, stage-spanning rainbow, built at a cost of £40,000, standing 29 feet tall, 40 feet across and four feet deep, lit from the inside by 3000 lights. In four readily distinguishable parts, the monster prop was based on a wooden version Ritchie took a fancy to at California Jam back in 1974.

"Initially it was my idea to have a rainbow," explained Ritchie, "because I did a thing called the California Jam which had a kind of fake rainbow behind us and that gave me an idea. I thought that looked quite nice. Then I forgot about it. And then we formed this band and with the name I naturally thought about, well, a rainbow would look nice above our heads with the lightning scaffold on the rainbow. Then we thought we should have an LP. So we made the LP and it started going from there, really."

The rainbow, built by See Factory in New York, took six months to make. Invariably such an albatross caused headaches, most notably electrical interference due to its huge draw, but it would live on for eternity, pressed firmly to mind by its presence on the cover of Rainbow's *On Stage* live album from 1977. Also on stage, there was a Rainbow logo, depicted in the gothic lettering that would carry over to the next record cover, and a backdrop image of the first record's album cover, namely the guitar-shaped castle. Cozy had his two bass drums with his name across them in the same gothic font now being used for the band name logo.

Songs from the first album played live were "Sixteenth Century Greensleeves," "Self Portrait," "Catch the Rainbow," Man on the Silver Mountain" and "Still I'm Sad." Surprisingly, there were no Deep Purple selections, nor did the band play the song that started the whole idea, "Black Sheep of the Family." What is eminently more notable is that in the short time between the new guys joining in the summer of '75 and the start of the tour in November, they'd managed to cook up and place within their set "Do You Close Your Eyes," "A Light in the Black" and "Stargazer," the latter two regarded as two of the greatest heavy metal songs of all time, soon to be on an album considered one of the greatest heavy metal albums of all time.

Chapter 3

Rising
"And he said so be it."

"The second one, Rainbow *Rising*," answers Ritchie, emphatically when asked to pick his favourite record of the varied, eventful Rainbow catalogue. "We had 'Stargazer' on it, and 'Stargazer,' I felt, was very reflective of where we were trying to go, with the orchestra playing away, and I think it was a good riff. And Ronnie sang extremely well. I think there are only nine tracks on it. And we were still having fun, whereas for the next one we started getting a little bit tired of each other. So it would have to be *Rising*."

Amusingly, in a separate chat with Ritchie (quoted later), he told me "There are only seven tracks on it," whereas, of course, *Rising* only holds six! I almost anticipate his throwing me a new total in the next chat I have with him, at which case, it will be confirmed that Ritchie was only amusing himself at the expense of a tiring journalist…

In any event, tallies aside, *Rising* is in fact, far and away the fan favourite as well. In a book of mine from way back in 2004, *The Top 500 Heavy Metal Albums of All Time*, a huge fan poll placed it at 39th—Rainbow did quite well in general, with *Long Live Rock 'n' Roll* taking #84, *On Stage* at #401 and *Down to Earth* at #487.

Even *Rising*'s symmetry is legion—four tracks on side one, and two on side two. Its cover is iconoclastic and anchoring, its critical emotional mass singular and steeped in a sense of confident, workmanlike mission. In fact the confidence that emanates from the record—and even, if you please, its black-and-white photography—is near Zeppelin-esque.

As alluded to in our last chapter, *Rising* would mark a changeover of more than half the Rainbow lineup, with only Ritchie and Ronnie remaining from the first album, the result representing what most fans would call the ultimate Rainbow configuration.

Explains the now departing Craig Gruber, "When the album was completed, we all went back to the States, obviously. Ronnie and I and Elf, we were all living in New York at the time. The label and everybody had decided, hey, this is going to be a super historic band. Whether you know it or not, it's probably going to be the next Deep Purple and probably bigger. You probably all need to get to the West Coast because Ritchie is there in Oxnard and find some houses and let's put this thing together."

"So we did—about two months later we relocated to Los Angeles and got some houses in Malibu. Ritchie was living in Oxnard which was about 30 miles west of us, which was great. And we got into rehearsal. The drummer, Gary Driscoll from Elf, was an incredible drummer and really had a great feel, but he tended to overplay a little bit. And Ritchie liked eighths and sixteenths, if you will, eighth notes and sixteenth notes, very clean, concise beats. And anything other than eighths and sixteenths, you're going to get that death ray. He looks at you like, 'What are you doing?' Gary modelled himself a lot after John Bonham, and John Bonham is a pretty busy drummer. Incredible drummer, but did a lot with the foot and the bass drum. Anyway, Ritchie wanted a clean, concise, Cozy Powell beat, which is what he ended up with. Eighth and sixteenths on one and four, whereas Gary consistently overplayed."

"Now I in turn," continues Gruber, "I'm half of it—I played along with him. Although I cleaned up my parts quite a bit, because Ronnie said, 'Listen, you're kind of overplaying the parts, you guys. It's just not… you need to open it up a little bit and play on the beat.' And we did. But through the rehearsals, it just wasn't locking in—it just wasn't. Gary and I were so wrapped-up in doing what we were doing. It worked in Elf and it worked in the studio for Rainbow and the album came out incredible, but when we got into rehearsals it just wasn't locking in."

"So they let Gary go, which broke his heart, and really upset Ronnie incredibly. Because Ronnie and Gary had worked together already incredibly for ten years, with Elf. So Gary was let go, very disheartened, and they brought in Cozy Powell. I love Cozy, incredible drummer. And then him and I *really* overplayed, because at that point he came from the Jeff Beck Group. And talk about overplaying—I mean, I'm a pretty good bass player, and when he did those double bass rolls and monster fills, I went along with him."

"So all of a sudden the rhythm section turned into a freight train—holy shit. And Ritchie went crazy: 'No, this isn't going to work.' So I was the next in line. 'We really need you to play straight parts, Craig. We talked to you about this in the past.' And I said, 'Look, I know where you're coming from, but if you're going to tell me what to play, I'm in the wrong band.' And he said so be it. And I said, 'Huh? Maybe I misspoke.' So we got into it, and I picked up my Fender Precision bass and threw it about 30 yards in the air and it split when it hit the ground. And Ritchie threw his Strat down. Now, Ronnie looked around, and Ronnie was the most incredible ambassador, if you will, as far as keeping bands together. I said some foul words. I was frustrated about being put in my place all the time and I just said, 'Look, it's better that I leave at this point, because sooner or later, Mickey Lee will be gone too.' And of course that happened too."

Rainbow's new 28-year-old drummer Colin Trevor Flooks, a.k.a. Cozy Powell, was a known though not famous entity, having caught Ritchie's ear through his work on Jeff Beck's *Rough and Ready* album. Cozy would record two records with Beck, and then move on to heavy rock act Bedlam, who managed one quite decent album in 1973—his somewhat adjacent and equally hopeful vehicle called Big Bertha never recorded—before Powell was to find surprise success first as a session man, then with a series of singles, most notably "Dance with the Devil." But Powell would now stand to gain stature through three of the very best Rainbow albums, enhanced later through work with the Michael Schenker Group, Black Sabbath and Brian May, and then achieve even larger legendary status—unfortunately as these things go—by dying in a high-speed car wreck.

Juilliard-trained California virtuoso Tony Carey would distinguish himself first through this record's memorable synth lines, and in the mid '80s, as a prolific top-selling solo artist with hits such as 1982's "I Won't Be Home Tonight" and two years later, "Fine, Fine Day" and "First Day of Summer." Tony also had what amounted to a vastly under-rated modern-ish prog band called Planet P Project, who released a self-titled album in 1983, and the double concept album *Pink World* in 1984, which drew a few favourable comparisons to Pink Floyd's *The Wall*. Tony now has over 50 album credits to his name and is also a prolific producer.

Bassist Jimmy Bain, as we've said, an unknown entity entering Rainbow, would, post-Rainbow, build upon his ranking as part of the classic Rainbow lineup through his integral role as Ronnie James Dio's most ubiquitous co-worker and co-writer in the highly successful Dio franchise.

"Jimmy Bain was a wonderful human being," laughs Ritchie. "He's such a happy-go-lucky guy. The only thing I could say about Jim was that he used to pick his nose a lot. Excellent guy, really nice guy, and I can see why Ronnie keeps him around. He's a very positive fellow to have around."

That should read "kept him around." As we've discussed Ronnie is no longer with us, but Jimmy has passed on as well, dying on January 23rd, 2016 in his cabin on Def Leppard's Hysteria on the High Seas cruise. Bain had been battling pneumonia, but the cause of death was determined to be lung cancer. Whatever the specifics, hard living, including years of heroin use, must have contributed as well. Taking a moment to reflect, fully three of five members from each of the two records discussed in this book so far have now died. All that's left from the debut are Ritchie and Mickey, and all that are left from *Rising* are Ritchie and Tony. Of note, in 1996, Mickey became Jon Lord's keyboard tech, having since moved on to become Roger Glover's bass tech.

"It's actually a crazy story," recounts Jimmy Bain, on his joining Rainbow, in one of his interviews with the author. "When I was living in London I was living with a couple of guys, roadies, who were Scottish. One of them worked with Jethro Tull and the other one worked with Ritchie; he was with a band called Badfinger before that. He ended up working with Ritchie. His name was Fergie. Ritchie decided to leave Deep Purple and planned to put Rainbow together, and he did it with Ronnie and the guys from Elf. But he didn't really like the bass player at all so he was going to be the first to get replaced."

"So I got a call from this guy, Fergie, from LA, and I was in London; it was about three o'clock in the morning on Wednesday. And he said, 'Ritchie's looking for a bass player' and blah blah blah, and the next minute he hands the phone to Ritchie and he talks to me for about an hour. And he basically asked me when I was playing next. And I said, 'At the weekend.' We had a residency at the Marquee for about six Sunday nights. So he said, 'Well, I'll come over and check you out.' And I was going, 'Yeah, sure, sure.' You kind of think that there is no way that that is going to happen."

"On the Sunday when I went down to the bar, just down from the Marquee, I walked in and there was Blackmore, Ronnie Dio, their manager and Fergie, and a couple of other people that had flown over from LA to check me out. So my band unfortunately, the two guitar players couldn't play a note, and the drummer, you know, he just drank too much Guinness or something like that. The band just completely sucked, you know? And I thought, 'Oh, there we go, there's my big chance to get into something good.' But then Ritchie took me aside after, and I was apologizing because the band really didn't play very well, and he said, 'Well, they made you look really good.' And a couple of weeks later I was in LA and I had gotten the gig with Rainbow. And then later he threw out most of the other guys in the band and replaced them with Cozy and Tony Carey, and then we went and did Rainbow *Rising*."

The band became a bit of an international entity with the new hirings, explains Jimmy. "Yes, well, I was in London, Cozy was in London, and when I got the call, basically, Ritchie was in LA and Ronnie was living in LA, and we just kind of moved. I moved out first because I was the first one that got a place, and then Cozy came out from England. And he kept going back because his wife was there. I wasn't married, so I kind of stayed out for the entirety, for the whole of '75 and most of '76 when we were on the road. I went back to London in '77. Ronnie had met Wendy around the time we were rehearsing in LA for *Rising*. I believe that's when that happened there. I believe they got married shortly after I left the band, '77 or '78, something like that."

Asked about Ritchie's reasons for doing all this, especially beginning Rainbow in the first place, Jimmy says, "It's funny, when I was about to join Rainbow I went into Deep Purple's office and I met Tommy Bolin, who was in the office about to go to Germany to start rehearsing with Purple. I was very interested because I was a big fan of Tommy Bolin's. I listened to *Come Taste the Band*. I thought it was different; it didn't sound much like Deep Purple to me. It was more like something else all together, and you weren't quite sure their identity."

"But no, I believe Ritchie, for one thing he was fed up with splitting all the songs five ways. He had a deal in Purple where he had to, I guess, split all the songs with everybody. And as he was the main writer, I think he felt a little bit... like he had to do all the work and everybody else could just sit around and basically pick up their 20% for nothing. So he was a little peeved with that. I know that for a fact. Plus I think he wanted to broaden his horizons, and maybe musically try it with a different singer. I thought Purple were a great band as they were, but he obviously had ideas to do something maybe a bit more colourful. I thought that from the first rehearsals we had. He was definitely into getting a more raw sound than he had before. Purple had become a bit commercial, I think, so he wanted to get back to that sort of rough edge."

On the subject of Glenn and David bringing the funk and the soul, Bain chuckles and says, "Absolutely, Ritchie didn't like that much at all. I made the bad move of putting on the *Stormbringer* tape in the limo one time and he took it out and chucked it out of the window. He wasn't too taken with that record. I really liked *Stormbringer*; I thought it was a great record, but he didn't like that lineup. He didn't care for that period of Purple at all."

Concerning his own influences, Bain says, "John Paul Jones and Geddy Lee were my idols, can I say, as far as bass players went. Those were my two main influences, I guess. I always listened to what they did and got some vibe from them. It was great. But I wasn't particularly into heavy music. The band I was in, it was a good time rock 'n' roll band. It had a heavy edge to it, but it wasn't that heavy. But when the opportunity came to get a job playing with Ritchie Blackmore, it was a dream come true. It happened in such a phenomenal way and I just jumped at the chance to get in there with him."

As for his take on the Elf angle to all this, Jimmy figures, "As I understood it, from what I heard at the time, Purple and Elf had toured—Elf had supported—and Ritchie had spotted Ronnie and heard the voice and whatnot, and the first record, *Ritchie Blackmore's Rainbow*, he played with most of the guys from Elf, minus the guitar player. Ritchie's idea was always consciously to take Ronnie and get rid of the other guys in Elf as he could—it was his plan. He had sort of figured it out. Nobody knew at the time but that's what he wanted to do. So when I came along, I replaced the first guy who went, aside from the guitar player, Craig Gruber, the bass player. I kind of took his job. Ritchie managed to get rid of each guy individually. Mickey Lee Soule left before he could get fired, but the other guy, Driscoll, got fired. And it wasn't because he was a bad drummer or anything; I just think Ritchie had plans for a different lineup. More of an individual, each guy in each position kind of thing. I mean, Ronnie must have figured out at some point, too, what was going on. He didn't object because it was going to make a better band. He was always interested in the best possible lineup. So we went for it. We were all into it that way."

"But I was a big fan of Purple," continues Jimmy, who drives home why this was such a special opportunity for him. "Not only were they the most innovative as far as music was, they went to new areas. They went to new territories that hadn't been conquered by rock 'n' roll bands. They were so cool; they went to Japan. And when I went there in '76 with Rainbow, it was almost like Beatle-mania at the airport. I couldn't believe it. There were thousands of people at the airport just for us. I'd never seen anything like it for a band. I'd seen it on videos and stuff, but never experienced it myself personally—and it was Purple that had created that vibe. And then Ritchie carried on with Rainbow. But Purple were a very important band at that time when I got the call. I was thinking, well I'm in heaven here. I get to play with Blackmore and do music like that; it's going to be great. And it was—it turned out to be fantastic."

Offering more appreciation for Blackmore's past, Jimmy explains that with Purple, "Ian Paice was phenomenal, a very high quality and technical drummer, and Roger Glover was really solid but Ritchie was the key. He was the one who wrote the songs and had the sort of presence that everybody kind of thought was bizarre. He wouldn't go out and talk to journalists and he wouldn't go out with the record company. He created this mystique about himself that I don't think he did intentionally. But it worked for him, because he became the first one that was associated with being a little crazy, simply because he didn't talk to people and wasn't that public about everything. And that helped the band, too—they fed off that. Great singer, too, in Ian Gillan, while Jon Lord gave them depth. The whole combination of personalities plus the strength of the material made them very much my favourite band at the time. I liked Zeppelin as well, because they had a different style and they jammed too, which I liked a lot. But Purple were the heavier band, I think, of the two."

"And Ritchie was definitely the main writer, for whatever reason, just about the only writer besides Ian Gillan. He came up with just about everything, and you'd never know from the credits because everybody's name on it. But he was the one who came up with it, from what he told me, anyway—that was why he got pissed-off. Because he was having to come up with all the material and then split it with everybody. It wasn't that he was greedy or anything like that. He resented the fact that nobody else brought anything to the table when it came to doing records, and he was left to do it because they got used to that fact that he would come up with the song. He felt that they should have maybe tried harder to come up with some ideas. I guess when you're dealing with millions of dollars, depending on whether or not somebody does or doesn't write can become quite a thing in a band."

"So it was really great to work with the guy," continues Bain. "The way he wrote, the way he'd come up with ideas and we developed them was really interesting. And the way I would go about it myself, and did so afterwards too with Ronnie in Dio, we came up with ideas and we developed them very much the same way."

The recording of *Rising*, due to extensive preparatory machinations, ponderings, rehearsals and live runs, took a scant ten days. The band gathered, along with Martin Birch, in February of 1976 at Musicland in Munich, although, oddly, the Rolling Stones mobile was set up outside and used instead of the German studio's gear.

The landmark album, as it would come to be, opens with a classic synthesizer flourish from the fresh legs of Tony Carey. Its moody, mystical, swirling quality immediately sets the stage for this most medieval of metal records.

"Tony Carey—very talented guy; very talented," recalls Ritchie. "And I didn't realize what a good singer he was when he was in the band; he never sang. But he's got a really good voice (laughs). And he's a great keyboard player. But my problem with him was that he lacked discipline at the time he was in our band. I think he has it now and he's doing his own stuff and he's made some good records on his own. At the time, I remember, he did this one solo, just off the top of his head, very quickly, and luckily we kept it. He said, 'Let me have another go at that solo; I could do it all again. That's not a very good solo.' And I'm saying, 'I thought it was a great solo.' I said to the engineer, 'Whatever it is you do, don't lose that solo.' He said, 'I've got you.' And then we proceeded to record Tony for the next, I think, whole day, and all the solos didn't match up with that first one. I was so happy. That was on 'Tarot Woman.' I'm so happy we kept that solo, because he couldn't follow it."

"And sometimes I've done the same thing," continues Blackmore. "You're just playing around, fiddling, doing a sound check, and if the engineer is clever, he'll say, 'Just have a run-through and let me get the sound.' And of course you're relaxed and you do a spontaneous solo, which is always the best. And that's happened to me many a time. Sometimes I've stayed up all night, only doing solos, and the very first one at seven o'clock at night is better than the one at four in the morning."

"They called me the gunslinger," says Tony, alluding to the role carved out for him in the band. "Cozy came up with that and it stuck. Ritchie wanted me to be there not so much to play the songs. And I'm talking about in the studio, because onstage was different. Because in the studio he would play three or four guitar tracks. He wanted me to do something that was unusual, so like the Minimoog introduction to 'Tarot Woman,' or the unbelievably crazy Minimoog solo on 'Light in the Black.' That was his thing with keyboards, like a Miles Davis thing—just blow. He didn't care much for rhythm keyboards or anything like that because he pretty much had that covered."

Tony tells the story of his joining Rainbow. "I bumped into Ritchie and Jimmy at a rehearsal hall in LA. I was rehearsing with my band; I had a band that had just signed a big deal with ABC/Dunhill at the time, and the band was being produced by Gary Katz, Steely Dan's producer. And we had Steely Dan's... back when Jeff Porcaro was on drums; David Paitch played some piano. And it was fantastic, but we couldn't get the record finished. There was too much cocaine and pussy, really. We were in Hollywood, at the Chateau Marmont hotel for nine months, the hotel where John Belushi died. We were there for months and months and months, always rehearsing, at this pretty well-known Hollywood rehearsal studio complex."

"And they were looking for a keyboard player. Jimmy and Cozy and Ronnie were scouting for keyboard players, and Jimmy heard me, like, through the walls, I think. In the rehearsal room, playing with my band. And he thought, ooh, that would be a good keyboard player for us. And he asked me if I would like to audition. I mean, if he had asked me a month earlier, I would've said, 'No, I've got my band signed.' But things just weren't going well with the band. It didn't look as if the record would ever come out. And in fact, it never came out. So I said, 'Yeah, yeah, sure I'll audition with your band.'"

As for the name of the band, Tony says that it was Blessings, which amusingly recalls—see last chapter—what Ritchie had said about recording the song "Catch the Rainbow." "Yeah, like you get from God. But a completely obscure band. Like I said, we had a record deal but we never released anything. And then the band broke up, of course, because I left. And I think everybody was relieved, because we were almost a year in the studio and we had like three songs done. Too much cocaine. You've got to remember: 1974."

"I kind of helped get Tony the gig," explains Jimmy. "Because I was at a Led Zeppelin rehearsal at SIR and we were looking for a keyboard player, and I heard this guy play Minimoog, just wailing away, and I asked somebody who the guy was who was playing. And immediately Mick Hinton, who was Bonzo's roadie, went in and grabbed Tony and brought him out to where we were playing pool. 'Oh, here he is, Jimmy.' So I sort of asked Tony if he was into coming down and playing with the band. And he wanted to, and I just gave him the tip of playing as much Johann Sebastian Bach as he could, and just that was all I said. And he came down and did just that, and we found that he could trade off licks. Anything Ritchie played on guitar, in a trade-off situation, he could copy immediately and play on a Minimoog. So he was hired immediately, too, because of that. I mean Ritchie didn't like it too much because he could play everything that Ritchie could play, but he couldn't help but know that the guy had all the chops. He had all the necessary things for a keyboard player, plus a few more—he was just a great keyboard player."

Once *Rising* took shape, Jimmy could tell that this was something fresh with respect to the role of keyboards in metal.

"Definitely—that was another element, I think, that just hadn't been used in metal, that gave it that thickness. Ritchie could wail away with a heavy rhythm section and the keyboards just layered the sound so much. And with these big songs like 'Stargazer' it was a huge sound onstage, live. And Tony was the boy. A lot of people came after him that did the same thing, but he was the one who was the innovator, the first one who did it.

He was a great player, and not just organ player, but he was into his Mellotron and all the different keyboards at the time that were really good. He was right on top of it as far as the technical side."

And Tony Carey knew his Purple. "Yes, well, California Jam was in '74, and I saw Deep Purple and I saw Ritchie trash his guitar and I was a complete fan," chuckles Tony. "Remember, he threw all his cabinets into the crowd, as it were, and the explosion knocked Paice's glasses off and all that at California Jam. So before Rainbow I was aware of what was going on. But to that point I had been a country western-type player, which I more or less am today, except hobby-wise I do hard rock. The sign of the times there was that there was a lot of music in the air. There was Keith Emerson, fast on the Hammond, and there was Rick Wakeman, my personal favourite, fast Hammond and some moves on piano and some of the early string machines."

"And they all came from a classical background, especially Keith Emerson and Jon Lord, who was the master. He played these classical scales, but then I come from a completely different thing. I come from blues and jazz. And what clicked with me the first time I played with Cozy and Ritchie and Jimmy and Ronnie was that we were a really fast, jamming, improvisational blues band. And Ritchie came in with his Arabic scales and everything—great. Ronnie came in with his spooky thing—great. But basically we were a kick-ass rock 'n' roll band and without very much of the classical influence. Because, I mean, I couldn't play classical piano to save my life."

"So yes, I always saw Rainbow—after I joined it, I mean—as a hard progressive blues band. Okay, we had those Arabic touches in the music with 'Stargazer' and everything, and Ronnie sang about exotic fantasy-type themes, but still the music, Jimmy Bain and Cozy Powell and Ritchie and I, we would go on for hours, and I always thought of us as a hard blues band. Ritchie comes from the blues. He was a session musician in England before any of this happened, when he was a kid, and that all started around the John Mayall era. I produced a record for John Mayall a few years ago and we discussed this at length. It's funny how one thing falls into another. For instance, I always thought that Iron Maiden was a direct evolution from Rainbow, without a keyboard player. Anyway, for me we were a hard rock, progressive blues band."

I asked Tony if he found it hard packing up and heading off to Germany with these older longhairs, at such a young age. "No, hey, that was a piece of piss; I loved it. I mean, there are people in the world who get homesick and there are people that don't. And in 1979, I moved back to Germany, and I was over 20 years there, and I don't get homesick (laughs). Pretty much where I am is where the party is for me, you know? Depends what's going on. I stumbled into all kinds of production work in Germany, and got to produce great people, great German artists plus John Mayall, Eric Burdon, and I was always busy. I did a bunch of films, a bunch of TV series stuff. I kept busy, basically. That's the thing. Now, if I had been there two years and didn't have any work, or wasn't happy or busy or having any success, that would be another story. But I came in '79, and started recording a solo album in '80. In '82, Planet P Project came. 'Why Me?;' that was #1 on American radio. And I said, okay, I'll stay (laughs)."

So yes, Tony and his synthesizer wizardry gets to open the *Rising* record—alone for over a minute—after which the band reverse-fades into opening track "Tarot Woman," in most dramatic fashion, Tony continuing with his ornate texturing right up until Ronnie's slashing, triumphant opening lyric and beyond.

Says Ronnie somewhat dismissively (this is not Ronnie's favourite Rainbow album—more on that later), "I think Ritchie said to me one time, 'Why don't you write a song about a tarot reader?' And I went okay, and that song became 'Tarot Woman.'" Elsewhere, Ronnie elaborated that indeed, the tale is of a man being warned by the tarot reader that his girl is about to do him wrong, Ronnie quickly penning an early example of what will be a multitude of evil woman tracks throughout his career.

"All of them took shape in rehearsal," adds Tony, with respect to the *Rising* writing process. "Nothing was finished. Ritchie comes in with a lick and they all take shape in rehearsal. I'm not saying he didn't write them; I'm not saying I wrote them. It wasn't really an issue. It was his band completely. He was the star, I was a kid—I was 22. I didn't care. I never thought I wrote this or I wrote that or where's the publishing or anything like that. What I did say is, you know, 'I want a piece of these records.' Just as a player, not as a writer. Just a royalty from these records. 'Oh, of course, of course, of course, of course.' And it was the '70s and I got fucked. And you know, they kind of laughed at me, I guess, and I never saw a penny."

"I should have gotten writing credit on anything we ever played live," figures Tony. "If you've heard them, you'll know what I mean (laughs). But you know, that's not the way rock 'n' roll works, and that's really not the way rock 'n' roll in the '70s worked. I never got a penny for any of the Rainbow records I played on. On *Rising* I am credited in the way that my picture is there; I'm all over *Rising* and *On Stage*. I'm not credited for *Long Live Rock 'n' Roll*, and I played that too. But the way it worked was that we would go into rehearsals, and Ritchie would have his ten songs, and we'd learn them and we'd learn them and Ronnie would put lyrics to them. But you know... who wrote 'Tarot Woman?' Ritchie or me? The introduction anyway. Well, I wrote it. And who wrote the solo on 'Still I'm Sad' on the live album? Well, I wrote it, of course, because I played it on stage live, you know (laughs). But that's the thing. With Purple it was pretty much the same way. Somebody would come up with a riff. Even if it was Ritchie, it was always credited as five songwriters. Like, 'Smoke on the Water' is five songwriters, and so is 'Burn' and all of their hits. The whole band was credited and that kept the whole band happy, because the whole band had a lot to do and a lot to say about the sound and, within the limitations of an arrangement, played whatever the hell they felt like playing, on that night. And that's composition."

Somewhat a novel way of looking at songwriting credits, but there you go. Also interesting or obscure is Tony's take on how "classical" Rainbow at this juncture was. As pertains to himself, he says he was "just bluffing. I'm a self-taught keyboard player. I learned string bass in school and played in orchestras so I like classical music, but piano, I learned through boogie-woogie piano. I taught myself. As far as having any kind of repertoire? I know that Don Airey now plays real classical music—I don't; I never did. It's all a bluff (laughs). Ritchie would say, 'Play something churchy.' 'Okay, Ritchie.' I'd just do something. Actually what I don't like—and I don't want to be critical of anybody; Yngwie is a great guy—but I don't like this Paganini thing. For me it's either rock or classical. I'm not really interested in these intricate, very fast classical styles, like Bach-type scales. That doesn't really interest me. I think B.B. King can say as much or more with one note than most people can say with 150 notes played in two seconds."

Concerning the ramp-up to *Rising*, Carey says, "I know that Mickey Lee Soule works for Purple to this day. He was the keyboard player on the first one. I had heard 'Man on the Silver Mountain' on the radio—that was a radio hit I heard in LA before I met up with the guys. I know it was called Ritchie Blackmore's Rainbow and I didn't know there was an actual band. And there wasn't an actual band. Ritchie found Jimmy and he found Cozy and he found me last. And I know Ronnie and Ritchie wanted to make a live band, and the tone of the first Rainbow album, there's some classic material there, but it's like they hadn't started the engine yet."

"Elf toured with Purple," continues Tony, "and Ritchie, who has an amazing ear for good musicians, as a talent-spotter, he grabbed Ronnie. But it was a New York band. And the New York thing is different. I tried to fit in. When I say blues and soul, I don't mean blues and soul exactly, in the strict sense of the word. What I mean is improvisational music, put it that way. So in that sense, I could also say free jazz (laughs). And that's the thing—we would improvise for hours on end. And no, I'm not a funk player either. We laid down a power beat. Live, my job was to lay down chords for Ritchie to solo over and play the verse with him."

"But even with Ritchie, it's kind of fake classical. He plays great solos with interesting things but I mean Yngwie plays real classical. I know that. You ask him who's the best musician? He'll say Paganini or Bach or something. And Ritchie just kind of fools around with it. Everything he does is basically fooling around. He's very clever, very, very clever, and he just has a good time with all kinds of different stuff. Before he was in big bands I know he did a lot of studio stuff. He could play anything. He could play country western, he could play 'Greensleeves' and he could learn Beethoven's 'Ninth,' but we didn't do that in those days. Instead he did a solo on 'Stargazer' that was absolutely amazing, this Arabic scale with a slide guitar on a Stratocaster. I'd never heard anything like it. I used to look over, 'What are you doing?!'"

"But again, I don't play anything other than blues, first of all. Or sing anything that isn't blues or country. And that puts a pretty unique aspect on it. Okay, here it is. On 'Man on the Silver Mountain,' the typical keyboard that would accompany Ritchie would double his lick on the organ. I didn't. I did the Jimmy Smith thing and just held the chord and let him play and let the bass play. That gives it blues tension, and all my fills and little stuff I do, it's also just pure blues. I can only speak for my… I know Cozy can't talk about it any more, and unfortunately Ronnie can't either, and I don't know where Jim is, but it'd be interesting to hear Ritchie's take on it. But my take on it is we were a hard rocking blues band."

Concerning Ronnie's place in the band as a lyricist, Carey reminds us that "Ronnie was a lot older than anybody else… well no, not anybody, just a few years older than Ritchie, but a lot older than I was or than Jimmy was. By the time he'd died, he'd basically spent 50 years doing exactly what he wanted to do, or 55 years. He didn't do anything he didn't want to do, Ronnie. So by the time Rainbow started he was already 35 and he was a mature musician and he had his own voice; let me put it that way. He didn't need to write somebody else's idea of what a song was or fill this cliché or fill that spot. Ronnie built his audience. He was really the first to combine this tarot card sorcery, *Lord of the Rings*-type thing, the wizard flying over and then a fist coming out of the ocean grabbing a rainbow, this whole fantasy thing with hard rock. I mean that in itself, I never heard anybody doing that until that point."

"But don't think of him as just a lyricist," qualifies Tony, "because he was a songwriter. Ritchie comes with a riff, or later Tony Iommi comes with a riff, and Ronnie puts the melody to it—he writes the melody. So Ronnie's not just a poet. We'd have a bottom track and we'd say, 'Well, this is a hot song' or whatever. Ronnie would be off with his little legal tablet writing reams of probably very poetic but never heard stuff, and then he'd come in and put a melody to it that was shockingly good. In the case of Elton and Bernie, Bernie writes the lyrics, as the way I understand it, and Elton does all the melodies and the music and they're a great team. But Ronnie wrote his vocal melodies as well, and that's not to be forgotten. He didn't write poetry and set it to an existing song. He invented the song with Ritchie."

Concerning the subject matter itself—call it medieval, Renaissance, fantasy or occult, which all just makes it evergreen— Carey figures Ritchie actually had a lot to do with the thematic direction Dio explored.

"Ritchie for sure. Ritchie is for real, by the way. He's not kidding with his Blackmore's Night thing. In the '70s he used to lug a cello around. I don't think he could play it very well, but he wanted to learn it, and he had his top hat on. Ritchie was Blackmore's Night in 1974. And Ronnie, of course, his bell bottom pants and his outfits, he looked the part too. And they wrote 'Sixteenth Century Greensleeves,' so that was there from the very start when I came into the band. Live—very different from my role in the studio—my job in the band was actually to be a second guitar player—you either have a guitarist or an organist—to be someone who backed up Ritchie when he soloed, and then to like tease him to make him solo more (laughs). Actually, tickle him a little bit, like a traditional call and response blues thing. But the medieval theme was more Ritchie's and Ronnie's thing. That's what they wanted to do. I read a lot that people are surprised that Ritchie is doing Blackmore's Night. He was absolutely in exactly the same place 35 years ago as he is now. That's what he always wanted to do—you could tell."

Tony also remembers the acoustic guitar Ritchie would cart around. "This is a great story, because he would take it without a case and everybody would be afraid to break it. It was a nylon-stringed acoustic, and it would come off the baggage ramp with all these big huge flight cases, this lonely little guitar. And it never got broken, even though, especially in the '70s, they used to throw luggage around and break everything, and everything had to be in big huge flight cases. And Ritchie's lonely acoustic guitar would come down and it would be intact."

"But no, in the '70s each band had a vibe. Led Zeppelin was there and Pink Floyd was there and they all had this spooky presence about them in one direction or another. Led Zeppelin was more Renaissance than anybody else at the time. They were kind of folky and then all of a sudden they had their heavy metal, heavy rock. And Pink Floyd were on Jupiter somewhere and then *Wish You Were Here* came out and it was just wonderful. So definitely, each of these bands had a vibe. Rainbow's vibe was castles and dragons and wizards. Ronnie thought it out. He was there with a yellow legal pad and we would be playing and he would be sitting there writing books that turned into his lyrics. Personally, we didn't talk medieval, but there was a lot of interesting sorcery and witchcraft and séances and all that."

"Actually Ronnie eventually got fed up with it," continues Tony. "All of a sudden there was this intense screaming pressure, during the *Long Live Rock 'n Roll* era, calling up the spirits and all this stuff. So he played the game until he didn't like it (laughs), put it that way. As did I. I left in the middle of that recording. It just got too wacky. I tell you what, I'm a musician, I like to play music, and everything peripheral to that like séances… I think you quoted me saying, 'Booze and girls, you do that in the eighth grade,' do you remember that? It's the same thing as with séances—do it on your own time. I'm here to play music, and to rock. That's how I felt when I was 22 and I think that now. It eventually got too much to take. I just booked a plane and left, actually without saying goodbye."

Jimmy similarly thinks Ronnie was partially following Ritchie's lead. "It started out with what Ritchie wanted. He got into that medieval thing because Ritchie liked that. But then I think he found a niche in there that he liked himself, and he enjoyed dealing with the supernatural and the mythical aspect. It was easier for him to write about than real life. He didn't write a lot of love songs, Ron, you know (laughs). It was easier for him to write lyrically about these subjects rather than the present day."

"And I don't think he believed it," continues Bain. "He's very much a believer in what he sees, and anything else is pretty much imagination to him. He didn't buy into the séances or any of that kind of shit. He was just too earthy for that. But he understood Ritchie real well in terms of what Ritchie wanted to see lyrically, and just slotted himself right in on that. He was very much into getting the feel that Ritchie wanted for a song. They didn't really discuss it so much, but Ronnie always seemed to come up with the right topics to write about in each of the songs, and there was never any disagreement about what direction he was going, because he always kept it right on the mark where Ritchie wanted it to be. He was always happy, Ritchie, with what Ronnie was doing; there was no doubt about it. Everybody just walked around with smiles on their faces at the recording sessions. It was just like this is really cool. I'm not sure why they fit, but they did fit, and it worked out great. It was just magical. For that record, it was the right songs and the right lyrics in the songs too—and good timing all around, I guess, on our part."

Second track on the *Rising* album, "Run with the Wolf," upheld the record's spooky mood, Cozy pounding out a plodding backbeat that, in conjunction with Martin Birch's boomy yet dry drum mix, evokes images of the big bashing of John Bonham. And as with certain Bonham methods, the drums had been set up in an echoey hallway, with a wooden shelter built over them to add to the bleed. Powell's groove is felt most richly and fully on the song's passion-filled chorus.

"Just a song about werewolves, really," offers Ronnie. "About that really dark... I probably saw a movie with Lon Chaney and saw werewolves somewhere and said, hey, that's cool. And obviously it fit the feel of the song as well. Which is how I usually write. The rhythm is there, and it inspires me to do something like that. I'm sure it was probably the music that first inspired me to write what I did, and 'Run with the Wolf' seemed to be apropos. We were a little more *Beowulf*-ish at that time anyway."

It's telling that Ronnie says "the rhythm is there." Indeed, many consider the musical heart of Rainbow to be, first, of course, Ritchie, but second, Cozy Powell. And it's true that Cozy had a certain style, centred around hitting the drums hard (and this despite holding his sticks traditional grip) and his double bass drum work, Cozy being one of the early practitioners in that field. But it can't be said Cozy had much of a groove. His timekeeping was technically accurate, but songs from that era moved a bit awkwardly. As well, much of Cozy's "sound," as alluded to, is down to the way Martin Birch recorded him.

And that ain't all good either—yes, there's a certain raw quality, but all told, *Rising* and *Long Live Rock 'n' Roll* also sound one-dimensional, cardboard-like, midrange-y, noisy, lacking in richness, parched, in the same way that almost every Led Zeppelin production seems parched. So yes, this is also part and parcel of the Cozy Powell sound. Of course, thankfully, all this got chucked out the window in a live setting, where Cozy shone and got very busy indeed, pounding out a note-dense barrage to the '1812 Overture,' choreographing the thing, lights and all, taking the art of the drum solo to new creative places.

Remarks Carey on Cozy, addressing this idea of getting him to switch over from Jeff Beck mode to more of a straight-line four-on-the-floor approach, "I never discussed that with him, but Cozy was so hard-headed. I mean, he was a really stubborn and hard-headed guy, that it would be hard to imagine anybody moving Cozy from one mindset to any other. Ritchie and Jeff are completely different. I mean, they're not anything alike. Jeff Beck plays with his fingers with enormous dynamics, and at that time Ritchie was playing through a 200-watt Marshall with a pick, and was really quick and clever. So the Jeff Beck Group and Ritchie Blackmore's group... a good musician fits in where the job is, you know? And I think that was more instinctive than anything. All of this stuff is more instinctive than having a discussion saying we're going to be spooky and we're going to be about dragons and wizards and Cozy, you're going to play four-on-the-floor and Jimmy, you're going to be the crazy Scotsman and Tony, you're going to invent a Moog sound. None of that was discussed. It just happened."

"Cozy... he had a belt—and this was before 9/11 of course—he had this belt that the belt buckle turned into this unbelievably lethal weapon. I couldn't believe it. And he had snakeskin boots and one knife in each boot. And he had his belt and we would go through airports and nobody would stop him. It was the old days."

Chocolate fanatic too. "I was actually not aware that he was a chocolate fanatic; maybe that was later. But he liked Silk Cut cigarettes. He wouldn't smoke anything else than Silk Cut. They had to fly them over from England."

And what to make of Martin Birch? As discussed, *Rising* is weirdly boxy-sounding, but then again so is *Physical Graffiti* and *Presence*. So were the Ted Nugent and Blue Öyster Cult records at the time. However *Sabotage* and more so, certainly, Aerosmith's *Rocks*... man, these records crap on *Rising*'s tones, frequencies and dynamics from a height of several miles.

"Martin was a fabulous producer and a fabulous engineer," says Tony, a unanimous assessment across approximately two or three dozen folks I've personally interviewed with regard to Birch, pertinently pointing to other necessary qualities in a producer beyond quality and quantity of bass. "He was easygoing too. I mean, he could put up with any amount of bullshit from any musician in any condition (laughs). He was cool, calm and collected and was like a team captain. Everybody would look up to him."

"When we went to Musicland Studios in Munich—which is how I got to know Germany, where I live—to do *Rising*, he wasn't satisfied with this typical '70s dry drum room, where they had rugs on the walls and everything like Abbey Road. So they smashed into a storeroom and made this concrete and tile room for Cozy—actually tore down the wall—and that's where that drum sound came from. And then Martin put the mics up and we had this unbelievable drum sound."

"But no, he was just a helping hand. The way the band would record is that Ritchie, Jimmy and Cozy would do the bottom track, and then I would do keyboards and overdubs and then there were the solos. Ritchie said, 'I'll be back in two hours to do a solo.' And then when *I* did solos, I said, 'Go away for two hours. I want to do a solo.' And then he would just let me use my imagination. I did actually two long introductions for the record. One of them didn't make the cut. There was also one for 'Stargazer,' not just 'Tarot Woman.'"

"Martin's a very astute guy," adds Jimmy, also asked about the mysterious Martin Birch. "He's worked with all kinds of different people. When people were getting a little edgy and stuff about trying to get something right or the orchestra wasn't working out, Martin brought this calmness to the whole thing. He was very experienced and you could tell he knew what he was doing and knew his way around the board better than most people. He just had that confidence that you knew you were going to get the best from him at every point."

And Martin was dealing with a band that had attitude. "Exactly," says Bain. "I was definitely aware of that, but first off I was so pleased to get myself in a band with a couple of people that actually had a name. I mean, Rainbow *Rising* was the first album I did, my first actual recording, so I was over the moon. And to go out to LA was blowing my mind. I walked around with a big smile on my face from ear to ear the entire summer that I was here at first. But in terms of that attitude, I did think there was a lack of really big bands with a big attitude that wanted to play in big venues. The Rainbow guys didn't want to play in shit little clubs. That was the attitude the band had, and pretty well that's kind of where it went too. We wanted to play in front of a lot of people and we enjoyed playing in front of a lot of people. That's what we were sort of told we should be doing and that's what we did."

Ironically, all of this was talking place at the same studio locale where Ritchie's nemesis Ian Gillan had just been floundering away on one of his ill-conceived Ian Gillan band albums, *Child in Time*. Jimmy remembers Ian being there, and that Deep Purple not too long previous had just finished *Come Taste the Band* there. He also says that, "We

went out to this go-kart club and rehearsed every day and wrote the whole album out there. We were staying at the hotel and then when it comes time to record, you just go down to the basement. It came together very quickly. Ritchie just took it to the next level, I thought. He played some solos that I'd never heard on a Purple record. He pulled out all the stops. He seemed to be really happy at the time and I think that helped. He was in a great studio, great place, he loved Germany, so everything was exactly the way he wanted it. And I think that's where you get the best from people, if you give them the atmosphere and the area they like to be in. He loved it there."

Back to the record at hand, "Starstruck" rocks and rollicks into view next, the track introduced with a bit of a Celtic run, before becoming somewhat of a modern metal blues shuffle— moat metal Foghat as it were. Again Cozy punctuates often and fills ornately, even occasionally using double bass patterns in a fill role. Ritchie's solo is classic, snaky, meandering, medieval and melodic, yet somehow modest if you like, serving the song.

"'Starstruck' was a song I certainly remember," reflects Ronnie, "because it was written about a real person, a girl who used to follow Ritchie around a lot. I think her name was Miriam (most earlier interviews have her as Muriel). And she followed Ritchie everywhere. She was from Paris. She would always be at the front of the stage and she would, at times, turn up at his house in England. She'd be in the garden somewhere and frighten the life out of him. He'd be walking his dog and she'd pop out from behind a bush. So it was a really heavy-duty relationship, I guess, heavy stalking. So I wrote that song about her and Ritchie."

"I found a girl in my garden once," confirms Ritchie (speaking with the press back in the '80s), on Ronnie's portrayal of the story. "I saw the bushes move and a little head popped up. It was a French girl of 18 who somehow followed me to England. I set the dogs on her. They're friendly dogs; they just jumped into the bushes and she came out screaming. It was strange how she found my house. She went around touching the walls, caressing the house."

Next, closing side one, "Do You Close Your Eyes" is the only party rocker on the album, the band pertly turning in a melodic foot-stomper built on time-honoured, pregnant-pausing chord patterns, save for the slightly baroque and fully successful, song-making pre-chorus and chorus sequence. Noted Ritchie in Circus, "I've been told by several people that it should be the single. It's got that hook that the postman can whistle as he does his rounds. It's a very simple rock tune that the public will take to, although it's not wholly representative of where the band is at. Then again, side two is comprised of two nine-minute tracks, and I'm not sure that this is where the band is at either."

"'Do You Close Your Eyes,' well, we needed something fast," says Ronnie. "And I decided to write that song about asking the question, well, when you're copulating, do you close your eyes? Simply that. I thought it was probably clever and it worked all right. The song was okay." Asked whether it was meant to lighten the album up at all, Ronnie replies, "No, not really. It's just what I felt like writing at the time, and I didn't get any opposition to it. But no, it wasn't meant to make levity of any part of it at all."

Out on the press trail for *Rising* back in 1976, Ronnie was asked by Circus' Scott Cohen to pontificate over his creative process. "It's usually a very long one," opined Dio. "It depends on what you've been doing recently. After being on the road for so long, and in the studios, you get damn well sick of doing anything musical; you want to get away from it. Like not wanting to take the bus if you're a bus driver on your holiday. You kinda have to get yourself in the state of mind to write. You have to say, 'Get off your ass and back to work.'"

"And then as soon as I go into my den, where I have all my gear set up, I put on headphones, put on my guitar and my tape recorder, and just wail away for hours. It starts with a little germ of an idea, and I'll lay it down on the tape recorder. Then I'll go and watch television for a day and then come back and pick up on that idea again. From the time I know I have to start writing until the time the song should be finished, it usually takes about six months. I'll tell you, this is really weird. I've always found that I've written my best songs while watching sports programs—football, basketball, anything that doesn't have music in it. Anything that has a constant bantering of words for some reason suits me. Sports soothes me. I'll watch any kind of sport, from ping-pong to chair throwing."

"I've always considered people in bands to be not unlike athletes," continued Ronnie. "Usually I use it kind of like a football team. I would consider a lead guitar player, especially one of Ritchie's calibre, as quarterback, although there are some bands where the lead guitar player doesn't take command of the band, and I would equate them with a wide receiver possibly or a really brilliant running back. I would equate the drummer to be fullback, because he's the crux of the offense, and I don't think you can think of a band being a defence unit. I think the singer, if he was going to be the one in charge of the band, would be quarterback as well, or else he could be the wide receiver. The lead singer and the guitar player are more of the glamour parts of the band. The bass player would have to be some kind of lineman, maybe the center, and the keyboard player would have to be maybe a tight end, or, if he plays synthesizer as ours does, could be the rest of the line."

In the same interview, Ritchie commented on one of his strengths, namely his rock-solid timing. "I was brought up on a metronome, so I always notice if someone's playing slightly fast or slightly slow. It's very important because when people dance to a record or listen to you, they don't know you're speeding up or playing slower. All they know is that something's wrong."

Cohen then asks if an affinity for numbers play a role as well. "Yeah, they have their place," mused Ritchie. "I won't stay in a room that adds up to 13, like if the number of the room is 607. I noticed it when I went down with hepatitis. Two weeks before I went down with it, I wasn't feeling too well, and did notice the numbers on my door. I tended to add them up because I was bored, and I noticed that in nearly every hotel where I stayed, I got a room that added up to 13. So the next tour... I'm very suspicious by nature; my mother taught me all that because she had a lot of gypsy friends. I can't cut my nails on Sunday, I won't cross anybody on the stairs, I won't... there are so many incredible things. I won't wear green on stage, whistle backstage, go out on Sundays, there's a million of them. I always believe in being prepared. That's why I never get too drunk. What I don't like is when people pull guns on me. I'm not too keen on that. Whenever I sit somewhere, I always sit with my back to the wall so nobody can come up behind me. And at night, I always sleep with various kinds of implements around my bed. If anyone broke into my house, they'd get a shock as to what they would find. I'm always on guard because I'm suspicious by nature."

Asked if there was a particularly productive place where he found that his creativity flowed, Ritchie offered, "Yeah, in cars and especially in planes. The altitude for some reason gives me... but I never have a guitar around to write. But I always get good ideas on long distance flights."

Cohen also looked at Blackmore as live performer, wondering if, on stage, Ritchie's fingers had a mind of their own. "No. When they do, that's when I play badly. As soon as the head has stopped controlling, you're in trouble. The head has to be in a good position and you have to be completely oblivious to your surroundings, which I am. Usually if I play well on stage, I could be anywhere. You can say that I astral project when I'm playing well. I'll go into all the corners of the actual theatre I'm playing in."

Back in the present day (and on an earthly plane), when asked by the author about memories of this first side of *Rising*, Ritchie is somewhat nonplussed... "Not particularly. I just felt that they were songs we made up on the spur of the moment. And I never had anything to do with lyrics in those days, so I can't even say what it's about. For me, it's just basic riffs put together at the last minute."

After side one's solid—if apparently spontaneously conceived—quartet of songs, the band open up for two eight-minute master blasters, the first languid and plush, the second panicked and manic.

"Stargazer" is quintessential Rainbow in every sense. The lyric is all Ronnie and Ronnie's superhuman concerns, Dio telling the saga of a people trying to come to terms with the death of their wizard. Just like the debut presented in the packaging one lyric only, so did *Rising*, the band printing the full "Stargazer" lyrics within the gatefold, to the right of the posed band portrait.

Clarifying the gist of the "Stargazer" story in conversation with Jon Tiven, Ronnie said that, "'Stargazer' is written from the standpoint of a slave in Egyptian times. He is serving The Wizard, who observes the skies and stars and becomes obsessed with the idea of flying. The slaves are building a tower of stone so The Wizard can jump off the top and take to the air. Finally this Wizard, this Stargazer, attempts to fly and, of course, falls to his death. The slaves are released, and this is where the song 'Stargazer' ends and 'Light in the Black' begins. The Wizard has died and the slaves are free, but all they've known all their lives is an allegiance to the Stargazer. They don't know where to turn or what to do until they see the 'light in the dark.'" It might be implied that Ronnie, an avowed atheist, is warning about people thinking their "gods" have special powers.

Adds Blackmore, "'Stargazer' features a 42-piece orchestra, Mellotrons and a string thing all playing this half Turkish scale. This is my favourite track of the lot. Then there's 'Light in the Black,' very fast rock 'n' roll, about nine minutes of madness and solos. The drums are heavy-sounding; in fact they are all through the album."

The music to "Stargazer" is panoramic and squarely Zeppelin-esque. "Yes, it was very influenced by 'Kashmir,'" answers Ritchie, point blank, when confronted with the possibility. "And I don't think there was any competition because Page was so big. Especially over here in the US; he was like a giant. When I first came across him in '75 I didn't realize how big Led Zeppelin was. In Europe, they were big, but we were probably holding our own against them in Europe. But over here, nobody came near. They were the band. They were the American band. Led Zeppelin—nobody was in their class as far as popularity went. So there wasn't any competition because he was too far upfront."

"I just remember that I wrote 'Stargazer' on the cello, the riff," continues Ritchie. "Because I was beginning to learn the cello. And it's amazing; if you take up another instrument, you start thinking differently about scales. You don't go for the obvious scales, the comfortable scales, you go for some other notes. I found it interesting that the chromatic... the run-ups, Ronnie Dio wrote the instrumental run-up, the ascending riff, which is unusual for a singer to do. But he just sang it, and the keyboard player worked it out. So that was refreshing, to have someone help with the writing."

"Ronnie used to play trumpet, so he knew. That's why he could sing... that's why you'll never hear him go flat or hit the wrong notes, because he knows how to improvise on the trumpet. I do remember the 'Stargazer' session; we ran out of tape. We had this gypsy violinist playing, and at the end there should have been like a minute fade-out of gypsy violin playing. And he started playing and we ran out of tape. And he did this amazing solo, which is not on tape. So that was a little bit annoying, that we'd actually been so silly as to record near the end of the tape. Because in those days of 24-track tape, analogue... and we literally ran out of tape and the spool was spinning around as this guy was playing this amazing gypsy solo, which should have gone on the end. But I mean, the rest of it worked. And he came in to hear this solo. He said, 'Oh, how did I do?' And we all felt very embarrassed to say, 'It was a great solo, but the tape ran out.'"

Past and future co-worker of Ritchie's, Roger Glover, still looks upon *Rising*, and in particular 'Stargazer,' as a pillar of Rainbow's career. "I think the era of Rainbow that really contributed most was the era before I had joined the band. After I joined them, I joined them with the specific brief to commercialize the band and sell more records—otherwise it was going to fold. So I think the real cult era of Rainbow was the first two or three records, Rainbow *Rising* in particular."

"I remember when Ritchie... funnily enough, despite our past, I didn't sort of hold that grunge against Ritchie. When I bumped into him in around 1976 in Musicland Studios, I hadn't seen him since I left the band in 1973, and it was, 'Hey, how are you doing? What's up?' And he said, 'I just finished the album; let me play you this.' And he took me into the control room and he played me 'Stargazer' and I've got to say it blew me away. It absolutely blew me away. I thought it was brilliant. And I think that kind of... I don't know, classical influence there, somewhat dark, gothic sound, monks going aah aah aah... I don't think I had heard that much of it before. So I think Ritchie's really got a lot to answer for there. That's really his direction."

Parallel to a point made earlier, in another book of mine, *Riff Raff: The Top 250 Heavy Metal Songs of the '70s*, "Stargazer" ranked #4, by fans polled around the world. "Kill the King" ranked #23, with "Gates of Babylon" at #29. "Man on the Silver Mountain," "A Light in the Black" and "Tarot Woman" also made the top 100. One can only conclude that *Rising* was like *Montrose*—an album moderately underground at the time that grew in resonance as its brilliance sunk in, across generation after generation.

Indeed "Stargazer" is renowned as a classic example of foundational metal at its most sweeping and panoramic, one of the cornerstones of today's huge power metal movement. Opening with a tornado of drums from Cozy, the song then settles in for a long, phase-shifted voyage through shifting dunes, the band crafting a folk song in the here and now that is as old as time itself. Passages build upon past passages, all the while Cozy driving the song with one of the most memorable performances of his distinguished career, even as it's one of his most languid.

"I'm now giving the drums all the power I should have done two years ago," explained Cozy, in conversation with Chris Welch back in '76. "With Jeff Beck it was impossible to whack the hell out of the drums because it wasn't that sort of a band. Now I'm in a band where I can do what I want to do, and unleash the power! They say Ritchie is a difficult man to work with, and he is at times. But he leaves me alone and lets me get on with it, which suits me. He's very demanding; he knows exactly what he wants and won't settle for anything less. Jeff Beck, on the other hand, brilliant guitar player—very difficult to know what he's thinking. You can expect to know what's going on in a guy's head, so consequently it's very difficult to play with him. Some nights would be great and other nights he'd just go off on a tangent and it was very hard to keep up. All guitar players are prone to that."

But with Ritchie, "We've got on very well since the band started," said Powell. "But I hate to think what will happen when we do have an argument. No, he s been very good. He more or less lets me have a free hand. I like it this way. It's nice to work with someone as good as Ritchie, and good for me to get back into it again after being off for a while. The first time we went into the rehearsal room in LA I went bananas. We just blasted away for two hours. And then it all fell into place. Ritchie had tried some English and American guys and basically they were all frightened of him. I'm not frightened of anybody and just went and steamed in. Exactly the same story with Jeff. I went down to the audition, and there were literally 25 drummers all there with the kit that was supplied. 'Is it my turn now?' Tapping away very lightly. I thought, 'Sod all this,' slung the kit out, got mine in and sat right in front and said, 'Right, you wanna play? Let s play.' You've gotta be a bit arrogant if you're a drummer. You've gotta give 'em a kick up the ass."

"It was the same with Ritchie. With a heavy rock guitar player, you know they want a hard, solid foundation. If they don't get that, you're wasting their time. But you still have to pace yourself, which is very difficult in our show. It's an hour-and-a-half of torture! Yeah, it's painful all right. My hands are really suffering. I've drawn blood many times. John Bonham is of the same ilk and I lived in Birmingham for a while and met my wife there. I got to know John and Robert really well. John and I are probably the only two drummers in England who play in that style. I like him because he doesn't play too many fills but when he does, it means something."

Significant in the metal world without a doubt, "Stargazer" had even greater resonance inside the band, with Tony explaining that, "When Ronnie sings, 'I see a rainbow rising' in 'Stargazer,' at that point we didn't have an album title. It didn't start off, 'We're going to do an album called *Rising*.' And then Ronnie sings, 'I see a rainbow rising' and one thing leads to another and another and we've got the cover of this fist coming out of the ocean and grabbing the rainbow, which I thought was great graphics, such a great graphic thing. And then inside, there's just a full-page spread of the band, just a black-and-white picture, taken by Fin Costello if I'm not mistaken. But that cover, I don't even think there was a plan B. I never saw any alternatives to it. It's the only cover I ever saw."

The *Rising* cover was painted by Ken Kelly, famous also for *Destroyer* and *Love Gun* by Kiss, Conan the Barbarian and myriad other fantasy works used in book and film, plus his depictions of impossibly rippling muscles on covers for Manowar. Ritchie recalls that the fist holding the rainbow was difficult for Kelly to get right, having gone through about seven renditions.

Back to "Stargazer" and its links with Zeppelin, Jimmy says, "I know that 'Stargazer' lent itself a bit to 'Kashmir' but Ritchie only listens to two things: Jethro Tull and Bach, unless he heard something on the radio. And if you played anything else in his company he would take it out of the player and throw it out the window. I mean, he was pretty radical like that. And we actually did a couple shows with Jethro Tull in the States during that period, and he jumped at the chance to play with them. We were supporting them kind of thing. So he wasn't looking to anything in particular, other than at this point he was into being heavy and heavy was good. He was enjoying the freedom of being away from Deep Purple and having other people contribute to the writing. It was nice to have Ronnie in there to do lyrics, and we all contributed a bit to the arrangement and music stuff as well."

"'Kashmir' was definitely an influence on 'Stargazer,'" agrees Tony. "Of course it was. As a matter of fact, I met Robert and John Bonham in the rehearsal studio, and they'd just come back from Morocco, and they both had auto accidents that summer. Bonzo had a broken leg and a broken arm, and he still played mean drums (laughs). Him on drums, with two casts, like a full body cast-type of thing, he was playing with his feet and one hand, and Boz Burrell played bass and I played organ. Crazy days."

Carey also agrees that the band chipped in on the music, specifically remarking on Ronnie, that, "Of course he did, because Ritchie is a riff writer and, well, Ronnie wrote the melodies. Listen, if I give you a riff, if I give you 'Man on the Silver Mountain' with a four-piece backup, you just have a piece of music. It's potentially a great piece of music, but a shitty lyric or a boring melody will ruin it. Or 'Stargazer.' And so very, very definitely, Ronnie contributed. I mentioned Elton John and Bernie Taupin, but in rock bands, the guitar player will put the riff down and the band will work out an arrangement. But it's up to the singer to come up with the melodies, the actual melodies. That's what makes a great singer. I mean, nobody could have told Robert Plant how to sing that early, really wild, folky, Lilith Fair-type, whatever, Renaissance music they were doing. That came out of pure cloth, and he channelled it from somewhere, as did Ronnie."

Asked about the orchestra on "Stargazer," Tony comments that, "These days I do that in five minutes on any synthesizer. You know, you get these orchestra guys in a rock studio, especially back then, and they're all sawing away at their violins and they're all looking at the clock and want to go home. Basically what they played was really easy; I don't imagine it was much of a big deal. I mean, it probably looked like a great album credit, but we had all gone home. Martin did that, I guess, with Ritchie, maybe with Ronnie too. But I was already back in LA. Don't overrate that. It's not like we stood there in a room with a hundred enchanted musicians. I know what session guys are like from classical organ shows. All they want is their pay checks. They read their music, and it's very, very simple. It worked well—don't misunderstand me—but it wasn't a magical concert."

Rising winds to a close with a quick cinch of the knot, "Light in the Black"—provisionally entitled "Comin' Home"—being a proto-speed metal innovator that, ironically, takes 8:12 to do its dirty work. Ronnie, again, has little to say in the song's defence. "Well, I just didn't... I thought, well, what am I doing here? I guess I have to sing some words here to cover this up, to lead to whatever else is going on. You know, if I had more time to think about it, I probably wouldn't have done it that way. But that's just the way it came out. They'll never go down as being my favourite lyrics on earth. They just filled a need."

Ronnie's curiously flippant attitude is illuminated by his remarks on the *Rising* experience as a whole. "I think that Rainbow *Rising*, although that's always looked upon as being the masterpiece, really, you know, one side of that whole album, was... 'Stargazer' was fine, but 'Light in the Black' wasn't my favourite thing to do. That was more of an exercise for the musicians, and that's cool, that's great, that's wonderful, and I thought they played brilliantly. But as a vocalist, you kind of feel out of the loop a little bit. So I look at that whole album and say, well, I was on the first side, and half of the second side, and not very much of the other part. So it just seems to me that there were better songs on the first album, although there were some good ones on the second one."

"But I think the first one always pleased me because of that," counters Dio. "I mean, I was involved on the writing on all of the *Rising* songs all the way through and I thought the first album blew the hell out of the other one. I thought the second one was amateurish and looking up people's asses, to tell you the truth. I thought the first album was populated with great songs, and, like I say, the second album was nothing but an exercise on side B for Ritchie and Cozy to do what they eventually did in the live shows, which was to relegate us to go behind the amps and have drinks and Ritchie to play a solo on every song, which he did on 'Stargazer' and 'Light in the Black,' and for Cozy to be what he wanted to be, which was a drummer who plays all by himself."

Conversely (and comically), Tony points to side two as the successful half of *Rising*.

"I remember playing those shorter songs, but that was the thing—they were so easy. We learned them in ten minutes and just did them, you know? Those weren't the important ones. The important ones for us were 'Stargazer' and 'Light in the Black.' 'Stargazer,' obviously, because it was right after 'Kashmir' and 'Light in the Black' because it really showed some soloing. There was keyboard soloing and amazing drums. Cozy had cool double bass drums going for 17 minutes or whatever it was (laughs). Unbelievable, the bass drum figure alone."

"And by the way, if I'd play 'Light in the Black,' and I was Cozy, and you said 'Good, Cozy, now can we try...' I would say fuck you (laughs), just like Cozy did. So he banged his way through that! And it was perfect rock 'n' roll. And if you didn't like it, the answer is, 'Get another drummer.' He used to throw drumsticks at me, but it was all good fun. It wasn't good fun; he was pissed, but I think he was a good enough shot that if he wanted to hit me, he could take my eye out. I would have drumsticks whizzing over my head. I think if he meant to hit me, he would've hit me. Like, 'Shut the fuck up,' you know?"

"'Light in the Black' was unbelievable," continues Carey. "We tried to play it live a few times. We *did* play it live a few times. But after 'Light in the Black,' Cozy was like a race horse that had run twice its length, twice its distance. It would just kill him. Here's a story. I didn't see Cozy's audition, but I saw him do this. Ritchie would say, 'Well, can you play this?' And he would start this amazingly fast shuffle, and he basically played 'til the drummer passed out, until the drummer just died. He would do this for like 20 minutes. And Cozy would do that double with both feet, for half an hour, at 130 DB, and so that's how he got the job (laughs). I mean, amazing energy. He's a wiry guy and he was a madman. He was a race car driver as well. He was hell-bent for leather, kind of a real cowboy, and with amazing energy. Now they play double bass drums with one pedal, on one drum."

"Double bass like that, yeah, maybe Cozy invented it, I don't know, but I'll tell you, today's master of it is Bobby Rondinelli, who later played with Rainbow. In fact, he wrote a book about it, *The Encyclopedia of Double Bass Drumming*. Bobby is amazing and he's got the same kind of power. I mean, double bass really drives a song. But the point is, the bass player has to really be clean at the bottom end. He can't play long notes, because it all gets mushy. You have to hear every click of each bass drum and you need to hear really short staccato bass notes. And Jimmy Bain was excellent in 'A Light in the Black.' Each duddle of the duddle duddle is a $1/16^{th}$ note, and that was Cozy with his bass drum. That's something I learned years later when trying to record other drummers and bass players, is how precise Jimmy and Cozy were together."

Jimmy agrees wholeheartedly with Tony's assessment of Powell.

"His energy was just absolutely phenomenal," begins Bain. "The guy's pedigree goes without saying, but the sheer fact that when we had auditioned drummers in LA, it was done very, very impersonally. We auditioned about ten drummers in LA, and we had a particular way of doing auditions. It was quite unique. Ritchie, we had set up in this huge soundstage—now SIR but it was called Pirate Sound before that—and we had our gear set up in such a way that the drummer would come in, he would set his gear up, we would be at the other end of the soundstage playing pool and we wouldn't say anything to the drummer."

"So the drummer would come in, set up, and we would let them warm up and then we'd come down and plug in. Me and Ritchie would start this really super-fast riff and that's basically how it started. The drummers, we'd try them playing for 20, 30 minutes, at which point if the drummer wasn't in shape he'd be falling off the drums or dropping sticks or whatever."

"At first, the drummer would kind of go, oh, okay, and he'd start playing. And he'd be fine for about ten minutes or 15 minutes or however long it took him to kind of tire or lose the tempo or something. About 25, 30 minutes later, it was very hard for somebody, unless they were completely fit and really on top of their instrument. They would kind of fall apart. And there was nothing really said. It would just all fall apart and the drummer would kind of go, oh, okay, again, and break down his drums and leave. And there was nothing really ever said. It was very impersonal, how it was done."

"Cozy came along, flew in from London, didn't go to the hotel, which we thought he would do. He came directly from the airport to the rehearsal. He changed into his wrestling outfit, this outfit that he would wear, the high-top Nikes and the tight pants and the T-shirt. He picked and put a drum kit together out of three or four kits that were there. When we came down he was rummaging around between three drum kits, putting his drum kit together from all these drum kits."

"Then he sat down at the drums and said, 'Okay, what do you want to do?' Ritchie did his normal fast riff. He played the riff for 35 minutes, and as soon as we were finished it, he was the first one who could actually complete the whole thing. Then immediately after we finished, Cozy goes into this super-fast double bass drum shuffle thing at an unbelievable tempo that almost made the first thing we had done sound slow. And we kind of turned around and looked at each other and went, 'Hmm, okay.' He just fucked us right up (laughs). So that was it."

"I mean, it was a case of, I think Cozy turned it around and really actually he auditioned Ritchie more than Ritchie auditioned him, kind of thing. He got the gig. I mean there was no doubt that the guy had stamina beyond anything that anybody else had brought to the table by miles, you know? It was night and day. And it was kind of funny, because he really did sort of turn the whole thing around and auditioned the band rather than they auditioned him. And that was the one thing the band didn't have at the time, was the oomph in the drumming. When Cozy came in, I just had the perfect partner for a rhythm section, because I just slotted right in with him and kept it simple and heavy and it was great."

Speaking of powerhouse drummers, "John Bonham came down, actually, to our rehearsals when we got Cozy, because Cozy and him were really great friends. So he came down and jammed with us. Robert Plant and Bonzo came down and played with us. Bad Company came down. A lot of bands came down and checked it out. There were a lot of visitors at that time."

Back to "A Light in the Black" and Cozy, Jimmy lauds the fact that Powell "really had the double bass thing down. He had that intensity with the double bass. He had these drum sticks, man, that were like baseball bats. They were so big. I mean I'd never seen drum sticks like that in my life. He hit the drums so hard. He was just a different kettle of fish, so solid and right on with tempo and everything. But he hit everything so hard. Some drummers that play heavy metal, they play quite lightly. You can tell, Martin, you're around them, you see them—they play very fast tempos and everything but they don't hit the drums that hard. I don't want to mention any names, but Cozy, if you were around his kit on stage even with all those amps, you could hear his drums. The air moved around where he played. It was just a great experience."

Another highlight of *Rising*'s climactic last track is Tony's soloing—Carey opens the album and he finishes it strong.

"'A Light in the Black' was this very quick Minimoog solo," recalls Tony. "I'd run my Minimoog through a guitar amplifier. It might've been the first time that was done, I don't know. But I said to Ritchie, 'What would you like here? Just a general idea before you go. Leave me here with Martin for two hours.' 'I don't know, something flashy.' I said okay. So I did what I did in an upper register. It actually started very similar to one of his guitar solos, through a guitar amplifier, on a Minimoog. And then he came back and said, 'Well I like it, it's cool, but why don't you play lower, way lower? In register, I mean.' I said, 'Okay give me an hour and come back.'"

"So I did it two musical octaves lower, and used the sweep knob on this Minimoog through a little guitar amplifier. And then he came back and I remember him saying, 'Oh, that's really good. You know, it's really good when somebody's creative.' Or some bullshit like that, with his English accent. So he liked it. Otherwise Ritchie never really had much to say."

"I didn't give it much thought. I mean, a Minimoog, if you just plug it in you get this Rick Wakeman sound which is a nice sound, and with Yes it fit perfectly. But Ritchie wanted to use synthesizers. The Minimoog then was an Arp Odyssey, and there wasn't much else on the market, and it just sounded too weedy and thin if you don't start the motor (laughs). But running it through a little guitar amplifier, all of a sudden, 'Where'd that come from? I'd never heard that sound before.' But it was in the air. It was the logical thing to do. We were an extremely energetic band! There was a power that the band could generate. Cozy was like a steamhammer. You had to stand next to him to experience what he was actually all about. He played tree trunks for drumsticks. And Ritchie of course wasn't shy either. And I was probably the loudest organ player—I still am—that I've ever heard."

"There was a lot of aggression in the band. Cozy Powell is an aggressive son of a bitch and Ritchie's passive aggressive. And I'm aggressive. And we wanted to play. We wanted to play fast and tough, and we did our best at it and there weren't really any weak links in our chain in the first live Rainbow lineup. I mean, everybody was really proficient at their thing. Cozy had the endurance to do it and I had the endurance to do it, and that was the vibe that was in the air. Let's rock, you know?"

And yet Tony reiterates that where Ritchie went with the vastly quieter Blackmore's Night is very much of a continuum. "Yes, I'll say it again: Ritchie was exactly the same Ritchie as he is now, but then he was doing what he wanted to do then, playing loud, quick, electric music, and now he's playing very, very clever acoustic music. But it's all the same roots. He was fascinated with castles, especially German castles and history in the Middle Ages and that hasn't changed. He used to lug a cello around. He used to play minstrel music and he'd say that was his favourite music. He meant it. He wasn't kidding."

"So if anybody thinks that Ritchie Blackmore is a poser, they're wrong. That's who he is and always was, which is important. I've read a lot of negative criticism about Blackmore's Night, from people who still live in the '70s (laughs), and it's just a logical natural extension of what he is. Just like Jon Lord went on to make wonderful classical records with orchestra. He was doing basically what he always did, mixing classical with rock beats, except he's got a real orchestra with him. And Ritchie is basically doing what he always did, playing his take on 16th century music, just in a different setting."

"He was born like 500 years too late, absolutely," chuckles Carey. "He thinks of himself as being in the 16th century. He'd walk around with his pilgrim hat or whatever he had. He'd dress up. In all his bands he'd dress up—he would always dress up in Deep Purple. Before that I guess he used to play with Screaming Lord Sutch and he wore a loin cloth or whatever. The point with Rainbow was I think he was like a kid in a toy shop. He found he could indulge that at 130 decibels, you know? And blow your socks off, like a kid with his first electric train. By the way, we *were* a 130DB band, and for those who don't know the term, that's too loud. And we *were* too loud. And then after Ritchie did all that, I guess he took it as far as he thought he could and now he's playing the same type of music but on authentic instruments, on lutes and acoustic guitar. But it's the same music and with the same thought process—when I hear him play, it's the same Ritchie."

Despite the long songs on *Rising*, the whole affair came in at a scant 33:43. "And we played it in about 40 minutes," chuckles Tony. "It went so amazingly fast. You get all five of us in the room and you turn on the motor and it would go. Rainbow *Rising* was done amazingly fast."

But the motor ran hot at times. "Yes, that was the trouble," remarks Jimmy, adding colour with respect to the band's fragile chemistry. "It was always the basic minimum amount that had to be done, and even at that, it was hard. We did it in Germany, and it was a lot of fun. Obviously because it was my first record, I was totally into it. But there were never any B-sides or any bonus tracks at that point. It was just 'Let's do this.' And I had no say in it, so I basically did what I was asked to do. During *Rising*, Ritchie and Ronnie were pretty happy with each other. Ritchie was definitely happy with Ronnie's vocals, having done the first album. He was happy with Ronnie, who had a really down-to-earth personality. And Ronnie could handle doing a bunch of interviews, which Ritchie didn't really like doing. He had this image of not talking to the press and he worked on that really hard. So Ronnie could sort of answer questions and was very personable. In essence Ronnie's lyrics are probably what he loved as much as anything about Ronnie."

But then eventually that wasn't enough. Ritchie and Ronnie would soon butt heads (or their egos would). And then Ritchie's patience with everybody else would wear thin as well. Almost comically, Tony—a mere keyboardist!—and Cozy (even lower on the food chain—a drummer), would find themselves up against Ritchie and his Blackmore-given right to be a petulant artist. Jimmy was another story—he was just too stoned.

But back to the music, Tony, less sure than Jimmy, is non-committal concerning whether there would have been any extra material left over from his time with the band.

"The only one who would know that would be Martin Birch. You never knew when he was recording, and we played a lot. So having said that, I really don't know about outtakes. Martin Birch would know, or Ritchie would know. I was just the keyboard player and they'd say, 'Let's play this now' and I played it now. And I was also naive about the studio at that age. I couldn't tell you if the tape was running or not. I wouldn't have had any idea if he was recording or not recording or what he was doing. I learned about studio stuff in the '80s."

"I think it sucks," says a refreshingly blunt Tony, assessing the sum total of the *Rising* album, although, granted, it's an opinion of his laced with affection. "No, I don't like it. Yeah, I don't like it. But you know, it's 30 years later and I get fan mail from that record. No, I don't think it sucks, but it's very naive. Side two was like two songs, like mega-long solos, both for me and for Ritchie. I don't know if that's necessary to the song. I hated the lyrics; I didn't like the lyrics. But what people react to and the emotional response that *Rising* invokes in people is because of the power, and the power is there. It was a rocking fucking band, you know? In the studio and onstage. And that's what people respond to. They aren't going to criticize too many solos or Ronnie's lyrics, which might be a little weak. All this shit about wizards and dragons and my eyes are bleeding and all that shit."

Offering additional comment on producer Martin Birch, Tony says that, "Again, the best thing he did is that he threw everybody else out of the studio when somebody was doing a solo. That's Martin Birch. He's a completely cool guy, completely relaxed, completely easy. I haven't seen him in 30 years. I wish him well. Is he still alive? He was fabulous, such a nice sweetheart. And he was really good with me. I was the youngest, you know? And I wasn't nervous, but, on the opposite extreme, I was probably cocky. And if anybody would sit there and criticize my solos, I would say 'Fuck you—do it yourself' (laughs). Much cockier than I would be today. Martin would have the brains to say, 'Okay, Tony is going to do a solo. Everybody leave and come back in two hours and we'll play it for you.' Same with Ritchie. When Ritchie played his guitar solos, everybody would piss off and come back two hours later. And if there were any comments to be made, they'd make them then. But first of all, it was, 'Let the kid work.' And that was Martin's strong point as a producer. I thought he was really good one-on-one with musicians."

As to the degree of drinking and drugging during the sessions, Tony says, "In the sessions, nah, not really, but, Rainbow drank all the time. We were always drinking whiskey cola. Ritchie didn't take drugs, Ronnie didn't take drugs, I took drugs and Jimmy took drugs. But not in the sessions, nah; they were loose, you know, but we were there to work. But no, there was no one laying around drunk. The nights after a concert, that's another story. But in the studio it was actually fairly disciplined. For the *Rising* album, we rehearsed in some farmhouse about 20 miles out of Munich. I didn't know where it was then, but now I know exactly where it was, because I lived there for 25 years since (laughs). But we rehearsed at some farmhouse, some little inn. The German guy would serve us lunch at noon; he had a little restaurant. Otherwise we would just rehearse all day long and then after we did that for two weeks, we went into the studio for three weeks. So we were there to get it done."

In response to accusations pointed from time to time at Cozy for laziness, i.e. not wanting to do too many takes, Tony comments that, "He's not lazy. That's not lazy. That's a little bit like cocky, but certainly not lazy. Cozy was a drummer that, when he was alive, he played his heart out every time he played. He thought he played every take well, that that was the best he could do, at least, if not that year, then that day. He came out ready, he warmed up, he counted the song off, 1,2, 3,4, and then play it. And with Cozy, it was a real energetic style, a little bit like Keith Moon; not as wild as Keith Moon but a balls-out energetic drummer. But there is nothing to really criticize. I mean, what were you going to say to him? That you sped up a little bit here, or that you slowed down here? 'Yeah, of course I did—that's rock.' What are you going to criticize? I never noticed a problem with that. But sure, Cozy played one time, or maybe twice (laughs) with the whole band, and then we would keep Cozy basically, and fix the other stuff. But that's the way you do rock records anyway. The first thing you want is the drum track."

Adds Ritchie, "Cozy could be very opinionated. He had two sides to him. An incredibly nice guy who would make you a cup of cocoa and get the chocolates out or he was gunning for you like James Bond. Two extreme sides to Cozy."

Maybe becoming a bit dubious on Cozy, Blackmore came to be dubious on what they did together as well, summing up *Rising* years later for me this way. "'Stargazer' was an excellent track, but there again, there was some stuff on there that was a bit strange. The first record was good. The first one was just Ronnie and I, really. And the second one was more of a band."

And then Tony affirms that the Jimmy Bain who would blossom as a writer in Dio wasn't the Jimmy Bain you got with the *Rising* sessions. "Not at the time, not in those days—he didn't write. What he contributed was a band camaraderie, esprit de corp. He was the glue that held a lot of it together, because he was the one with a sense of humour (laughs). Ronnie and Ritchie and Cozy were really serious about everything. And Jimmy was kind of loose-y goose-y rock 'n' roll and I loved the kid. I really, really loved the kid."

"But as you know, after the *Rising* album, they fired Jimmy; Ritchie fired Jimmy. And Jimmy was really great for the band. He was a fabulous bass player and he knew just how to play with Ritchie, and he fired Jimmy and he hired Mark Clarke, who had played with, you know, The Hollies or something. He was not right for the band, not at all. Jimmy played a Gibson Thunderbird bass through about 5000 watts and was beautiful onstage, fantastic onstage, always smiling, always there, always solid. I really loved Jimmy Bain. I thought he was one of the greatest guys I'd ever met in the world."

Ultimately the importance of *Rising* in heavy metal history is not disputed, and yet surprisingly, the record never reached a certification level in the States, although it did go gold back in the UK. It peaked at a lowly #48 on Billboard, fairing better in Britain, reaching #11.

There's an interesting wrinkle to the crediting of the songs across the record. The record label (US issue) states "All selections written and arranged by Ritchie Blackmore and Ronnie Dio," implying a 50/50 split—more than generous, really, on Ritchie's part. But the gatefold specifies: "Music Written and Arranged— Blackmore/Dio" and "Lyrics—Ronnie James Dio," which implies something closer to a 75/25 split in favour of Ronnie. In either case, of course, Ritchie was putting himself out as a true team-mate and co-leader with Ronnie, albeit leaving the rest of the guys somewhat out to dry.

In any event, all five can be proud of contributing to a record that indisputably made heavy metal history, even if Tony fumbles to articulate the record's hold upon millions of rock fans the world over. "I can't. Because I can only look at that whole period of my life subjectively. Ask any music critic. He knows more about it than I do. I was just there. It went by real fast. We were a real shit-hot rock 'n' roll band and the idea was to get the songs done fast, which we did. What butterfly effect or whatever it had on the rest of the world, I have no idea."

Jimmy, who spent his life in heavy metal right up until the end, essentially dying while at a gig, understood all too well the appeal of *Rising*.

"It was actually heavy," begins Bain in his summation, stating the obvious, and yet a point that cannot be stressed enough. "It was one of the first heavy, heavy albums that came out. I mean there were so many cymbals in the goddamn thing, I thought people might be reticent to buy it. And there wasn't that much music on it. You know, six tracks isn't much to do on a record. But people are still coming up to me and telling me it changed their lives and shit like that. The first Ritchie album didn't get as much airplay, and I think when he got the band together with Cozy and me and Ronnie and Tony Carey, especially when we went out and played live, I think that helped a lot too, because we could play both records live really well. A lot of bands can't cut it when it comes to the live thing. We were out there just killing them with the live thing."

"With six tracks on the record," reflects Jimmy, "that's not a lot of songs, but judging by the popularity of the thing, it's stood the test of time. Everybody likes it to this day. It was exactly what people were looking for at the time. The timing was perfect for the band. We hit it right on the head as far as timing went, as far as the style went, the music, the whole vibe of the band. And we had Ronnie's voice, as well, which was not too shabby. I mean the guy, I'd never seen anybody perform like that—just phenomenal. He took it to another level, two or three levels higher than anybody else. And with the heaviness of the bass and drums and guitar and keyboards, his voice just slid right on top. It couldn't get any heavier, but he had the pipes to just sit right on top of that heaviness."

"But the main thing was the material. They were really hardcore songs. When they were written, they seemed to have that edge, and when we recorded them, they had an added nastiness that really good metal should have. It has that edge to it you get when everybody's playing flat-out. You got that in the recording, and of course you got that when the band played live as well. I loved it because it was the first record I made. I didn't know at the time, but it turned out to be a classic. Everything just seemed right. The right lineup, the right people playing and the best performances from everybody, even a great title."

"But yes, in particular, 'Stargazer' and 'A Light in the Black' were just heavier than anything that I'd heard up until that point, which just seemed to be right at the time. And I'm not sure if it was a conscious thing or whether it just happened that way, but we did retain that in the performance. If there was any lightness to the songs, they lost the lightness when we went into the studio and recorded them. It went bye-bye."

Ronnie victorious. © Rich Galbraith.

Portuguese issue of "Man on the Silver Mountain"/"Snake Charmer."

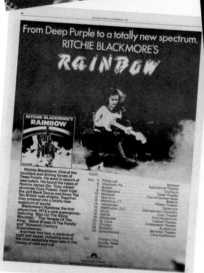

US ad for the debut with iconic gatefold live image.

Ritchie, white Strat and reel-to-reel. © Rich Galbraith.

Cozy Powell. © Rich Galbraith.

Ronnie James Dio, in fringe, like Oz; Oklahoma. © Rich Galbraith.

Ronnie James Dio and Bob Daisley, Tulsa, OK, July 7, 1978. © Rich Galbraith.

Ritchie looming over another guitar he's just killed. © Rich Galbraith.

Note the name of the band: Blackmore's Rainbow.

Ronnie, Shreveport, LA, July 22, 1978 (headliner was REO Speedwagon). © Rich Galbraith.

UK 7" live EP.

Ronnie and Bob, Shreveport. © Rich Galbraith.

Ritchie Blackmore, Cozy Powell and David Stone.
© Rich Galbraith.

Cozy's righteous drums, plus
two strummers. © Rich Galbraith.

Ronnie throws his shoulder into it.
© Rich Galbraith.

Ritchie, amused. © Rich Galbraith.

Bob Daisley, *Long Live Rock 'n' Roll* tour,
Shreveport. © Rich Galbraith.

On Stage ad from Melody Maker.

Canadian David Stone in action.
© Rich Galbraith.

Colour ad from Circus magazine.

Ronnie catching the rainbow. © Rich Galbraith.

Ritchie communicating with Shreveport.
© Rich Galbraith.

Bob Daisley and David Stone, Oklahoma
City, July 8, 1978. © Rich Galbraith.

Ritchie and his righteous platforms. © Rich Galbraith.

Chapter 4

On Stage

"You'd wake up to somebody axing your door down."

The *Rising* tour proper limped to a start in June of 1976 amidst various cancellations and other debacles, including a riot at a festival in Idaho when the money ran out. One such cancellation was a hiccup in the scheduling of the band with Thin Lizzy, a bill set up to put two struggling but promising acts on a ticket together.

"I think that was because Thin Lizzy were going to be on the bill with us, and Phil came down with hepatitis," recalls Ronnie. "In fact, I remember seeing him at this club here, The Rainbow, before the gigs. Ritchie and I were sitting at the table, and Phil came over and said, 'We're going to kick your asses all over the stage.' 'Oh, okay. Good for you, Phil.' (laughs). I liked Phil; he was a good lad. He meant it in a positive way. And the next day we were told he had hepatitis. So we all had to go out and get... what are they called, haemoglobin shots? Which was the worst part. We felt bad for Phil, but we felt bad for us too, because those needles hurt like hell and they give them to you right in the muscle. So we had to get those things, and I think that's why we had to cancel those gigs." Apparently both Scott Gorham and John Bonham were at the Rainbow to corroborate the story.

But the show went on at least for Rainbow, as they delivered songs from their two albums into late June and July across the States.

Support for Rainbow wasn't much of a constant either, with Max Webster, Angel, Gentle Giant, Moxy, Roy Buchanan, Savoy Brown, Don Harrison Band, Henry Gross, Man and Mahogany

Rush collared for the job, along with Rainbow backing up Jethro Tull and Blue Öyster Cult on occasion. The band was supported by Stretch in September of '76 in the UK. A September 8th concert at the Hammersmith Odeon was attended by Roger Glover, Ian Paice, David Coverdale and Jon Lord. AC/DC warmed the crowds up late September into October in mainland Europe while November dates in Australia saw support from legendary (and very collectible, with respect to their records) Oz heavyweights Buffalo. The tour wound up with an extensive jaunt through Japan.

By the time it was all done, the band would have their material for the *On Stage* live album, as well as tracks to be used years later on the *Live in Germany* release. *On Stage* would draw from shows played in Germany and in Japan exclusively, two markets that were massive for Deep Purple and proved to be friendly toward Rainbow as well.

Given how big double live albums were at the time, Rainbow and management sensibly thought they would throw their hat into the ring. Remember, this was the era of *Alive!*, *On Your Feet or on Your Knees*, *All the World's a Stage*, *Frampton Comes Alive!*, *Double Live! Gonzo!*, *Live and Dangerous* and *Strangers in the Night*, not to mention the much celebrated *Made in Japan* and *Made in Europe*, the latter being the lone restrained record in the bunch at only single-vinyl length.

And as with select bands from the above list, it was often considered premature to be making live albums, especially in this case, with Rainbow only having two studio records to its name at this juncture. In any event, here it came, big arcing Rainbow over the fragile band, a band that consisted of the same players who penned and played *Rising* and not that long ago. Compiled and edited (bluntly) in March of '77, *On Stage* (suggested title *Chase the Rainbow*) would see release four months hence, July 7th, 1977, rising to an impressive #7 in the UK charts and a more modest #65 in the US.

On Stage kicked off in explosive, exciting fashion, with a sample from *The Wizard of Oz* ("Toto, I have a feeling we're not in Kansas anymore. We must be over the rainbow") echoing off before "Kill the King," a fast, flashy, pure metal anthem that had yet to show up on a studio album. But first the band would briefly play live their patented "Somewhere Over the Rainbow" theme, and then ease into the song proper with a more melodic version of the song's classic intro, as portrayed next studio album out. It's a perfect concert-starter. In fact "Kill the King" (provisionally titled "Got to Get Away") was written, unsurprisingly, with the stage in mind.

Says Tony of "Kill the King," We didn't play it in the *Rising* sessions, but yeah, we had it, and by the time *Rising* was done, we really had it. It came just a little too late to be on the album. I know Ritchie and the way he thinks. He needs a real crack-'em-up starter song, and later, for years it was 'Spotlight Kid,' very, very up-tempo number. And he was very concerned at the start of the tour, 'What do we open with?' We don't want to do 'Speed King,' we're not going to do 'Highway Star,' what do we open with? So we wrote 'Kill the King.'"

And the rest of the album? A huge disappointment to this writer, with all those hot-clocking rockers from *Rising* ignored, save for a tossed-off "Starstruck." Indeed, "Do You Close Your Eyes" and "Stargazer" were highlights of the band's touring at the time, but instead we got a dreary 15-minute "Catch the Rainbow," tired, barely written Deep Purple blues "Mistreated" at 13 minutes, "Still I'm Sad" (a cover, albeit an appropriate one, melodically, for Rainbow) at 11 minutes, and then granted, the two key tracks from the debut, namely "Man on the Silver Mountain" and "Sixteenth Century Greensleeves." To add insult to injury, for a double album, it was actually quite short in duration (this offers a shred of mercy, I suppose).

From all angles the math is horrible to the point of career suicide. For all the internal concern that *Rising* only had six songs on it, well, *On Stage* is a double record with six songs. Two potential valid selections, "Man on the Silver Mountain" and "Starstruck," are diminished in importance by being part of a medley, mashed together with something called "Blues" no less. "Mistreated" is torture at any length, but here it gets an entire side; likewise "Catch the Rainbow." And the third longest song, at 11 minutes? It's both a cover *and* an instrumental. There have been some clueless live album set lists in the history rock 'n' roll, but *On Stage* has to take the prize for very worst of all time.

Explained Ritchie on playing "Mistreated," "It's one of my favourites. I was inspired by B.B. King to do that one. Not that I like B.B. King but I like the song, and it wasn't typical of what Deep Purple did. It was very guitar-orientated and there's actually no room for the organ. I thought it wasn't a song that represented Deep Purple. If we did 'Woman from Tokyo' or anything like that, that's just copying a Deep Purple song. But 'Mistreated' wasn't a Deep Purple song in my opinion. The lyrics were written by David Coverdale, but I mean there's not much to the vocal on it. It was just a guitar riff I had in my head."

In other words, because it's not a typical Deep Purple song (whatever that means, given the wide scope of that band's material), "Mistreated" got an exemption from the rule not to cover Deep Purple. Instead, as we go for a hot dog and a bathroom break, we can each—and for a long, long time—debate Ritchie's love/hate relationship with the blues.

Drawing the contours of Rainbow in a live setting, Ritchie says that, "We have two sides to this band. We have a clowning side and a very aggressive athletic side, a musical side against a laid-back just plain, havin' a good time side. It depends on the audiences just what we want to put across. Some nights we obviously do an encore. We'll be very aggressive and be more of a hard rock band. Sometimes we'll be laid-back, and that's what we do a lot in Japan because they want to listen. If we find an audience wants to listen, then we give them the material that's nice to listen to."

On Stage, therefore, on top of being built mostly from performances in Japan, must be the record Ritchie imagines the fans in Japan to prefer.

"It's no good thumping out God knows what if the audience has come to listen," continues Ritchie, on this curious theory, speaking of a show he had just finished in Australia. "Some audiences come to watch and you can always feel that within the first minute or ten seconds by seeing the audience. That's why tonight there was no breaking of guitars. It was just a very plain set, but I enjoyed it because it was different to most of the sets we've been doing in Europe. Europe was kinda hectic. I don't like to be predictable. I like to go from one extreme to another. The next time we play in Sydney, it'll be the complete opposite."

Further compromising these opinions, it's hard to believe hundreds of people at any given concert, from those pressed against the stage to those in the cheap seats, ever act with one consciousness. Being unappreciative (no encore) to wanting to hear 13 minutes of "Mistreated" (Japan?)… who does this? How could it possibly be that some "audiences" come to listen and some come to watch? Individuals, yes, hundreds of people in lockstep, no. And when does "come to listen" mean that you play the quiet songs, or that you jam, or both? Is "Tarot Woman" a song for seeing but not hearing? How do you know a certain crowd wants to see you smash a guitar and others don't? And again, how or why would a bunch of people who don't know each other suddenly think the same? Personally I never want to see Ritchie smash a guitar, unless he's threatening a 20-minute version of "Catch the Rainbow." Then I'd prefer they all smash their tools and go home so I can go home.

"Oh, I don't know, it depends what we're talking about," shrugs Tony Carey, on the subject of doing the short snappers versus the endless jams. "The thing is, you know, you hear them on record, some tinny little recording from the Budokan or whatever, and if you're not there, you don't have it, you know? But if you're there, and you're in the tenth row, and you're a kid, and these gods of rock are on stage blasting it out at you for 20 minutes, it's a different thing—it's the experience."

Oh really. So Tony is admitting long jams are no good on records, but somehow they are more enjoyable live. I would think that if something is enjoyable on record, it likely was more enjoyable live as well, versus, well, most of *On Stage*.

"Charlie Parker would play 20-minute songs too, but they weren't his records, really (laughs). They were his performances. His records were three minutes. But the thing is, I'll tell you one thing, a Rainbow show never lost energy; let me put it that way. People would go into a song excited, and at the end they would be just as excited as they were in the beginning. I think that's the way you judge it. You're playing for kids. In the '70s—I'll use this word loosely—virtuosity on an instrument wasn't even considered show-off-y; it was just something you did. There was always a drum solo, a bass solo. When was the last time you heard a bass solo? And you know, a long keyboard solo, a long guitar solo.

Everybody leaves the stage and the one cat sits and shows off. That was a uniquely '70s thing. And it doesn't happen anymore—thank God! (laughs)."

Yes, thank God. Even if Tony spends most of that championing the idea of the more boring bits the better, he ends it with a "thank God" that bass solos are over with. Go figure. Bottom line, Rainbow *On Stage* is why punk happened.

And this is indeed when it was happening, sure, as a reaction to progressive rock, but just as much as a reaction against bands that deemed their audiences unworthy of encores, because they apparently weren't listening.

"Nobody really noticed it, per se," comments Jimmy, on the punk craze that was forming around time the *Rising* tour was concluding. "Although we were all annoyed by it because it was, okay, if you're ugly and you can play a C chord on the guitar you'll get signed by a record company. That was the vibe at the time. I didn't care for it. It didn't do anything for me. The energy was good but that was about it. There was nothing subtle about it. It didn't last that long, so I didn't think it was that necessary. I like all kinds of music, but punk and rap I'm reticent to say anything good about them because I don't honestly care too much for them. But I'll put up with anything for five minutes."

Asked about bands he remembered playing with on those Rainbow bills, Tony recalls, "Well, we backed up Jethro Tull once, and that was fantastic. I was very impressed by Jethro Tull. We supported Heart in America; that was a mismatch (laughs). And AC/DC opened for us and that was with Bon Scott and they were still doing 'Whole Lotta Rosie;' that was their first hit. They would play, and I would watch them from backstage every night and I thought, they're going to be big. I guess we did the best in England and Europe. The crowds were absolutely crazy."

Famously Ritchie complained in the press about AC/DC, vehemently lamenting that they were destroying rock 'n' roll.

"Ritchie hated everybody. You can't put Ritchie and Ronnie in the same sentence. Ronnie is a typical East Coast American kid, and he talks typical East Coast American and he thought typical

East Coast American, which is a little bit like, you know, we're all in this together. There's not really a competition vibe in New York, among bands. There were millions and millions of bands but nobody is jealous when one of them makes it. You wished the competition the best. And Ritchie was pretty much jealous of everybody (laughs). But that's his insecurity at the time. I don't know, he's probably better now. You're only insecure if you're not sure how good you are. If you're scared of the competition, that means you're doubting yourself. Especially if you're headlining. Because people have paid their money to see you."

"I had everything you could have at the time," continues Tony, indulging in some gear talk. "I had three Mininoogs, which was the first monophonic synthesizer. And I had an Arp Odyssey string machine, which would make these beautiful strings sounds. I had something called a Polyphonic Orchestron, which was like a precursor to the laser disc, and it would make these crazy choir sounds, like Mellotron sounds, like the Moody Blues sounds, a little bit. And we used them for colour."

"But what I played basically is second rhythm guitar. I would play rhythm guitar to Ritchie's solos. And that means, I would have my left hand on a Clavinet, sitting on top of the organ, through a guitar amp, so it sounded exactly like guitar. And my right hand played Hammond organ. And I would play chords, you know, just accompaniment—I played what Ritchie played. His riff, that's exactly what I would play on the organ. The effect would be to double his riffs, which is actually fairly unique, that a keyboard player could double a guitar riff. And it gave the band like a two-guitar attack, because the sound of my really distorted Hammond organ and my distorted Clavinet on the bass end sounded like maybe five rhythm guitar players—really big. And that means when Ritchie took a solo, I wasn't sitting there playing cocktail lounge. You know, I kept playing the guitar riff that he had been playing before he went into the solo, so there was continuity there. And I was very solid and fucking loud! (laughs)."

When asked to name personal highlights of the live set, Tony goes with, "All of it. I didn't like any of the songs particularly better than any of the others. They all had the same animal energy. Heavy metal is not my music. It wasn't then. And I didn't sing, you know? And since 1979, I haven't really done anything that I haven't written and sung. It was like an apprenticeship, but the vibe was the whole thing. We were loud and fast and aggressive and it drove audiences crazy. And that was the whole buzz of the thing."

"Ritchie had such an aura about him when he played, that you couldn't help," remembers Jimmy, also addressing what Rainbow was like live. "Even when you were onstage with him, you constantly were watching him because he was such a character onstage. He didn't do anything that anybody else did onstage. He had a character all his own and a charisma all his own, and the audience just were glued to him the whole time you played with him."

"And it was like being in the Marines. The physical energy you had to put out to play these songs at the intensity he wanted them played was pretty heavy, and you had to be in good shape. I remember Cozy and I would look at each other onstage thinking, 'Is this song ever going to end?!' It was such a fast tempo and it was so really heavy at the same time. You couldn't slow down or stop playing. You just had to go at it until the end and it was sometimes pretty intense physically. So it was a very demanding gig, but we all loved it. We gave it everything when we played. Live shows were more like events when we played. We never had bad shows, although we got better as we played more. You'd go up onstage and just kick ass every night. It was phenomenal. Cozy Powell was just the best, and Ritchie just went from strength to strength as far as his playing went."

But there was still time for fun. The tripartite theme on the road with Rainbow, according to Carey, was "sex, drugs and rock 'n' roll. You've got to remember, we were kids and nobody was married. I mean, anything you heard about the '70s, just put it this way, it was true, and then add 20% for Rainbow. We were a fairly wild band. But what are we talking about? We're talking about getting high and having sex, basically. And who doesn't do that? Everybody does that in the eighth grade when they go to parties. A little bit more freedom and probably the pussy was better."

The band's key prop, the rainbow of lights, pre-dated Tony in the ranks, but he remembers it well, to the point of distraction even. "This guy named Tony, who had a company in upstate New

York had built it. It wasn't the same one used at Cal Jam, which was just a prop, like a cardboard or plywood prop. The one we used had 3000 light bulbs and was computer-operated, whatever that meant in 1975. We had some problems with that beast. Some of the halls we played in weren't high enough to accommodate it, and there wasn't really very much room on stage when we did fit it in, between the two corners of the rainbow. That thing was huge. It was really tight; it was like playing in your living room. I was never more than two feet away from Jimmy and ten feet away from Ronnie."

Jimmy says that on tour, Ronnie and Ritchie were marked contrasts in terms of fan interaction. "Yes, well, Ronnie very much had an earthiness to him, and he just loved his fans, and would spend hours and hours in the cold and wet just hanging out with them and talking to them and stuff, which is why he still has such a great fan base to this day. He never let the fans down, which I think was one of his big secrets. Plus his voice was straight from heaven. I never heard him sing a bad note once in all the times I played with him. He was perfect. He's very British in his determination. He's got an earthiness to him that Americans don't usually have."

"And Ritchie was very shy. I mean he developed a reputation for being unapproachable. It was just that he was very shy. That was to the press and the record companies and the fans, but within the band itself he was a prankster. He was pulling all kinds of nasty things to the band behind the scenes. But he didn't show his face very much in public, per se. And every time we did an interview, he would just pass the question on to Ronnie, and Ronnie would be only too happy to answer it. Ritchie was just very shy and nobody really kind of knew that. They just presumed because of all his behaviour onstage and the showmanship that he would be like that off stage, and he wasn't at all. He was very withdrawn."

Back in 1978, Ritchie offered Circus' Jim Farber a few musings on hitting the road, beginning with another example of his documented early ambivalence with US audiences. It must be said also that everybody was pretty disappointed with how the record had not sold like gangbusters in the States. Basically, in both departments, it was not going well, although Europe and Japan had been encouraging.

"I'm not going to go blue in the face trying to win America. We'll play our best and if they come along, fine. Otherwise, I'm not going to worry. I definitely think my playing has improved. In this band, I play with other people, rather than in Purple, where I'd just have a blow and then hold back while the other four members had their showcase. Although there was a nice sense of competition in that, here I play in a better atmosphere."

Although Ritchie was now an American resident, "I'd really rather live in England," noted Blackmore. "But I guess LA is all right. I don't really have a set home anymore—no permanent relationships. I've just been wandering these last two or three years. I've gotten used to it now. I can no longer settle down with anyone or anything. I just have to move on; otherwise I get bogged down."

Of note, at the time of the interview, bassist Mark Clarke (Colosseum, Uriah Heep, Tempest, Natural Gas… more on him later) was tentatively in the band, Ritchie remarking that, "Jimmy Bain just wasn't working out. The music we play may sound simple and straightforward, but every now and again, there is a very intricate part and Jimmy just couldn't handle it. Mark can. I think he's very talented."

In the final analysis, barring the hideous track list, the sound quality on the *On Stage* record was more than acceptable, and the usually restrained Cozy Powell gets to step out a bit, due to the unbridled jammy quality of the album. Songs were spliced from different shows (sometimes a world away, Japanese and German performances showing up on the same track), and bits were cut out, including the drum solo (again, thank God). But all this mellowness and meandering, as well as all these solos, vocal exercises included… it was all too *Made in Japan* and not enough *Unleashed in the East* for this writer's liking.

Ronnie disagrees, and why wouldn't he? Like never before, Dio is given huge expanses over which to display his mastery. "I really like that album, as a matter of fact. That's the first live album I'd ever been part of. Martin Birch and I did that one. Ritchie came into the studio once. We were in the studio for I think, 16 days. We did it in a studio that at the time was owned by Ian Gillan, a studio called Kingsway in London, where we had done three Elf albums as well, so we knew the place pretty well. When we mixed it, Ritchie came down one day out of the 16 days, I think on the eighth day, and said, 'How's it going? Okay, fine, see you.' And he left. He wasn't really that much into live albums."

"But I think the proof of that all is, what you hear is what you get. It's not an album we went into and Ritchie played more guitar or put a bass in or we fixed a vocal. We just let it go as it was. And that's why it was so easy to do and why it worked. I just remember it being, again, my first live album, a really good first live album I thought, and a hell of a learning curve for me. I learned so much in the studio just being immersed with Martin for 16 days without any outside influences to come in and go, 'Hey, can you do that?' It was just a great time, a great 16 days."

"Pretty well everything that was in the live show went on it," adds Jimmy. "It's quite a long record. It was just a lot of fun to do. That came out after I was out of the band, so that was kind of a bonus for me. I liked doing the live stuff obviously, and it came out after I had been let go. I can't recall anything funny that was done recording-wise. I mean, it was all funny at the time, because Ritchie was pretty neurotic to say the least at the best of times."

"There was all kinds of stuff that went on, but not on stage," continues Bain. "You'd come back and your room would be completely gone. You'd come back to the hotel and there would be nothing there, just a light bulb, no dresser or anything and it was all in the bathroom. They would spend hours and hours and hours trying to keep you away from your room so they could do all this stuff to you. And there were a couple of instances where we got kicked out of hotels in the middle of the night because of something one or the other of the guys had done. You'd wake up to somebody axing your door down. It was crazy, but it never really affected your performance or the records. It was always done on the side."

"But no, I don't think they really did any doctoring to that record or anything. What you hear is actually what happened. I'm not even sure they even got together to do much to it at all. Basically it was produced and mixed by, I think, Martin Birch. I don't think Ritchie would ever consider going in and overdubbing or anything like that. After listening to it, I thought it was pretty well what it was."

"Kill the King" was the only track from *On Stage* with even a remote possibility of making it as a single, and thus it was trotted out, with edits of "Man on the Silver Mountain" and "Mistreated" as part of the package. The song loudly rocked its way to #44 on the UK charts before dropping out of sight.

When the album was issued in July of '77, the band hadn't toured since the end of 1976, having taken a short break at the start of the year before beginning work on a third album, May through July of '77. The main touring cycle in 1977—whether one calls this the *On Stage* tour or late dates on the *Rising* tour is a moot point— took place in late September through to late November, all of it in Europe with a pronounced emphasis on Germany and the UK, in fact, the most extensive German tour, as it were, that I've seen out of any archival itinerary. Support through both the mainland and the UK came from Kingfish.

With what was to be *Long Live Rock 'n' Roll* wrapped up in December of '77, the band jumped on a plane for another extensive blanketing of Japan, where Ritchie by this point had become an almost mythical figure.

Chapter 5

Long Live Rock 'n' Roll

"It was turning violent and unpredictable."

For Rainbow's highly anticipated third studio album, Ritchie famously was out shuffling his lineup again. Tony Carey, mentally battered then sacked, then quietly brought back to handle select keyboard chores for the record, was to be replaced by Canadian David Stone, who himself would soon be sent marching, last to be heard as a slight guest on Max Webster's stellar *Universal Juveniles* album from 1980. Stone, ex-of obscure, forgotten Canadian prog act Symphonic Slam (one and arguably two albums—long story), was picked for the job after Ritchie had considered, variously, Vanilla Fudge's Mark Stein, Matthew Fisher from Procol Harum and Roxy Music's Eddie Jobson, the latter soon to find success with prog supergroup UK.

On the bass front, Jimmy Bain was on the outs, replaced for a time by a returning Craig Gruber as well as the aforementioned Mark Clarke from Uriah Heep, hard prog masters Tempest, and failed fusion blowhards Natural Gas. Clarke actually played live with the band, and after an attempt to secure Musicland Studios in Munich failed, actually recorded three tracks with the guys at the set-upon locale of the Chateau (d'Herouville) studios in France (again, using the Rolling Stones mobile unit), home base of not great records from David Bowie, Pink Floyd, Mahavishnu Orchestra and Elton John. But Clarke in Rainbow was not to be, with Jimmy Bain back as a band-aid solution (Tony Carey was even called back for a… spell), with a reported 40-bassist tryout eventually ending with the hiring of Bob Daisley.

"Well let's see, I had left Rainbow for the second time in

1978, and that's when Bob Daisley stepped in," explains Craig Gruber, picking up the story—which ends with a surprising offer. "I started working at the Record Plant. I was living in Hollywood, so Andy Johns was working at the Record Plant as an engineer and producer, and Andy and I became good friends. He did Led Zeppelin and Bad Company and he's a really great guy. He said, 'Listen, forget about the road for a while. Why don't you come in? I'll get you some work at the studio. That way you can go home every night, you can work and make really, really good money and get off the road and get away from the brain damage with Rainbow and all that stuff.' And I said, 'That's a great idea.'"

"So I did, and I stayed there for a year, and then in the spring of '79 came out, and that's when Ronnie left Rainbow for the last time. So that was the exact moment that Black Sabbath let Ozzy go, the spring of '79, February or March, right in there. So back to the Record Plant. I was still recording there and doing sessions, and Ronnie gave me a call out of the blue. I don't even know how he got my number. It's an unlisted number and I hadn't talked to him for a year-and-a-half prior to that. And he said, 'Listen Craig, how are you?, blah blah blah, I just joined Sabbath and they let Ozzy go and Geezer has left also.' And I just went, 'And why are you calling me?' I wasn't interested, truthfully, in the very beginning. I said, 'I'm doing well here at the Record Plant, I'm making huge money, sleeping in my own bed.'"

"And he said, 'Listen, we've written some really, really good material. They've got a house in Bel Air, they're rehearsing out there, please come up, I really want you to hear some of the songs before you say no.' Okay, anyway, after a couple more phone calls I agreed to it. So they came and picked me up and we went up there to the home. Way out there they had a full setup, and we went out to the garage and we played 'Wishing Well,' 'Children of the Sea' and like a blues jam. We played for about four hours and it really kind of rocked, felt really good, and they said, 'Think about the possibility of you coming in, you and Ronnie, replacing Geezer.' It wasn't called… the album didn't even have a title yet. So I said I'd think about it. And a week or so went by, and Ronnie gave me a couple more phone calls; we talked money, opportunity, talked long-term, so that's initially what brought me into Sabbath in a nutshell."

But we all know how that ends: Geezer soon after came back, Craig was out, but Ronnie was still in, and the world got out of the collaboration an immense record called *Heaven and Hell*.

Back to the Rainbow situation, "I had left in the fall of '75," relates Craig. "You know, all of us were fired, one at a time, and I just kind of quit playing for about a year. Past the brain damage, I made some money, so I had a house in Malibu at the time. We all did. We all bought condos at the same time out there, so I stayed out there for about a year and just kind of hung out. And then I went back to New York, bought a house in New York—upstate New York near a winery—just to chill. And it was cheap. It was like 80 grand or something. I just stayed there in this house for about nine months."

"And then I got a phone call from Colin Hart, Rainbow's tour manager, who was also Elf's tour manager and Deep Purple's; I've known Colin very well for years. And he said, 'Listen, we've let Jimmy go, we've tried Mark Clarke, we tried a couple of other guys, and Ronnie asked me to give you a call. Would you like to come out and give it a blow?' And I said there are some financial issues we need to go over from the last time, some residuals for writing some stuff. He said, 'Just come out and we'll talk about it.' So anyway, I came out, stayed three months, and the same stuff started up again with Ritchie and Ronnie and rehearsals. I would drive in from Malibu, 30 miles to Hollywood, to rehearse, and there was nobody there. Miserable."

"This is right in the midst of *Long Live Rock 'n Roll*. Ritchie actually played bass on the album, and then they brought my buddy Bob Daisley in right at the very end, and I think he played on the song 'Long Live Rock 'n' Roll' and maybe one more. 'Gates of Babylon'—I think he played bass on that too. But Ritchie played bass on the whole album except for two songs and then they brought Bob Daisley in. Bob is a great bass player, super nice guy, easy to get along with, and that is who replaced me. So Bob stayed with them until I think they brought in Roger Glover in 1979."

Sydney, Australia native Bob Daisley had worked with Chicken Shack, Broken Glass, Mungo Jerry and most recently B-level supergroup Widowmaker.

"I was looking for a steady band, but I was always sort of looking to 'climb the ladder' a little bit," recalls Bob. "I don't mean socially or fame-wise; I mean to get into a band that was fully professional, without any headaches, and without any personality clashes, and with somebody really at the reigns, and that didn't really happen properly until the Rainbow thing."

"I worked with Broken Glass, with Robbie Blunt. Robbie Blunt and I, with Stan Webb, formed Broken Glass, but I left to form Widowmaker with Aerial Bender and the rest of them. Broken Glass did actually do an album but I didn't play on it. The Chicken Shack album was enjoyable; that was the first album I did back in England in 1972, not long after I joined Chicken Shack. That was another experience for me, having joined a blues band. Widowmaker made two albums, a self-titled and *Too Late to Cry*. I didn't like hopping bands that much, but I just wanted, like I said, to get into a band that was going somewhere, and the Rainbow thing was, I think, a strategically placed step forward for me at that time. People warned me at the time, 'Oh, don't work with Ritchie Blackmore; you'll end up as a sideman, or you'll last three months and get fired.' But it worked out pretty well. Ritchie and I got on okay, and I think it was definitely the right thing to do at the time."

"With Widowmaker," continues Bob, "if everybody had kept their head together a little bit better, and kept their feet on the ground, I'm sure we could've gone further, especially with the second album lineup, when the band was the same but the singer was different. The first album had Steve Ellis and the second album had John Butler, who I preferred. He had a bit more warmth in his voice, like a Paul Rodgers or John Waite. But there were just so many clashes in the band, with people getting out and falling out with each other and it just got too much. So when I was offered the gig with Rainbow I took it."

Daisley gets specific on the ramp-up to his joining the band. "I was in Los Angeles after the second Widowmaker tour, in the summer of '77, probably around July, and a friend of mine had come over from England and was living in Los Angeles. He was there for three months with his family, having a look around. His name was Dick Middleton, and I had worked with him in Mungo

Jerry; he was a well-respected guitar player. We were a pop band, '73, '74 and we had some big hits. Dick was from way back, the '50s and the early '60s, and he was a mate of Ritchie Blackmore's. He said, 'Ritchie Blackmore is looking for a bass player for Rainbow; would you be interested?' And I said yes because things weren't going too well with Widowmaker. So I met Ritchie with Dick and we went out and had a few beers. We had a bit of socializing first because with Ritchie, he likes to get to know the person and make sure, regardless of how good you play or whatever, that he can get on with you. So we went out a few times and got on fine and he said come down and have a play with the band. Cozy Powell was there and Ronnie and I think they had just gotten a new keyboard player then too, David Stone, from Toronto."

Offers Bob on the subject of living loud drummer Cozy Powell, "Cozy was a nice bloke. He was down-to-earth, a fun person, and we used to have a bit of a giggle on the road and during the recording as well. Always into cars. I did one of the European Rainbow tours in Cozy's Ferrari; he had a Ferrari, and on the autobahn in Germany, there's no speed limit. So every day we were zapping along at 140 miles per hour, on this car about two-foot high (laughs). And Cozy always had, in the boot of his car, in the trunk, he always had his packets of Corn Flakes, in case he couldn't get them in hotels; he always wanted that for breakfast, as well as the things he liked from home like chocolates and Smarties."

Continues Bob on the tale of his hiring, "So yes, I auditioned at a film studio in Los Angeles, and Ritchie put me through the paces of various things to try out on the bass. He wanted a bass player who played with a plectrum, and I did, and he liked that, and someone who could play fast right hand stuff as well as having a left hand to do all the right notes. And he put me through various exercises (laughs), playing things and what have you, and at the end of the audition he said 'Okay, you've got the gig if you want it.' Because they auditioned lots and lots of bass players at that point, something like 40, and they couldn't find anybody who fit the bill all the way around. And that's when I joined, end of July, maybe August '77. Because I know during rehearsals with Rainbow, Elvis Presley died, which would have been August '77. It was a great experience for me; Ritchie Blackmore is a great player."

"Bob is a lovely bloke," says UFO's Neil Carter, at this point a future band mate of Bob's in Gary Moore's highly successful metal-directed solo act of the mid-'80s. "He's very… it's funny, being Australian, it's very funny with Australians. Bob is quite a go-getter. He really wants to go out and do it. He keeps his mind on things; he's very focused on things. And he's a great bass player and he's very fun to have around. His sense of humour is hysterical. And he and I were actually very good friends, really. He and I tended to hang out a lot together when we were on tour, a tremendous amount. And Bob, apart from Gary, was the constant in that band through the time I was with Gary. I was with Gary six, seven years and Bob was the bass player for most of that time."

Before we move on, Bob's predecessor, Jimmy Bain, gets to leave his stamp on the new record, however modest.

"I like the first album," opines Jimmy Bain, referring to his first album with the band, *Rising*. "We had to learn a few songs and everything, but I think that the Rainbow *Rising* album was more of a band effort. I mean, the first album sounds like it gelled and the songs are good. I thought *Rising* was a little bit short in terms of tracks, but I really liked being involved with it. It had great potential and I would have liked to have been around a little longer because I had just started getting into writing with them on a couple of songs that didn't make it until the album after that— 'Kill the King' for one. I was involved with the writing of that with Cozy. That was the first band thing that we did."

"But by the time that it came out, it was just Powell, Blackmore and Dio," says Bain, "but I was involved in it too. If I had been in the band, I think I would have gotten credit for it. But we were starting to do things like that. Unfortunately, I don't know… Ritchie would wake up one day and he wouldn't hear Rainbow on the radio, because they weren't playing anything as hard as that, and he would decide to change one of the musicians. When I got fired, I was in shock. I went over to see him and he really couldn't give me a reason why he got rid of me. He just sort of looked every which way but at me. I had gathered from that that he had made a decision and he had to stick by it. Because, you know, the management (Bruce Payne, 40 years on, still managing Deep Purple) had got hold of me and fired me, and then I went to see him. I don't know if he had second thoughts about it, but that's what happened. I know they had a little bit of difficulty replacing me because the guy that they got didn't work out, Mark Clarke. And they gave me a call and I said, 'I don't really think so. After you got rid of me once, it would be quite easy to get rid of me again, so why should I bother?' So I went on to do Wild Horses with Brian Robertson."

"So yeah, I was only in the band for a couple of records, but '76, '77, we toured extensively: Australia, Japan, Europe and America, and it was going along pretty well. I had great plans to be sticking around longer than I did, but Ritchie had this thing where he wanted to change people quite a bit, and I unfortunately was one of the first ones he wanted to change. I mean, we still remained pretty tight since then; we have no bad feelings about it. And he gave me my first break, so I have no animosity towards him."

"Maybe I was a vampire in an age gone by," quipped Ritchie to Circus, years ago, "because I thrive on new blood and adrenaline—new people. I get very bored with people, which is probably my fault. But I'm not a Dracula sort of person; movie vampires get tedious."

Mark Clarke's tracks would eventually be erased, with both Bob and Jimmy appearing on the album. As Craig alluded to, even Ritchie plied the fat strings.

"The tracks I played on were 'Sensitive to Light,' 'Kill the King,' 'Gates of Babylon' and maybe another, I can't remember," recalls Daisley. "I know Ritchie played bass on some of it before I had even joined, because they had some of the tracks done. That album was done over a period of a year. But Ritchie as a bass player is a great guitarist (laughs), and that's the end of my comments as far as that goes. I don't like guitar players that play bass; it's just a different way of playing. But yes, Ritchie played some of the bass tracks on that album, and I did what was still being recorded. We went to a place in France called Le Chateau, finished recording, and that was released very early in 1978."

"I think 'L.A. Connection' was Ritchie," adds Bob on the bass credits mystery. "But Ritchie, he doesn't think or play like a bass player. He's very precise and he knows what he wants, but to me, as a bass player… he doesn't sound like a bass player. But of course, on guitar he's an innovator and very unique, and anybody where you can recognize his playing after playing just a few notes has obviously got their own style. Yeah, he's a great player."

"I immediately liked his voice," says Bob, upon experiencing the vocals of Ronnie James Dio for the first time. "He has this huge voice coming out of this little bloke. He's only 5'4" or something. He's a little bloke with a fucking great big Italian voice coming out of him; that is what he was known for. Before I heard him sing live at the audition, I had tapes that I had a listen to and I really liked his voice. He has a great, great voice."

"I got along just fine with him," says Daisley, turning his attention to Ritchie, the volatile, mischievous, undisputed leader of Rainbow. "That was my first big, big break. In Widowmaker we toured the world and I had been in great situations but Rainbow was the first big break into an arena band. I just put me head down and did the job and didn't rock the boat. I got on fine with Ritchie. I didn't pull any strokes or anything. I knew I was being paid to do a job so I did it; it was great. I don't think I ever had any fall-outs with Ritchie. Some of the others did but I didn't."

"It was called Ritchie Blackmore's Rainbow when it was formed in 1975. It was still very much Ritchie Blackmore's Rainbow when I was in it but they had dropped his name. Ronnie and Cozy didn't like that anymore. It was called that to put the band on the map and by the time I joined they were on the map so they dropped the Ritchie Blackmore part and it was just called Rainbow. But it was Ritchie's band and always was. I remember that Ritchie was very particular about how things were done; I think that was a good thing. He was very serious and tenacious about his music and that was a good thing as well. It was a little difficult for me because a couple of drum tracks were done and I had to overdub a couple of bass tracks over the drums and that was not that easy at the time. But I got a handle on that pretty quickly and it didn't cause any problem at all."

Recording in France (chosen in part because Cozy liked that studio's drum sound) turned out to be a process of distraction. Ritchie commented that all the band did for the first ten days was play football.

"Ritchie had quite a few séances and I sat in on quite a few," adds Bob. "He would always get this negative force named Baal. I really can't remember that much about them." This prompted the "No Thanks to Baal" credit on the back of the album cover, as did declarations by Ritchie that things seemed to go okay in the daytime, but as soon as the sun went down, the place, and the equipment in it, became haunted. Séances conducted by Ritchie, Ronnie and a roadie called The Ox (says Bob, "a mate of Ritchie's from New York, big, beefy guy—I think he just went along because he was Ritchie's mate"), apparently elicited brief conversations with the being who promised chaos and doom upon the project, but no meetings with The Chateau's previous owner, Chopin. Meanwhile, Tony Carey was being tormented and tricked upon, ostracized and otherwise mentally victimized. He would be replaced by Stone (and Clarke by Daisley) in time for the interim tour dates in the fall of '77.

"I'm interested in odd things that happen, especially ghosts," said Ritchie speaking with Richard Hogan back in 1981, on his psychic pursuits. "I'm not interested in extraterrestrial beings, or Aleister Crowley, sacrificing little children and things like that, tearing heads off chickens, Satanism, no. I just like ghost-hunting. From the research I've done, I'm inclined to think there are ghosts. When we formed Purple, we had a bassist called Nick Simper. He used to do all the séances. I was totally opposed to all that, until I saw what was going on. I got intrigued with it all out of curiosity. I believe more in religion because I see what goes down in an evil sense. I don't practice evil stuff, but I see how effective it is."

"You can't be very tired," offers Ritchie, when asked what the ideal circumstances were for a séance. "You can't have weak personalities present; otherwise, you'll get possession. You need very strong, receptive personalities. A friend of mine, a guitarist, said, 'Ah, I don't believe in all this rubbish. I'm not scared of you ghosts; I'm stronger than you are.' The next moment, he was knocked out of his chair and was foaming at the mouth—he was unconscious. He had to go to a priest the next day, and the priest said, 'Don't do that again; this is possession.' You can go crazy if you're not careful. A lot of people go too far, too soon. Mental hospitals are full of people who are actually possessed by trouble-making spirits. In this business, I can come to meet a lot of people who have weird experiences. Usually it's a girl in the bedroom saying, 'What weird experiences have *you* had?' I must meet a hundred witches a month. The real ones are very reluctant to come forward with their stories. You can tell when they're sincere. Unlike these people that push their way backstage with their tits hanging out going, 'I'm a witch.'"

Adds Bob on Ritchie's supernatural pursuits, "Ritchie's got the reputation of being a bit like Jimmy Page and all that, but he wasn't. He was actually quite spiritual and more into the spirituality side of things and not the dark side of things. Sure, he was interested in séances and the other side, but he was quite a positive sort of person."

Back to the world of the five senses, Rainbow had a record to launch. Housed in an elegant parchment-coloured gatefold sleeve, *Long Live Rock 'n' Roll*'s visuals were summarily diminished by a pointless and off-message inner crowd shot, actually taken at a Rush show, reversed left right and otherwise heavily doctored to remove the Rush-ness (Geddy Lee flipped his lid when he heard about it). The front cover was classic however, featuring a detailed line drawing of the band, similar to what Aerosmith had done with *Draw the Line* only not in the least comedic. The album was released on April 9th, 1978, 11 months after the hijinks at The Chateau began.

Two days earlier, April 7th, Ronnie married Wendy Gaxiola, who would become his mate and manager for life, faithful to the end and beyond, now the custodian of Ronnie's legacy. The nuptials took place in New Canaan, Connecticut. Manager Bruce Payne was Ronnie's best man.

Once inside the record, the album kicked off with the somewhat folksy, plain-speaking title track. "It was a great song but when I first joined the band and first heard it, I thought it was a bit commercial," comments Bob, adding, "I was into much heavier stuff."

Indeed both the sentiment and the chorus are a bit sing-songy and quick to irritate, and, as with the gatefold, off message, in that by this point Rainbow had become a serious, inscrutable, myth- and sorcery-type band. The concept of "rock 'n' roll" seemed somehow beneath them, as did all this communion with the common rabble of the band's public. Rhythmically, the song stumbles along as a boorish shuffle, Cozy's lack of groove and his ill-advised bass drum pattern not helping matters. The track did some business in the UK as a single, backed with "Sensitive to Light," also from the album. Released in Europe a month before the record's launch, the single was eventually issued in the US and in Japan two months later, in May of '78. In the UK, the song hit #33 on the charts, failing to chart at all in the US.

"I never really came up with lyrics," offers Ritchie, "but that was the only lyric I had to explain to Ronnie. I said, 'Look, I've got this kind of riff, very straightforward, and maybe if you can sing something like long live rock 'n' roll...' And at the time I said, 'I know that sound corny, but it fits with the riff. I'm sure you'll come up with something much better.' And I was surprised, because he liked it. 'That's fine; I'll sing that.' And I was actually quite proud of the fact that I had written one line, for a song."

Adds Ronnie, "Yeah, that's right, Ritchie actually came in and said, 'I've got this riff here (sings it); long live rock 'n' roll keeps going through my mind. Can you do that?' 'Sure.' Okay, so we did (laughs). Yes, that was Ritchie suggesting that. I think it was more of an anthem; it was a good thing to sing for everybody to sing along with. And the message I guess was certainly important to people who were not able, perhaps, to listen to rock 'n' roll. We're talking what, '77? It probably really struck home with kids from Eastern bloc countries who weren't able to listen to records anyway. Or if they did, it had to be black market and bootleg stuff, but they still cared about it. So it's more in that vein. It's kind of us against everybody else. We love rock 'n' roll, but nobody seems to be accepting it. Remember, again, 1977. I mean, it wasn't that bad, but, yes, it was more of an anthem."

In the context of the times, there's those resonances and more. Indeed, this was before the Berlin Wall came down, so there's that, pronounced, because Rainbow were so intent on playing in Germany all the time. As well, this was the age of punk, which was threatening meat-and-potatoes "rock 'n' roll," which in Rainbow's headspace meant hard rock played with a certain level of craft. Finally, let's not forget that the band was not selling boatloads of records in the States, despite touring there, although not as exhaustively as the likes of Rush, Aerosmith, Ted Nugent, Blue Öyster Cult or Kiss.

Addressing the topic of lyrics in general, Ritchie comments that, "Again, when it came to lyrics, I was never a lyric man, unless I was listening to Bob Dylan. Lyrics to me were almost superfluous. I know that sounds a bit like a girl we knew once who said, 'What's the point of an instrumental without words?' She actually said that. And I was aghast at that. I'm thinking, she actually believes instrumentals are just not valid, because they don't have any words to them. What's the point?"

"And I thought that was a peculiar way of looking at music. That means that anything by Bach or Beethoven was just redundant, because it didn't have any words to it. But I know that it sounds like... because I used to kind of remove myself from that point, from the words, and leave that totally up to the singer. So the singer kind of had free range in there with their ideas. Now, with Blackmore's Night, I'm much more involved as far as, Candy and I would sit down often and think, what does this riff or chord progression represent? What's the visual? Let's think about what might be the right perspective. So we'd often talk about it, before she goes to write it. Most of the time, she's in the right area. But every now and again I would go, 'Mmm, I don't see it that way. I think the song should be about that.' But with Rainbow I didn't reject anything. I didn't listen; I did my part. The song worked, I'm happy, let's go down and kick a ball around."

Track two on the album, "Lady of the Lake," was much more up to scratch, as Ronnie attests. "'Lady of the Lake' was obviously a song that was really going to suit, in my mind, anyway, what Rainbow was supposed to be all about, that kind of medieval attitude that Ritchie purveyed and that I always liked very much. So it was written simply about the Lady of the Lake, who gave the sword that came out of the water; again, something I thought was very apropos."

To my mind, "Lady of the Lake" owes much to Led Zeppelin's "The Wanton Song," in riff, in pregnant pause, in Middle Eastern tone, even in guitar sound and compressed, claustrophobic recording. Perhaps at the literary end it's a bit obvious and trite—in this respect, it compares with Ronnie's "Lady Evil" lyric from Sabbath's *Heaven and Hell*. Still, along with "Gates of Babylon," it keeps the roaring *Rising* fires burning, its malevolent mass and the poetic, voluminous Arthurian lyrics from Ronnie capturing well the mystique of Ritchie and his otherworldly new franchise. Ritchie's slippery, dead simple, asp-imagistic solo also adds to the song's pure mystical quality, as does the new agey keyboard backwash.

"L.A. Connection," which Daisley calls "a bit like Rainbow wanting to be Bad Company," lightened the mood again, a bit too much in my opinion, perhaps sounding somewhat like similar vintage Nazareth or even Ronnie's old band Elf, especially come honky-tonk piano time for the close of this wry, mischief-ridden track.

"That's another true to life story, that one," laughs Ronnie. "That song is about Tony Carey, our keyboard player who at the time came back to the band, after being pretty soundly thrashed verbally by Ritchie, and fired unceremoniously. But we couldn't find another keyboard player. So it was left to Cozy and I to speak to Tony and see if he would come back and do the album. And he did come back, and nothing changed in Ritchie's eyes, so he was put through a whole bunch of purgatory while we were in France. We recorded that album at The Chateau about 30 miles north of Paris, and Tony wasn't allowed to leave his room. Tony couldn't record when the rest of us did; he had to be all by himself. Ritchie really put him through a lot of things (laughs). And eventually—I won't tell you the whole story, because it's very, very deep— eventually Tony was able to escape and got himself a ticket back home. And before he left, someone called the airport, while he was on his way to the airport, and said he had a kilo of cocaine on him. So of course, he was stopped at customs for a long time, just to make it worse. But 'L.A. Connection'… he lived in LA. He made an LA connection to get a ticket to get back home."

In this light, it's actually quite a cruel lyric, written less about Tony Carey, but more from the viewpoint of Carey himself, who laments failing to pass the test, as if he himself—all of 22 years old at the time—was the cause of defeat. All the while, the song stumbles around, like a goofy teen at a kitchen party, melodically saccharine but again, stilted and awkward due to parched recording values and a lack of groove from Cozy, who most definitely lacked the sweet science touch of, say, Deep Purple's Ian Paice or Thin Lizzy's Brian Downey. "L.A. Connection" was the album's second and last official single release, seeing European issue only, rising to #40 in the UK charts.

"You're kidding!" says an incredulous Tony Carey when told, 25 years later, the story behind the "L.A. Connection" lyric. "I've never heard that. Yeah, well, I didn't have to make an LA connection. I just had to get away from the crazy English people (laughs). It was a nasty situation and it was turning violent and unpredictable and I just left. There was a lot of violence surrounding both Deep Purple and Rainbow, and I draw the line. Let's just make great music, let's make cool music, but violence is not part of my makeup. And somebody was going to get hurt, so I left."

Asked whether these were practical jokes that turned violent, Tony reflects, "I didn't see it that way. Who knows? Nah, I don't want to get into it. I don't know. And I don't even want to say anything bad about Ritchie Blackmore. He taught me a lot. I respect his musicianship and his talent and his charisma. People loved him. He was a rock god in the '70s, and more power to him. But it just wasn't something I felt comfortable doing. And besides which, I saw myself in Rainbow as a stepping stone. I'm not a hard rock keyboard player. I knew at the time I was a lyricist, composer and a singer. And those three jobs were shared by Ritchie and Ronnie. Nobody else ever wrote anything. I mean, I didn't have that long of a life expectancy with the band. I would have liked to have spent two or three more years with the band, just to see if we could get as good as Led Zeppelin. Because I thought we were on the way."

I suspect however, that Ronnie wasn't really part of the problem though… "Ronnie's great; he's a great guy. He was a lot older than I was and he was a complete perfect gentleman. Both him and his wife Wendy, who I think, still manages him, or did for years and years anyway. They were terrific people, super. Cozy was a complete gentleman. Jimmy Bain was my best buddy, at the time. And who does that leave?! (laughs). Yeah."

And as Tony saw it, any problems there were within the band were never overt, noticeable. "No, never. No, never. It wasn't like that. The fights didn't happen to your face. I also never... nobody ever yelled at me or told me anything, but I got fired twice, you know? And then the third time I left. I was too chicken shit to fight. Which was another thing about it not really being a band, you know? Like, the cool guy would go into the dressing room, he'd get drunk and he'd be unhappy about something, but nobody really knew what it was. There was never any confrontation, let's put it that way. And in a band, like a marriage, you need confrontation."

A bit of a mystery (akin to the ol' "Who plays bass and drums on Scorpions' *Love at First Sting*?" conundrum) is the breakdown of keyboard work on *Long Live Rock 'n' Roll*. Here's Tony's response. "Well, I've only heard it once. But most of them are mine, anyway. Everything I heard, I recognized. But I left... Ritchie fired me twice and the third time I left. And I left in the middle of the *Long Live Rock 'n' Roll* sessions in France, at the Honky Chateau, outside of Paris. And the keyboard parts had already been pretty much finished. And I kind of left in the middle of the night (laughs)."

"Yeah, sure, all that shit," says Tony, on the subject of séances. "That was the chateau thing, that whole black magic thing. So one person's black magic is another person's practical joke. Yeah, I saw all that shit, and it was interesting and sometimes scary, always spooky. But it's not a great thing to get into. I don't want kids to think it's cool—it's not cool. It's nothing I really want to talk about. I was on the outside looking in. I wasn't into that black magic bullshit. I remember, a priest came down to bless the studio. Which was about the day before I left. I thought hey, this is getting too weird."

On the particular vibe recording at the chateau, Tony repeats the word: "Spooky. But it was great to record in. It was spooky, a stone castle, from the 1200s or something, 600, 700 years old; I don't know. It was a miserable, old, drafty stone place. You know, Elton John recorded *Honky Chateau* there. Everybody was there; a lot of people were there recording. Atmosphere up the ying-yang, and the equipment was good and the studio was good. And we were there in the summer anyway, so it wasn't too cold. I wouldn't like to have been there in the winter; it would've been too drafty. But it was this ancient castle that had connecting passages between the kitchen and escape passages into the garden and all that. It was fascinating, very fascinating. You've got to remember, I was 22, second time in Europe. I loved every minute of it."

"It was very old and it had a nice vibe to it," adds Bob on his impressions of Le Chateau. "It was out in the middle of nowhere, in France, so there were no distractions. It had a great big fireplace with this huge wooden beam across the top of it. I mean, you could go and live in this fireplace, it was so huge. I think I've got a photograph of it somewhere. And I remember one night, Cozy and I built up the wood and the flame so much in this huge fireplace, that we got it so hot that the beam at the top of the fireplace started smouldering (laughs). But no, we hardly did anything. David Stone, myself and Ritchie used to go out jogging a lot during the day. Because otherwise we were just sitting around in the studio and we wanted to have some exercise and air and all that sort of thing before we started working in the studio at night." Not Ronnie? He used to be a sportsman. "No, he was a smoker in those days. I don't remember Ronnie coming out jogging."

Tony offers an interesting response when asked if Ronnie was known, or thought, to have a fairly big ego in those days. "If you're going to get up and sing in a studio, you have a huge ego. If you're going to get up in front of 20,000 people and act like you're the boss, you have a huge ego. Now, how that manifests itself... that mellows over time and this and that. Or it doesn't and gets worse, or gets better. But to ask about any musician that's made any kind of breakthrough, does he have an ego? Yeah, he does. And the reason he broke through is because he has that ego. Because if you're not convinced that you own that stage or that you own that recording studio and they're all saying 'We're not worthy' to you (laughs), if you're not convinced of that, you won't give a performance that convinces anybody. That's very important to know."

"Ego is not an issue," continues Carey. "I love the people with the huge egos; I love it. Because, you know, you either laugh at them or fight with them or go along with it or don't—it doesn't matter. But those are the people I really wanna know. Those are the people that really take it seriously. They think they're the best. Some of them actually are! (laughs)." And Ronnie? "He's the best! He's cool! I'm not going to tell you how old he is, and I know how old he is. Next time you talk to him, tell him hi from Tony. Tell him T.C. says hi. Tell him I'm proud of him."

Closing side one of the original vinyl was the album's enduring offering, "Gates of Babylon," perhaps the band's most medieval and Zeppelin-esque song of the catalogue. Its riff is pure Arabic or Middle Eastern magic, as is the locale and context of its lyric. Triumphantly, in under seven minutes, the song manages a level of epic grandiosity a trace above that of "A Light in the Black" or "Stargazer"—perhaps "Gates of Babylon" deftly borrows the best of those two worlds then quietly, or at least abstractly, excels over those tracks due to intelligent, disciplined editing. Its parts, transitions, breaks and shifts are many but logical and fitting, and to the end (not continuously through the years, mind you), Ronnie and his Dio band presented it live, even if it never saw the stage with Rainbow.

The *Music of Erich Zann*-evocative cello at the end is said to be played by Ritchie himself, although strings are credited to the Bavarian String Ensemble, as conducted by Rainer Pietsch. Ritchie has been known to cite the guitar solo as one of his favourites, both for musicality and degree of difficulty. It's also one of Ritchie's favourite Rainbow songs, Blackmore, adding that "it worked well," while quickly adding the album's title track as perhaps the other very good song on the record.

In 1981, Ritchie had the following to say about his rock tastes, and more importantly his classical tastes, which bear great importance with respect to this very ornate Rainbow classic. "I like Jethro Tull, Ian Gillan, Jimi Hendrix, The Strawbs, Randy Hansen, Robin Trower, Bad Company, Led Zeppelin and Jack Bruce. Judas Priest? They have a good drummer. Eddie Van Halen is excellent technically, but he doesn't have the emotion that's supposed to go along the same lines as the vocal. I find The Who exceptionally average."

"I listen to Bach all the time," continued Blackmore. "I like his minor modes and his regimented way of arranging triplets. I love German baroque organ music. All I do on the guitar is emulate a violin, which takes from 16th and 17th century organ, which, from a rock 'n' roll viewpoint, I suppose, is horrible. But I really think melody in a solo is more important than technical dazzle. Three hundred years ago, composers weren't writing for the Top 20. The music came from the heart of the musician. Maybe that's why I keep going back to that type of music. If a rock station is on, I like to hear my own songs; there's no point in writing them if they're not heard. If I switch a radio on, I turn to a classical station. Thank God there were no FM stations in 17th century Germany!"

"That's my favourite from the era," notes Daisley on "Gates of Babylon." "I liked the bass sound on that, I liked the way Dio sang it, and I loved the middle section. Actually David Stone wrote that middle section, and they just bought it off him and didn't credit it to him."

"We were in France at the time," adds Ronnie. "I know we wrote it in the studio, in the chateau in France where we did that album. I remember that because the middle bit we worked on with our then keyboard player, David Stone; David was in France with us at the time. The song itself, I just wanted it to be really dark. Because it was so eastern in nature right away, to write to it was not so much simple, but it led me to where I needed to go. It was just hard to find what I was going to use as a title for this very, very eastern song. There were so many choices. But perhaps some of them were a little too silly, too jolly, too stupid. But this seemed to work really well. I remember looking at a map when we were writing the song. I was in my room looking at an old map of the Middle East, and saw Babylon and thought, well, there you go."

"Because we don't live in that area of the world, I think it's a very mysterious place to us. Of course, it has been mysterious through our history, with all the writings from the Middle East, the Bible, all of the Biblical stories—from all religions, really. I think that that's one thing that I like to do: I like the idea of having to use your imagination to think for yourself what that area is all about. And that's just from a historical aspect. But I love the Middle

Eastern scales and just the attitude of the music as well. So a piece is written that's very influenced by the Middle Eastern music—that I think is the only thing you can write about."

"'Gates of Babylon,' I was pleased with," says Ritchie, getting the final word, giving nod to the song's heavy Middle Eastern vibe. "And there's more of a Turkish solo. I've always been interested in Turkish and Egyptian scales, Moroccan scales. 'Perfect Strangers'—there was a heavy riff that had that kind of chromatic tone that was almost like a heavy Turkish riff, again. But yes, I was always more into the arpeggio classical Vivaldi stuff. So when it came to a solo, I wasn't so preoccupied with blues. You know, I liked the blues playing of certain people, but I also like classical music. So I wasn't 100% into blues."

"It might sound condescending, but I find them a little too limited," was Ritchie's remark on the blues, in a 1978 interview. "I like to play a blues when I'm jamming, but then I want to get onto other things. I listened to B.B. King for a couple of years but I like singers more than guitarists. Albert King I thought was a brilliant singer; that depth, which comes out in Paul Rodgers too. I do like a blues base to some things—that can be very interesting with classical overtones."

Side two of the original *Long Live Rock 'n' Roll* vinyl opens with a second now timeless Rainbow classic. "Kill the King," credited to Ritchie, Ronnie and Cozy, first saw the light of day as the heart-racing opener on the band's live album, but here it takes on a crushing insistence. The introduction is pure dynamics and drama, with Cozy turning in a simple yet highly memorable set of fills to announce the coming of a speed metal classic, a track that pushes and shoves its way forcefully between "Fireball" and "Burn." Ritchie's solo is old school shred, played over a nicely classical musical passage propelled by Cozy's double bass drums. Once done, Ritchie turns to a melodic phrase that revives the intro's pattern, the whole thing fitting somewhat the composed elegance of his solo from "Highway Star," arguably the man's most impressive from both a purely accessible and structured standpoint.

"I loved that song," recalls Bob. "That one was ballsy and I loved playing on that. That is the epitome of what Rainbow should have been doing. 'L.A. Connection' and 'Long Live Rock 'n' Roll' were good and well-played but 'Kill the King' was the epitome." Indeed epitome it is. Ronnie is on fire, savagely ranting about what he knows best, killing kings and such, spells and charms, rainbows and power, although in interviews, he remarked that really, the song is about power struggles within the game of chess.

Asked to address the subject of being a "speed demon," coming up with the likes of "Fireball," "A Light in the Black" and now "Kill the King," Ritchie agrees in principle to that label. "That's right, because I noticed that every band, especially Led Zeppelin, everything was at the same tempo (bom bom bap, b-bom bom). They were very mid-range songs. And I used to wonder why nobody ever did anything fast. And I mean, it was peculiar. You're talking about ten years of nobody ever recording anything that was really fast. And I almost looked at that after awhile as being a negative. I thought, maybe we should just write what everybody else writes, just medium tempo, because the fast stuff doesn't seem to be accepted by the radio, because it's too fast. We were told that a lot of times. But 'Kill the King,' it just got thrown in. Normally everything was written in the studio, but I think 'Kill the King' was written before we went into the studio, so we had an idea of it, in rehearsals."

Next up is "The Shed (Subtle)," which was provisionally titled "Streetwalking," due to that word being a prominent feature of the chorus. Opening with a spacey solo from Ritchie, the song transitions to a malevolent stomp, albeit with a bit of funk, providing a cogent extension from the heavier bits on Rainbow's first album through say, "Run with the Wolf" from *Rising* and this record's "L.A. Connection." The song fits well the premise of the album, striking at the workmanlike mean median average of the record's emotional palate, providing reconciliation between the happy songs and the melancholy grinders.

"There's this place… let's see, I think it's the Chelsea Football Club," recalls Ronnie, when asked about the curious full title to the song, "The Shed (Subtle)." "I talked about this one once and I thought it was the Fulham ground, but it wasn't. I think it's the Chelsea ground. If you put that down, there's going to be somebody who's going to slight me for this one, because they're going to know which one it is (no worries, he's right). Anyway, The Shed is the end of the stadium where the real supporters go. You know, you don't pay a lot of money to be in that particular end. In Liverpool it's called the Kop End, and I hope in Chelsea, it's called The Shed. We didn't have a title for the song. And I think Cozy was mentioning to Ritchie one day, about the Chelsea football team, and mentioned The Shed and Ritchie said, 'That's a great title; let's call it "The Shed."' He goes, 'But we have to put "Subtle" after it,' I guess, the reason being that, The Shed has really no connection with the song, so it was meant to be a subtle title."

If "The Shed (Subtle)" tended to pound the listener black and blue, "Sensitive to Light" scrapes him off the ground for a quick escape from the football hooligans. Somewhat similar in riff to *Stormbringer*'s "Lady Double Dealer," the track is an upbeat riff rocker at the party metal end of things. Ronnie offers this amusing take on the song's lyric. "That was just about somebody... that was just another way to say, you know, I get burned all the time. It's always me, isn't it? I must be sensitive to light, because light… at least 12 hours a day, we're going to see that. So no big shakes on that one either." Ronnie's extrapolation to a wider universal is commendable, although on the surface the track seems to take that attitude within the more constricted realm of sexual politics.

Closing the record is "Rainbow Eyes," the band's first ballad since "Catch the Rainbow" two records back. It's a dark, moody, almost Renaissance minstrel-type song, and is typical of what a serious heavy metal band might provide as quieter fare in the late '70s. The song features a delicate Dio vocal, along with a string quartet, lots of flute and no drums. It is the record's longest track and feels like it. Amusingly, Blackmore called Ronnie's ballad voice a "girly voice," Ritchie coming to the conclusion that he'd best stay away from writing ballads if Ronnie was to be the singer of them.

Years later, Ritchie and Candice would revive the song, reinterpreting it on the seventh Blackmore's Night album, *Secret Voyage*, issued in 2008.

All told, *Long Live Rock 'n' Roll* will always be considered second in line and limelight to *Rising*, in the pantheon of Rainbow's greatest albums. Its production, once more at the hands of Martin Birch, is quite simply worse than its predecessor, lacking in both bass and treble and yet at the same time is not hampered by an irritable degree of mud. Over the years, fans have come to view the album as being not quite so purposeful, deliberate or focused as *Rising*. Which isn't surprising—it's easy to come across determined and clear when your record has six tracks on it, even more so when none of them are ballads, even more so when there are four of equal length on one side, two of equal length on the other—it's just reassuringly tidy.

Ultimately, *Long Live Rock 'n' Roll* is an album of songs. And really, more than is remembered—perhaps also triggered by its regal cover art—it's quite often upbeat and leaning commercial.

Tellingly, as Ritchie explained to Sounds as the band were assembling the record, "We're trying to make this a party LP too. I'm pleased with the results. I've laid a little bit low on the guitar playing because I don't like to be totally brash and upfront all the time. I've done that on the live LP. I'm trying to make it a more musical content sort of thing; I'd rather have better songs. But as soon as these songs get played on stage, then I'll solo on them. I'm thinking about the end product. I'm not thinking about what I'm going to play. I've proved that I can play guitar; I don't want to keep playing just to satisfy guitarists. I want to satisfy the people, the guitarists and myself all in one."

Championing this sort of music, Ritchie added that, "I'm in a heavy band because that's what I feel. I like extremes, escapism too. As you know, I only listen to classical music. The only band I really listen to is Jethro Tull; I like to hear a bit of Zeppelin because they play it so well. But then I like to go mad, and go to the opposite end of the scale to out-and-out hard rock and that's it—I don't like anything else in between. It has to have out-and-out drama and intense feel like all my favourtite composers like Bach and Tull. I can relate to heavy metal, but heavy metal has been abused by a lot of bands. But I do like to play it, because it is valid—after playing guitar for 21 years, I can still turn around and say it's very valid."

It's interesting that all this talk about heavy metal is taking place in the venerable Sounds music weekly. Four months later, Ritchie would be back in the paper's pages, as well as on the cover abusing his Strat, flanked by a headline that simply said, "Kerr-aaannnngg!!!" It would take another four years, but in 1981, Sounds would spin off from their pages a new magazine called Kerrang!—if not Tony Iommi, who better to be part of the naming saga than Ritchie Blackmore?

Back to the band, like Ritchie, Cozy also sensed a mainstreaming taking place within Rainbow, telling Chris Simmonds, "It's a lot more commercial than anything we've done. The first album I wasn't on, of course—that was Ritchie's solo album and all the rest of it. Rainbow *Rising* was the first band effort, which possibly was a little self-indulgent. That was exactly what we were into at the time, and while it sold well over here, it suffered in the States because the tracks were too long and the short tracks that were on the album were neither one thing or the other."

"No-one in the band really wanted the live album to come out at all; that was a political move by Polydor as they needed something to come out then." Indeed Powell spoke elsewhere as well about his disdain for *On Stage*, decrying the performances, too much soloing and then overall, how the album was short for a double. Ronnie also complained about the sonics of *On Stage*, implying it was a real patch-up job to get it to sound good.

"I don't think live albums are a good idea for a new band," continued Cozy, "which Rainbow still is. It was also overpriced—£6 or something—and we were a little shocked when we discovered that. Anyway, that's past now. The new one, as I said, is more commercial, a lot stronger and the songs are more to the point. It's a hard, driving album, probably one of the few straight rock 'n' roll album out this year."

"Not the best studio in the world, but it was fun," continued Cozy, commenting on recording at the Chateau. "We were there a long time—changing personnel halfway through didn't help matters. It ended up with Ritchie and myself doing most of the backing tracks with Ritchie playing bass. Musicland is totally different, much more clinical. The Chateau's maybe not so good technically, but it's got a better feel. As we had Martin Birch with us, engineering and producing, he was able to correct most of the problems. I'd like to go back there again."

"It's difficult for a keyboard player in this band," mused Cozy, on Rainbow's game of musical chairs. "I wouldn't want to be Rainbow's keyboard player. The band is based around what Ritchie writes which is very riff- and guitar-orientated, so a keyboard player has to provide chords under that and also be able to take a solo when needed. It's down to laying a good foundation for Ritchie to solo on. They're hard to come by these day—they either want to be like Keith Emerson or Chick Corea. But you need those colours, even in a rock 'n' roll band."

Cozy closed the conversation with Simmonds talking about how the guys stay sane, essentially by leading separate lives when not recording or touring. "I like it that way, because I'm a miserable bastard at the best of times. We're all into different things. I've got my racing, Ritchie's into playing his cello at four in the morning. Ronnie likes watching the telly, whatever. Yeah, Ritchie's even brought his cello 'round to rehearsals a few times and I've put me boot through it a few times. He's quite a good cello player actually; I think he's having lessons from the fellow in ELO."

Proving, sure, that there must be something to it, Ronnie framed the record in "similar terms to that of Ritchie and Cozy, telling Sylvie Simmons, "I think we went for a concept on this one, being, you can put this record on at a party, and certainly you could listen to seven tracks out of eight and not have to take it off and worry about any drastic change in music. You can dance to it, because it all has a single thread going through it for at least seven rock 'n' roll tracks. The ballad—they can either take it off if they don't like it, or slow dance or slow rude to it, whatever they want to do. I think it's a very good album. We set out to make it as commercial as possible, but we're still being honest with ourselves and doing the kind of music we want to do."

"I honestly think that we as a band haven't written or performed our best material yet," continued Dio. "I just think that even though we've been individually in other bands for a long time that have had great success, we're relatively newcomers as

Rainbow. It's been not quite three years yet, and I consider that to be the beginning, and in no way should we think we've made it. I think we've got our best years in front of us—no, this is not the album that's going to put us on top. After this tour there's going to be another album. I think it will be kind of the same LP as this one. It has to maintain that same sort of rock 'n' roll music. That's what we're all about. We're out to prove that—quote—'heavy metal'—unquote—is not dead. We're trying to make rock 'n' roll a lasting idea. I'm pleased. I'd like to say this is the ensemble that's going to last. But with this band's past reputation I couldn't say. I'm only speaking for myself. It's Ritchie that has to make most of the decisions as to bass player and keyboards player—he has to work with them a lot more than Cozy and I do."

And yet... "*Long Live Rock 'n' Roll* was, I thought, a very unhappy album," surmises Ronnie, looking back decades later. "I thought it was an album where Ritchie obviously now wanted things to change drastically. So it became an album where I thought there were some tunes that were good on it, but an album where I thought that the end was coming. I think that you have to look at all of them as a whole, but also in their temporal context. The first album was done with all the guys in Elf, with the exception of Ritchie. And the second album was done with a whole different band. It's the perception of it. Your perception is as valid as my perception. But as far as writing goes, Ritchie and I wrote all the songs. We threw a few crumbs to Cozy, just to keep him in the ball game I guess. But as far as his writing goes, he was a warm body I guess; that's about the end of it."

"Ritchie wanted to go in a different direction," continues Dio. "He wanted to be more of a pop band. After I left they did one or two songs written by a guy named Russ Ballard. That was not the kind of band that I wanted to be in. I wanted to be in a band that wrote its own material and invented itself and carried on with that. At that particular time, Ritchie felt he wanted to be connected to a pop audience so we just went, 'Okay, see ya!'"

"Rainbow was a real drudge, a real drudge," sums up Ronnie, looking back 20 years after the fact. "I had all the opportunities to write what I wanted to write. But I didn't have the opportunities to have control of my life or work on parts for the band. I wasn't stupid enough to realize that it wasn't Ritchie's band nor that Ritchie's success with Deep Purple wasn't what put us on the map in the first place, aside from the fact that we were a good band, we wrote a good album, and people eventually… even though we were relegated to underground status, people finally discovered us well after the fact. We never knew what Ritchie wanted to do. The only thing bad that I thought about Ritchie was… because I always got along well with him, I never had a problem. Those who attacked him and said that he's the most difficult man to work with is perhaps the way they found it."

"But I didn't; I was able to work with him, I respected him, he respected me, and when you have that kind of respect, it's not that difficult. But that's as far as it goes. It's still Ritchie's band and he calls the shots. And I just found that live, we became so damn self-indulgent, that it made no damn sense to me anymore. Every song began with Ritchie, every solo became an extended work of Ritchie's, and every song ended with Ritchie's solo as well. So when you do 14 songs a night, compound that by three, you have a lot of solos. And that's not what a band is about. I didn't want— and never wanted to be in—those kind of bands."

"A lot of little things added up to that," says Ritchie, of the unfortunate parting of ways with Ronnie. "I think, in a way, with Ronnie, I put a lot of the aggravation down to his wife, Wendy, who used to go out with Ian Paice, and was married to Aynsley Dunbar, the drummer. So she's been around, I suppose. She used to kind of pick on him a lot and say, 'You should do more in the band.' He seemed to be very comfortable within the band until she came along and got into the picture. Then she started irritating things by saying he should be a bigger star, blah blah blah. There was one front page we did for a magazine and for some reason they put me on the front page and it should have been three of us, and the other two went berserk. And for me, I thought it was so petty."

Quite a revealing comment, that last one. Ritchie's ego manifested badly in some ways, such as all that live soloing, of which Ronnie correctly complains. But it's quite believable that Ritchie did not crave magazine covers, or interviews, over and above the other guys, while it's also believable that Ronnie and Cozy did. We also mustn't forget the generosity with respect to songwriting credits. There's also some truth in the snipes at Wendy, who always believed Ronnie should be featured more. Both she and Ronnie finally got their way with the Dio band, and in a sense were proven right, given the quality of the material we got from Ronnie as more of a "solo artist," even if, again, much of the brilliant music was generated by the guitarist, in the beginning, Viv Campbell.

But again, Ronnie's gripe is entirely valid. Whether he was talking from the point of view of a singer on the stage with Ritchie, or from the point of view of a concert-goer, it could be pretty dull dealing with the extended ramp-ups to songs, the solo spots in the middle and the jams at every turn, jams that leave no place for a singer, unless you want to mimic guitar solos like Ian Gillan, which never sounded good. Ronnie found himself having to ad-lib scraps of new lyrics, repeat things, hum along, again, just like Ian, none of it exactly working.

Asserting his status in the band, Cozy told Pete Makowski at the time, "The thing is with me, Ronnie and Ritchie, all three of us have got egos. All three of us have got different kinds of egos, so consequently there's a battle already there. There isn't any room for anybody to say, 'Well I think it should be done this way.' I think the identities of the three of us have been already established, that we're running the show sort of thing. Well, Ritchie's running the show in the first place obviously with Ronnie, then I came along and stuck in my two penny's worth and now it's three of us running the show and there's not a lot of time or room for anybody else. Say, for example, a Keith Emerson and Jack Bruce suddenly emerged from somewhere, we wouldn't last a week—there'd be an almighty punch-up and the band would cease to exist."

"I'm always flattered by tributes," says Ronnie, speaking specifically about Rainbow tribute albums, Ronnie then going on to marvel at the lasting influence of the Dio-era of Rainbow through the years. "I think it's something I never expected. It's just saying thank you. So to judge it… I judge it by the thank you as opposed to what's in it. But they all do a really good job of it because they all love Rainbow so much. There's all these kids who grew up that way, wanting to be the singer in Rainbow wanting to sing 'Kill the King' or 'Man on the Silver Mountain.' Just as I always wanted to sing 'Smoke on the Water' or the things that you grew up with—that's what you want to do at some point in your life. So they do it with care and they imitate very well, I think. But you know there is only one original."

"And the other part of the question, our impact on power metal… like I said before, and especially in Europe, it's had an incredible effect on so many people. I've spoken to a lot of people in my life who were stunned by the first time they saw Rainbow and went on to become what they became, not because of Rainbow but because they wanted to be like that. I know Lars Ulrich is one of them and Yngwie Malmsteen is another. I just know so many people who I've spoken to in Europe who are in bands and even bands you'd know very well who go, 'Ooh, I saw Rainbow and for me that was ohhhh…'"

"It's just amazing how that band affected people," reflects Ronnie. "We were always huge in Europe but we weren't that massive in America, at least the Rainbow I was in at the beginning of the band. I think we were more of an underground band at that time; I don't know why. I remember playing in, I think it was Toronto, Maple Leaf Gardens; they had to cut the place back pretty drastically because I think we only drew like 1500 people or so. I thought, 'Well, this isn't going to work.' Then we started to do a little better here and there but we were smart enough not to play massive places like that."

"Then 25 years later it has become this band that everyone saw at Maple Leaf Gardens (Ronnie may be remembering that very first show in Montreal, not Toronto). There must have been 150,000 people there and I didn't see them. That's what happens. But it's been a very important thing especially from the 'duo' combination aspect, which works so well all the time. From Mick Jagger and Keith Richards to Perry and Tyler; there are many more of them. I don't say we were on that level, Ritchie and I, but we created something very unique just as Tony and I did in Sabbath as well. You connect as two musicians who are necessary to make it happen and it's a magical thing. Rainbow just had an impact on everyone because they hadn't heard anything like that before."

"I was 22 and I'll be 51 on Saturday, as a matter of fact, and it's almost 30 years ago," reflects Tony Carey, on what was and what could have been. "The whole Rainbow experience was exciting, but I was the keyboard player. And over the last 30 years, I don't consider myself a keyboard player. I compose and I sing and I write the lyrics and I usually play all the instruments on my records, including the guitars and bass and drums and everything."

"But I mean, as a stepping stone, as an introductory course into rock music, it was probably the best training anybody could have. We were a loud, fast, exciting band. And we could've been very, very good. I never thought we got really good. We *could* have been, but Ritchie liked to keep changing the lineups. And in my opinion, a band has to stay together for at least 150 concerts before it's on the same page even. And I've heard all this live stuff that we did in Germany and Japan, *Rainbow Over Europe* or whatever it's called (indeed the name of a bootleg Rainbow live album), from our '76 and '77 tours. And when you listen to it, you hear exactly what I mean. There are spots of really, really cool jamming, and then there are spots where it could be better because the band didn't have enough experience playing with each other."

"I don't like any of it," reaffirms Carey, curiously, on the material he recorded with the band. "But I see Rainbow as a great unfulfilled prophecy; it could've been a really great band. And Ronnie went on to be a really great singer (laughs). I was good, Jimmy was good, Ritchie was good, everybody was good. It could've been a really great band. But to have a really great band, you've got to give it five, six, seven years. And not change bass players every ten minutes and change keyboard players every ten minutes. Because you just water down the creativity and nothing has a chance to solidify and to gel and to grow, you know?"

"So I don't have much of a feeling either way about any of the recordings that I've heard. It was a great learning experience for me. What can I tell you? I'm grateful I was there. But as far as me taking it really seriously, what I take more seriously is the quantitative leap in quality between my first and my eighth solo album. Each one got better, and by my third one I had two

American Top 40 hits. That's what means something to me, taking a germ of an idea and letting it grow. Because the concept on my earlier albums was always the same. It was Tony writing and singing. And I learned the craft. The first one was unspeakably bad, the second one just came out in Germany as a really, really limited edition. The third one had a radio hit, 'I Won't Be Home Tonight,' but didn't sell so much. And then *Some Tough City* had two Top 40 songs. And then Planet P came and made a really big splash. So, I would've liked to have seen that happen with Rainbow, you see what I mean? This starting from the cradle and then developing together. Instead of one guy who is so neurotic that he can't take competition or is jealous of the keyboard player or whatever."

Bob Daisley agrees that things were imploding, alluding more so to times post-Carey. "Ronnie and Ritchie were starting to not see eye-to-eye, and on the American tour in 1978, Ronnie was beginning to sort of hint to me that he was about to form a band at the end of the tour himself. And David Stone the keyboard player was really only brought in as an emergency to do the world tour. Ritchie always had this funny thing with keyboard players; I think he kind of picked on all keyboard players, and David Stone was no exception. David Stone had the right name—he was a little bit of a 'stoner' (laughs). But he was a good player and I got on okay with him. He was sort of laid-back, and I think he felt intimidated by Ritchie. He seemed to be, I don't know, picked on, if you know what I mean. And David was a very good musician. He was classically trained, and he used to be in a band called Symphonic Slam, which was sort of like a rock band doing classical music. But yes, Tony Carey had gone by the time I'd joined. David Stone had joined at the same time as I did, in Los Angeles, in '77."

Continues Bob, "A lot of people refer to that lineup as the 'classic' lineup. And we only did one album, and then after the world tour Ritchie went on to put together another version of Rainbow. And they had a lot of success as a slightly more commercial version of Rainbow. But I tend to agree that that was more or less the classic Rainbow lineup."

"There's a little story…" adds Bob. "The way things turned out was quite ironic, which is quite funny. Towards the end of the American tour with Rainbow, towards the end of 1978, we had been touring quite a lot, and Ronnie pulled me aside and said, 'Look, I wouldn't be at all surprised if Ritchie changes the band soon.' He said, 'If that happens, would you be interested in getting a band together with me?' And I said yeah, I would. So we talked about that and then the crunch did come. Ritchie wanted to change the band and he got rid of everybody; I think he kept Cozy Powell for little while, but then Cozy went as well. But Ronnie said, 'Hang in there. I'm looking for guitar players and we're going to get this thing together.' And then one day I picked up a magazine in England and it said 'Ronnie James Dio joins Black Sabbath.' And I thought, well, he didn't even tell me. Here I am sort of waiting around for the so-called band to happen with Ronnie. But the ironic thing was that Ozzy had been thrown out of Black Sabbath and Ronnie joined. Instead of forming the band with Ronnie, I formed a band with Ozzy and it worked out even better."

Daisley, of course, would go on to write a heck of a lot of the music and most of the lyrics for the first two Ozzy Osbourne albums, *Blizzard of Ozz* and *Diary of a Madman*, which became smash hits, as well as much of the work on the third and fourth Ozzy albums as well. Years later, massive lawsuits resulted over the crediting and subsequent payment of royalties for Daisley's crucial work on those huge records.

"Ritchie didn't fire me particularly," notes Bob, wrapping up his plight with Rainbow. "I think he just wanted to get a whole new lineup. Did he make the right decision? I don't know. I would have liked to have seen Ritchie in a heavier band than with the version of Rainbow that came after us. I thought our version of Rainbow was the best he ever had. Cozy, Ronnie and myself... I mean shit, what was wrong with him?"

"I don't know; I think it was politics," adds Bob, when asked what caused the eventual rift between Ritchie and Ronnie. "It was a bit of a hierarchy, that band, a bit of a totem pole. Ritchie was at the top and then Ronnie and then it was Cozy, because those were the three that sort of formed that band. But it was always Ritchie's band; as I've said, originally it was called Ritchie Blackmore's Rainbow, and then they dropped his name, by everybody wanting it dropped. But it still remained a hierarchy. And then underneath Cozy was me, and then David Stone last. We were the new kids, and David was the keyboard player and like I say, Ritchie had a thing about keyboard players (laughs)."

"Oh, a lot. God, I toured and toured and toured," says Bob, offering a glimpse at his time on the road with the band. "We started off… when I joined, end of July, beginning of August of '77, we rehearsed in LA for probably at least a month and got the show well together. And then we did the pre-production, last minute rehearsals in England and started touring in about, I think, September, in Scandinavia. The first show was meant to be Finland, but then it got cancelled because something happen with the gear getting there or the trucks or something. And then the first show we actually did was in Stockholm, Sweden, and then that tour went all the way through Scandinavia, Europe, England, everywhere."

Ritchie had this to say back in 1978, to Trouser Press' Jon Young, on the eve of the band's attempt at rock domination stateside. "It's just that the other markets came first, Europe and all that. We took advantage of it rather than just playing around America as a small-time band. Now the only market left is America and we're the underdog. Most of the time we're sharing the bill with REO Speedwagon, and Foghat is topping the bill in some places. It's not like starting again. A lot of people feel that, but it's just something you do. I'm quite looking forward to it. It means I can get back to the bar afterwards. If you're a top-billed act you get back to the hotel and everything's closed. (Deep Purple's audiences) were too big sometimes. It was moving too fast. It's funny how sometimes it will escalate and turn into something that big, when you know you're just the same as any other band. All these people are turning out to see this band and next year they'll be turning out to see some other band equally as bad or as good, whichever way you look at it. The way it's been going I think it's been getting worse. In America you have some very strange big groups."

These opinions are supported by the band's touring history. Many dates were played in '77, but none in the States. This was rectified in 1978, but still, Rainbow remained a mid-tier proposition. Punk had come and gone, replaced in the States by "new wave." Whether that was the stake through the heart or not, almost all of the big hard rock bands of the '70s were having a hard time in '78 and '79, running on the fumes of their successes in '76 and '77.

"In Purple I was happy to have any audience," continued Ritchie. "In Rainbow I come off stage quite confused sometimes. There are certain numbers we do that are very intricate and I know they've missed them. But I can't expect them to catch on. They're not musicians, it's Friday night, they've finished their work, they want to have a good time, they want to see someone break a guitar. I can't expect to educate people because if they'd wanted to become educated they would have become musicians themselves. At the same time I do like to listen to certain quiet parts that we play and get on to the party at the end. I don't understand an audience that's stomping all the way through and saying, 'Let's boogie man; let's get it on.'"

Blackmore's fighting a couple things there. Like I've ranted, no, the "blue jean army," as Aerosmith calls them, don't want to hear a 20-minute version of "Catch the Rainbow" and no, they don't want to listen to tons of solos. And it's also been a proven truism that dense, speed metal writing turns into an impenetrable wall of noise when up against the crap sound of a hockey barn, especially back in the '70s. The mob will rock out, to be sure, but they will not be able to discern the intricacies of "Kill the King" or later, "Spotlight Kid."

Ritchie went on to offer a glimpse into his creative process, which tended to manifest itself live. "This is gonna sound very cocky, but I think I can improvise better than any rock guitarist. My failing is composing; I really fall down in composing. I can come up with riffs and I'm good at improvisation, but I'm not very good at putting a song together. I have done, but there's nobody else around to do it anyway. I feel very frustrated in my songwriting; I think it's terrible half the time. But improvising for me is no problem—in fact, it's something I could do all the time. That might sound slightly weird. I have a very bad technical memory, so I can't remember, if I write a tune, exactly what the notes are. It's really exasperating, 'cause I'll write one and, 'That's great, I'll play it again and record it.' And I'll play it again and, 'Oh dear, I've forgotten it. What did I play?' It's really annoying. I don't like to write; it's a chore for me. I do it because there aren't a lot of other people around me who do it. It's not knocking the people around me—songs are a letdown half the time."

"Cozy and I, we're always trying to outsmart each other," said Ritchie, when asked by Jon Young about the loud pairing of Powell and Blackmore. "He's a very fast person, him with his cars. Me, with my medieval music, he hasn't got a clue where I'm coming from. So we have our differences, but when we're on stage we click because he wants to be the best drummer and I want to be the best guitarist. It works to a certain degree. Sometimes we do tend to get a little carried away with being aggressive when we should slack it off. I find to record we should tone down everything. We have to mush it up a little, put some icing on it to make it sell. In Europe and Japan they're more into adrenalin, but in America they wanna hear safer things. I've never really studied American culture as far as music goes, but I've been listening more and more. We're going to concentrate more on a back beat. We'll be playing more slow songs. I know what the American people are looking for—I don't really care what the American DJs are looking for; they piss me off to no end."

Asked about the nagging lack of respect issue that's plagued Blackmore back since the Purple days, Ritchie opines, "Some people know I'm good. Some people I want to know I'm good. I'm not into being a personality, a Johnny Carson, a Rod Stewart. I'm very thankful for as far as I've got, and I really don't think I should have any more than I have. If I hear other bands and I hear how bad they are, I get a little bit upset that people are buying their records in the millions. But I know my limitations. I think this is more than I deserve. I can't believe that people take as much notice of me as they do."

"I just think there's such a poor standard in rock 'n' roll. I think it's disgustingly low. Because of its limitations, rock 'n' roll is very difficult and classical is very closely related to rock 'n' roll. It's very disciplined; the modal structure is similar to rock. But I'm talking about progressive rock, not the Rolling Stones. When I play I always incorporate classical runs from violins and things like that. (Being called heavy metal) is better than punk, which means inferior. It suits us fine. I know I can play a bloody concerto any day, so it doesn't bother me at all. It would bother someone who was sensitive and knew their limitations. Sometimes I feel like I own the stage completely, on my own for an hour. I'm just going crazy. The adrenalin is so much that all my musical upbringing is thrown into intensity on stage rather than being a musician. After 22 years of playing it goes instead into a mood and comes out as an aggressive bulldozer. I don't know why; I often wonder why. I'm not an aggressive person offstage. I don't know why I am on."

Wrapped up in all that is possibly the best explanation of why Rainbow is so darn jammy live. Ritchie likes improvising more than composing. Coupled with that, the wild bucking bronco of creativity just overtakes him in a live environment. Singer, step aside. Which he did.

Finally, Ritchie comments on the sacking of both Tony Carey and Jimmy Bain. "Tony was a bit of a raver so he got a bit too heavy. He was asked to leave the first time and he was asked to come back. After a while he left of his own accord. He couldn't take the pressure. We were coming into contact with unforeseen psychic phenomena, which is kind of another story. It's just kind of a hobby of mine, psychic phenomena. He couldn't take that, 'cause we were playing at the Chateau in France. It got very heavy spiritually and he backed out. He thought I was completely mad. He thought I was trying to kill him. I don't know why he thought that. Jimmy Bain was a great guy, fantastic person, but his bass playing left a little bit to be desired."

Back in the present, Jimmy's successor Bob Daisley reflects upon the set list from all those many years ago. "We didn't do 'Gates of Babylon.' We did do 'Kill the King,' 'L.A. Connection.' We didn't do 'Lady of the Lake' or 'The Shed (Subtle).' I think in about December, we started recording more. Because the tour went through September, October, November, all around Scandinavia, all of Europe, England. And then by about the end of November, into December, we were back at Le Chateau, in France, where we did the album. We recorded there up until Christmas. And then just after Christmas, we went straight to Japan for a Japanese tour. And the Japanese tour… like, most bands go to Japan for about, I don't know, ten days, two weeks. We were there for about five weeks! Because Rainbow were huge there. And I think the album went to #1; it did very well."

So to reiterate, the band sort of toured for a long spell even before the album was finished. "Yeah, and that's probably why we didn't do that many songs off it. But in general, we stuck to the set, which was fairly worked-out. It was a little flexible; there was some improvisation during the songs, but it was fairly worked-out. Any arguing about anything or anything like that was usually done at rehearsals, then established. And once it was established—everybody being pretty professional—there weren't really many screw-ups. I know that after Japan I came down to Australia for a holiday. After that, we went to America. We were in America for a long time, where we played with a lot of different bands—I remember J. Geils—because some of the shows were outdoor festivals."

Before he leaves us, Bob adds a humourous slice of life on the road with Rainbow. "One comes to mind in Scandinavia. There was a promoter there called Eric Thompson. You might notice that his initials are E.T.; he looked a bit like E.T. He looked a bit like a light bulb. He had a weak and narrow chin that went down to his neck like a light bulb. The top of his head was sort of bulbous. Once Ritchie pulled the photograph out of his passport and replaced it with a picture of E.T. When Thompson went to go through customs, he didn't know and gave it to the guard and they just all fell about laughing. There were always practical jokes on Eric Thompson. Once in France they got a harness and the roadies got Eric Thompson behind the stage during the Rainbow concert. We used to have a huge rainbow that went over the stage and changed colours during the set. They stripped Eric Thompson naked and they put the harness on him and strung him up on the rainbow during the gig. They let him down because he was going red in the face. They thought the harness was on too tight and he was dying. After they let him down he told them that he was only going red in the face because he was trying to shit on Cozy!"

"But yes, somebody was always doing something to Eric. Whatever band was touring, and Eric Thompson was the promoter, somebody would always do something to him, like tying him up in an elevator naked (laughs), whatever it was."

This took place at the band's show in Paris on October 27th, 1977. The hoisting up on the Rainbow replaced an original plan, which was to take an unconscious Thompson, shave his head and strip him naked, stick him in his car and put it on a ferry to Iceland. There are no more pranks to come, however, as Thompson passed away on May 20, 2006. Of note, the Paris hijinks came five days after Ritchie had been arrested for kicking a security guard in the face, breaking his jaw and leaving him bloody, down in the pit during a nasty crowd surge. The Man in Black (stripes?) spent the night in jail, after being collared trying to escape the Viennese venue by being loaded on the truck in a flight case.

The irrepressible Joe Lynn Turner, vocalist on three Rainbow albums after Graham Bonnet's short sojourn (more on both those situations shortly), adds his views on why Ronnie's days with Rainbow were perhaps numbered from day one.

"Ritchie is a song guy, believe it or not. People think he is a riff master, but at the same time he was all for the song. And traveling through America, you had Loverboy and all these hit bands, and Ritchie's ear was just remarkable and he picked up on it. In his own way of course—I don't think he ever sacrificed or compromised himself—he likes very hook-oriented, melodic rock. Bluesiness from a singer's point of view, but at the same time he likes the song."

"So there was no forcing Ritchie into any sort of square peg/round hole thing. He was all for it. What I would do was… he would give me a master tape with all kinds of jamming, different riffs, parts, and I would say, 'Okay, this is the beginning, this is the middle'—in some cases, not in all cases. I would sort of be an arranger a little bit because I was also writing the melodies and the lyrics. So he gave me that freedom; a terrific collaborator really. Because he would give you all the freedom to hang yourself. Because if it sucked, he would tell you straight out, 'I hate that; go somewhere else.' And I would always come in with two or three sets of lyrics and different melodies and we would pick the best one that really suited the song and felt like the music. We always tried to capture what the Beatles had, which was basically the music sounded like the lyrics and vice versa. They always had that magic. Some songs, the titles and the lyrics just don't fit the music."

"But then again Ritchie was indignant about being popular," continues Joe. "In the back of his mind, he's the kind of guy who was just like, 'If that's popular, I don't want any part of it.' There was a certain kind of popularity he wanted, meaning more to the left of center. He wanted popularity but on his own terms. I think he was getting it and he always gave me a lot of accolades and respect because he felt we had a really good team. And it was a whole different vibe from the Dio thing or Bonnet. It was a completely different demographic. The audiences that we picked up… well, for the first time in their lives, they had girls in the audience, which the roadies thanked me a lot for. A girl demographic came in, MTV opened it up, and the 'Stone Cold' video obviously portrayed that and brought me into that; whether I liked it or not, that was the role I was playing. That's the way it went and we just followed it in a natural progression. One more album and I think we would have cracked the commercial rock market."

"Oh, a great guy!" says Joe point blank, when asked for his impression of Ronnie, who is leaving both Rainbow and our story at this juncture.

"Great singer, great writer—I love that guy. Ronnie's a gentlemen. He really is a gentleman and never has a bad thing to say. And don't take me wrong, I'm not deprecating Ronnie; I'm just saying a fact is a fact. He's still into this *Magica* thing, where there's trolls (Joe is referring to Ronnie's concept album called that, issued in 2000). It's like *The Hobbit*. He just took *The Hobbit* and rewrote it. And he's probably got two more albums he's going to squeeze out of it. *Magica* is going to continue. I'm sure there's going to be *Magica 2*. You know, I mean, because this is just *The Hobbit*, taking the characters and giving it different names and things."

"Ronnie, as a person, to this day, I saw him last year in Vegas, he's just great. He's always warm, he's always cordial, he's always friendly, he's always proper, he's never arrogant, he's never obnoxious, he's never any of those things. He's just Ronnie and he's just great. He's down-to-earth and I have nothing but respect for this guy. You know, I love the way he sings. I loved him when he was in Elf. I think he's got one of the best blues voices ever, and it obviously shows, because he's just going as strong as ever. You know, he's never let down from his past."

And so something had to give. Rainbow spent a large chunk of their May through August 1978 tour of the United States in support of vanilla-flavoured "Midwest rock" act REO Speedwagon—and doing it without their electric rainbow. Toward the end they did some theatre-level headlining, supported by the likes of Black Oak Arkansas, Cheap Trick, Eddie Money, The Cars and finally AC/DC at the end of August. Ritchie topped off his year by jumping on stage with Ian Gillan's freight train of a band Gillan, at the Marquee back in London on December 27th. Blackmore's finicky rainbow of many lights would never be seen again.

Chapter 6

Down to Earth

"Oh my God, they're a scruffy-looking lot."

As we leave the problematic, difficult *Long Live Rock 'n' Roll* record, here's a comment from someone who has, interestingly enough, never been in a band with Ronnie James Dio, yet has always been in the same "Deep Purple-related" orbit. Roger Glover would figure prominently on Rainbow's next album, the stellar *Down to Earth* (it was time to leave the realm of heavy metal fantasy and bring the band "down to earth"), fronted by a then 32-year-old Graham Bonnet. Glover would begin as producer and shadow bassist on the record, ending up as fully-fledged band member. Here he charts the transition from Ronnie to the magical one-off lineup and record—this writer's favourite by a long shot—that came next.

"I was brought in as a producer first. I started my production duties when Ronnie was still in the band, and it quickly became apparent that they weren't actually on the same page anymore. I had become a go-between, between them. Their ideas veered madly. I was a huge fan of Rainbow. Ritchie played me 'Stargazer.' I bumped into him at Musicland Studios when I was over there doing Rory Gallagher or something like that. And they were just vacating the studios, having finished Rainbow *Rising*. And Ritchie said, 'Come on and listen to this track' and he played me 'Stargazer' in the control room and man, it blew me away! And when he said, 'Do you want to produce us?' I said sure. So the next thing that happens is Ritchie and Ronnie exploded, and Ronnie leaves, and the whole thing falls apart. I don't know what it was between them, to be honest. I think Ronnie was more kind of groove-oriented, and Ritchie was more music-oriented. I can't remember some of the ideas now. There were bits and pieces of cassette demos that I would ferry from place to place, and they didn't seem to sort of marry together."

Fleshing in a bit of detail, Roger, in a separate interview, explained the situation thusly. "I joined the band when Ronnie was still in the band. Actually I wasn't in the band yet; I was just the producer. They were looking for a bit of extra help and it became clear to me very quickly that Ronnie and Ritchie weren't talking; they weren't on the same wavelength. Rehearsals were horrible. Ronnie would sit in a corner and scribble down words, but wouldn't go to the mic and actually try anything. And I found myself a go-between between Ronnie's house and Ritchie's house with tapes, you know, 'Ronnie, this is Ritchie's latest idea,' and then over to Ritchie's saying, 'This is Ronnie's latest idea,' and it exploded and Ronnie left, and the only person left was Cozy. And I was really there helping just as a friend and as a producer, trying to put the band back together again, going through auditions with them and sorting it out."

Seasoned veteran Don Airey joined the band in December of 1978, having, along with the Purple connections, played with Cozy in Cozy Powell's Hammer, joining that consortium in 1974. Airey then moved on to Colosseum II for three ponderous prog albums, alongside his brother Keith, who was a guitarist in the ever-evolving franchise. Session work was still in the talented Manchester College of Music man's mix, (the Lloyd Webbers, Gary Moore, Black Sabbath), and then, after flying to New York and impressing Ritchie with his classical skills, Don Airey became part of Rainbow.

Continues Roger, "They actually had a bass player, but he wasn't very good, so I actually ended up playing. It was actually easier for me to play the parts than teach him what to do. Not that I'm such a great bass player, but he was worse. And we didn't have a singer. We started off with a singer, but I forget his name actually. He's one of these guys who's been in a bunch of bands and I don't want to embarrass anybody by telling you his name, but I can't remember it anyway."

"Anyway, it became really apparent, and I went to Ritchie and said, 'This guy isn't really in your league. You shouldn't be working with a singer like this. He's not in your league, he's third-rate, he shouldn't be playing with you.' Then he said, 'Well, then sack him.' And I said, 'What, me?' And he said, 'Yes, you—you're the producer.' Hmm, okay. I went to Cozy, borrowed his bottle of Remy Martin, got this guy and said, 'Could you come into my room for a second?' We were in a castle in the south of France—Ritchie loves castles, always has, feels right at home in them, loves old settings. And I poured a couple of stiff brandies and said, 'You're fired,' but a bit nicer than that."

"And then we proceeded with writing songs, but we needed to find a singer," continues Glover. "We were auditioning over the phone, and we thought of Graham Bonnet from The Marbles who had that huge hit with 'Only One Woman,' and what a voice! Soaring voice! So it was like, why not try him? So we tracked him down and him, along with about half a dozen others, auditioned, and he amazed us with his voice; it was stunning. And I found myself doing all the writing chores and producing, and playing bass, and I wasn't in the band. And right at the end of the album, Cozy came up to me and said, 'Why aren't you in the band?' 'Because I haven't been asked.' So he went to Ritchie and said, 'This is ridiculous,' and so Ritchie said, 'Okay, do you want to join our band?' And I said okay. But come next album and the following tour, it became apparent that Graham wasn't really hard rock material. He had a killer voice, and I don't want to be nasty to him, but it's just that he wasn't the right material, wasn't resilient enough to last the distance, not with us."

Adding flesh to the tale, Don Airey had once explained that Graham's name came up from a game of "name that tune" instigated by Cozy, who challenged the band with a snippet of Bonnet's schmaltzy single.

Likely an exaggeration, other accounts have the band auditioning approximately 50 singers, including Brian Johnson, Marc Storace and Lone Star belter Kenny Driscoll. Early in the process Trapeze's Pete Goalby actually recorded "Since You Been

Gone" with the boys, and would end up in a greatly revitalized Uriah Heep for that band's classic *Abominog* album. Ritchie had auditioned Goalby over the phone, and he indeed spent a few weeks with the guys before disagreements began to flare. Also considered was Chris Thompson from Manfred Mann and Roger Ferris from No Dice, a band that had supported Rainbow on tour the previous year.

All the while the band was spending $2000 a day in France—most of it without a vocalist—tinkering away on the Maison Rouge mobile studio. Before Glover was cajoled in, bass players bandied about as a replacement for Bob Daisley included Jethro Tull's John Glascock, the Sensational Alex Harvey Band's Chris Glen (later of MSG), Jeff Beck's Clive Chaman (recommended by Cozy), Gordon Rowley (from Strife, later of Nightwing—he lasted one day after Chaman had a go), and Pretty Things' Jack Green, whose orbit in the band would also include an extra go 'round up into the Joe Lynn Turner era.

"I came over for a day, to France," recalls Graham, with respect to the audition process. "I had to go to the store to buy Rainbow albums because I'd never heard of Rainbow (laughs). Oh, you see how sheltered I was. So my manager (David Oddie) said to me, 'You better go out and buy some albums and see what they do.' And I saw all these longhaired guys and looked at my girlfriend, and said, 'What do you think?' She's like, 'Oh my God, they're a scruffy-looking lot,' blah blah blah. 'What kind of music is it?' And I said, 'Well, here it is.' 'I don't like it—do you?' And I said, 'Not really; I'm not really into this stuff.' And then I think Ritchie said, 'Learn one song, called "Mistreated."' And I said okay. And that was my audition piece. I went over there and sang 'Mistreated' and they said, 'Do you want the job?' And they said, 'Can you sing it again?' I think we did it about four times."

"But yeah, I never listened to that kind of music, to be honest with you. I get my influences from stuff I played over the years, which is jazz and R&B and pop songs, you know, since I was a kid playing in a dance band when I was 14 years old and having to sit there all night strumming along to cha-chas and waltzes and bonitos and whatever else, playing to dancing, but at the same time picking up all kinds of interesting chord sequences and singing songs I wouldn't normally sing at that age, when the Beatles were around. Standing up to sing 'I Left My Heart in San Francisco' was not my ideal, but it taught me how to construct songs, and really, it's a great lesson, you know, chord-wise, and melody-wise."

"That's absolutely true," answers Graham, asked if Roger's recollection as to how his name came up was accurate. "Ritchie had seen Marbles in the past and he asked Roger, 'What is that Marbles singer doing these days?' and that's how they found me out." In terms of others up for the job, Ritchie had even asked Ian Gillan to join at one point. Gillan declined and asked Ritchie to join his band instead. However Graham says, "I never saw anybody else because I was there alone with the band then. I knew that they tried many others before me but I didn't see anyone else. The audition was very brief. I only did that one song and right after they asked if I wanted the job and I said, 'I have to think about it' because I wasn't completely sure if I really wanted to do it or not, but I'm glad I did."

So Rainbow found themselves with a top-flight singer. But as they found out soon, they hadn't—as they might have assumed—gotten a lyricist along with the package.

"He's definitely a different type of singer," ventures Ritchie. "It's hard to explain Graham. Graham is in another world. He's a very nice guy, and obviously this man could sing up to an F sharp above top C, and in full voice, which is very high. But I always found that Graham wasn't too bothered about music in general. He wasn't highly motivated. I'll kind of leave it at that. So consequently there was a lot of work done behind the scenes to get him to sing the songs, much more so than any other singer. Most singers give their input and come up with their ideas, but Graham was just content to sit back and be told, note for note, what he was going to sing. And we'd often say, 'Graham, do you have any ideas?' 'Not really.' And it was like, my God! And that was really difficult to do. So we only made the one record. But he was a nice, easygoing guy."

"And another trouble with, I suppose, Graham, was he didn't have particularly too many interests. You couldn't socialize with him particularly and get into depth talking-wise. Because he didn't have too many interests outside of walking with his dog—that was his thing. But as a person, he was great. Like I say, he didn't have too many ideas. He was just like the cherry on the top. He had this amazing range, very high for a guy. So on the one hand, he wasn't a troublemaker like some of the people in the band, yet he was a bit wishy-washy sometimes. I could go into great detail, but... there's something not motivated there."

In his defence, Graham offers that, "Roger did all the words. At that time, I wasn't really writing anything. I was actually never given any credit on writing any of the songs at all. But I would get a basic idea from Roger about the melody and then I would sing it my way, whatever—Frank Sinatra there—and kind of twist it around to the way that I thought it should go. Roger did, at first, say though, 'Well, you're a singer—you make up the words.' And I said, 'Well, not really.' I've usually only kind of added things to people's songs. I'd never really gotten into songwriting."

"And Ritchie would listen to what Roger had written and we'd sometimes put down one song three or four different ways, different words and different melodies and then Ritchie would come in and choose the one he thought was the better of the bunch. That's kind of how we did it. Roger was surprised that I didn't write. To tell you the truth, I was nervous of writing anything with this band because I didn't really know what they were all about. I was new, and I thought maybe the things I did wouldn't be quite right, or too corny for them or something. I was really intimidated by this different style of music that I was suddenly plunged into. Because before that I had been doing R&B stuff and pop stuff, which was totally different."

It's quite a plausible explanation, because having gotten one heavy metal band onto his resume, Graham quickly went on to become actually an uncommonly *good* lyricist, starting with his work on Michael Schenker Group's *Assault Attack* album and then into Alcatrazz and beyond. Bottom line: he proved himself to be a fast learner, once the concept of being the literary engine of the band crossed his mind.

Much of the credit, however, goes to Roger for making *Down to Earth* such a barnstormer of an album. As lyricist, he was (mostly) rock-solid, and as producer, he turned in a tone painting that successfully artfully reconciled the band's Purple-like instrumentation while simultaneously courting a dry yet tough heaviness. The end result was a marked improvement over *Long Live Rock 'n' Roll*'s noisy, almost addled, midrange values, and in essence, the album's old school feel triumphs over all three of the Joe Lynn Turner era productions, even if *Straight Between the Eyes* and *Bent Out of Shape*, at face value, were fatter, warmer, more "accomplished."

Writing for the record began in December of '78 at Ritchie's new place in the Northeast, Ritchie working with Cozy, Roger and bassist Clive Chaman. However the assembly of the album found the band in France again, but at the Chateau Pelly de Cornfeld, a castle renamed for Bernard Cornfeld, the British financier who bought it.

Explained Ritchie, speaking with Armando Gallo from Sounds, "We recorded it in France in a place called the Chateau de Pelly, which was a castle, because I love recording in castles. I don't know why; maybe it's reincarnation, but I just love mucking around in castles. So we got together in this castle just outside Geneva and we hired the Maison Rouge Mobile. Ian Anderson—well actually Jethro Tull, the group—owns it. I was slightly biased there, because I think he has one of the best bands around, so I wanted to use the sound that he had. It's a very good sound, very clear, very powerful."

"The Mobile is like a lorry, so we took it along to the castle and just passed the leads through the window and played in the old dining room, which was a massive dining room. We got an excellent drum sound; I'm very pleased with that. We all lived in the castle and got up to our usual pranks. It was haunted as usual—it has to be haunted, otherwise I don't go there. It would be much cheaper for me to record in America, but I don't like to. I have to get back to Europe to get the feeling. America's a great place but I can't take too much of it, because it lacks the culture. I'm not trying to be snobbish but it drives me crazy."

Concerning the departure of Ronnie, Ritchie told Armando that, "It's very easy to put someone down if they're not there to actually back up the other person. Every time I pick up the paper, if it's someone I've worked with they usually say bad things about me, so I don't like to talk. It's very hard. Usually if a band has gone different ways then obviously you've had some kind of confrontation so far as not getting on. I think Ronnie thought he could do better, and I wasn't particularly interested in taking him along with what I was doing, so we gradually grew apart and he's into other things. So I thought it was best if he went his way and I went mine. He wanted to change his music and get into other things; let's just say that."

"After three or four years I tend to get tired of the people I'm working with and I tend to change a lot. And it's nothing detrimental to them. I'm just trying to get the best band I can for the public. I'm not trying to be a moody bastard. I could play safe and just stay with the same lineup and think who cares, just keep playing. But I don't like doing that. That's why I left Deep Purple. I just couldn't be bothered with the same people all the time. I wanted to do something new. I do the same type of music all the time, but I like to do it with different players. I think you have more initial excitement if you have a new band."

As Cozy explained to Geoff Barton, "We'd just begun rehearsals for the new album and Ronnie was sort of humming and hawing about this and that. His heart didn't seem to be in it; something wasn't quite right. So he'd come to rehearsals and we'd be bashing away at the backing tracks, waiting for him to come up with the vocal lines and nothing was really happening. So after a couple of weeks of this Ritchie Blackmore said to me, 'What's the deal? Have you noticed anything different?' And I said, 'Well, yeah. He's not exactly 100% into it, is he?' And this went on and on and I just think Ronnie had either lost interest in the band or interest in singing our particular kind of music. So, like, the writing was on the wall."

"The thing is, with Rainbow we don't accept anything less than total conviction from the people in the band. Ronnie wasn't giving it as far as we were concerned, so 'Pfft!' It's as simple as that. It wasn't a case of him not singing very well—the guy's a great vocalist and he always will be. It's just that he'd become disenchanted with us and we'd become disenchanted with him and rather than just keep going, plod along like a lot of bands do, we decided that it would be best to take the trouble right out at source. So we asked him if he wanted something else and he said, 'Yeah, okay' and left. He didn't get fired; we asked him to leave. You can read into that what you like."

First bassist to be part of the recording was Jack Green, but he was soon sent packing, with Roger taking over and the band still without a vocalist. Once Bonnet was secured, vocals were captured at Kingdom Sound Studios on Long Island, New York, where Graham found himself the victim of racism, an experience which years later he turned into a song called "Long Island Tea."

"I was out there with my ex-wife and we were staying at the Holiday Inn, at that place called Hampstead in Long Island. We went out for a walk, and I said to her, 'God damn, it's hot today.' She says, 'Well, we should stop in the bar and get a drink.' I said okay. We walked into this bar and we were suddenly looked at by all these people. I thought, well, what's wrong here? And I went over to the barman and I said, 'Could I get a… I'd like a beer, and Jo, what you want?' 'A glass of wine, white wine.'"

"And the guy behind the bar says, 'I'm sorry sir; you can't come in here.' And I said, 'Why?' And he looked at my feet and said, 'Well, you're wearing Converse sneakers.' He said, 'We don't allow sneakers in here.' And I sort of looked around the room and saw everybody was in like Nike sneakers or whatever. Everyone was dressed casually. There's no tuxedos and ties. And then I realized that Jo—Josephine my ex—Jo and I were the only people in the room that were white. And it was like, oh, I get it. And I said, 'You mean we can't stay? I can't buy drinks from you? We're really thirsty.' He says, 'No, sir, I'm sorry; you'll have to leave.' And all these people, all these eyes in the room looked at us when we walked out."

"I said, 'You realize what just happened to us, Jo?' 'Yeah, racial discrimination. We're not black' (laughs). It was funny to be on the other side, being on the outside of that that game of black and white. I couldn't believe it. Now I know how it feels to be black (laughs)."

Thirstiness notwithstanding, the voyage across the sea to work in a proper studio turned out to be of utmost importance to the preservation of the team. Bonnet was going through a bout of depression at the castle and it had affected his voice. Also, it was winter and it was cold and furthermore Roger and Graham couldn't find a room to record in where they were both happy with the results. Ritchie, who craved dramatic working environments, was amused but perplexed that Graham wasn't soaking up the castle atmosphere, but Bonnet was adamant that he needed a proper studio to work in to get things done—and progress turned out to be swift at Kingdom Sound.

Down to Earth, released July 28th, 1979, arrived on record shop racks with graphics so fresh and positive, all but the most dedicated Rainbow fan would miss it with a fast flip. Gone is the gravitas-intense gothic lettering for the logo. The three records with Ronnie looked as medieval as Ritchie's beloved moat music, each cover being timeless and serious and epic. *Down to Earth* looked like a disco record, inter-stellar similarity with *Fireball* and *Who Do We Think We Are* notwithstanding. Also somewhat bright and cheery, the first 10,000 copies in the UK were pressed on clear vinyl. But it all made sense—the messaging matched the musical narrative written by the arrival of Roger, of Graham and of "Since You Been Gone." All of this seemed to serve as a reminder that the band was called Rainbow, not Rain.

Once past the wrapper, the album opens with "All Night Long," which begins with a tough freight train of a riff somewhat evocative of "Man on the Silver Mountain" that quickly gives way to a series of poppy progressions further signalling that the above described change of attitude had taken place within the very grooves of the album. To be fair, the chorus was still strongly metallic, but the verse was unmistakably sing-songy, a bit of a letdown against the snarling opening (and chorus) riff, and rhythmically awkward to boot. But all is forgiven each time the chorus kicks in. Indeed, the song's working title was "Once More with Feeling," and that's how it felt every time Ritchie tore into those menacing chords.

Turns out that this is the only song Graham feels he might have deserved a bit of writing credit on. "'All Night Long,' Ritchie played it to me in the studio one night before we went home. He got his acoustic guitar and just started playing that old Mick Jagger song called 'Out of Time' and he said, 'Remember this song?' 'Yeah, yeah, yeah.' And he said, 'Could you kind of base the melody around that?' And I said sure. So that's what I did on 'All Night Long.' That was the only one I kind of had full melody control, but as I said, I was never credited for doing anything on it. I kind of lost out there, being the new kid on the block. 'Oh, just glad to be here!' (laughs)."

In fact, 'All Night Long' represents a rare bit of a lyrical idea from Ritchie. However, although it's somewhat improved by Roger in the final analysis, it's still a crap lyric, Blackmore explaining that his idea revolved around playing a gig, catching the eye of some bird, deciding she might be worth meeting after the last splinters of his smashed axe settle in the front few rows, end of the evening.

After this somewhat nose-wrinkling introduction, *Down to Earth* proceeds big-time to earn its supper, beginning with the intelligent medieval metal of "Eyes of the World," a belligerent, deliberate force of nature chock full of classy, classic, classical metal manoeuvres. "No Time to Lose" is next, Ritchie turning in one of his time-honoured note-dense riffsters in a style similar to "Lady Double Dealer" or "Sensitive to Light." On the 2011 2CD deluxe expanded edition of the album, there's a delightful alternate version of this song—pretty similar at the music end but completely different lyrically and vocal melody-wise—called "Spark Don't Mean a Fire." Graham sings it an octave lower than he does on "No Time to Lose" which gives the song a real bar room Whitesnake vibe.

"Makin' Love" closes side one, and to this writer's mind, it is the band's smartest and most successful ballad thus far, given that it actually floats on a full band arrangement, has parts that are not crutched on ballad clichés, nor does it rely on clichés of the Renaissance or dungeons and dragons nature so easily embraced by Ronnie and Ritchie working together. In fact, this track was central to Roger's stated goal of bringing a bit of sexuality into the band's bulging literary canon. The song's working title was "The Plod," which is an exact description of the song's rhythm, a novel sort of slow-motion gallop.

Side two opens with even more controversy than did side one. "Since You Been Gone" was the band's first cover since the debut, and it was an incendiary pop track, even a somewhat well-traveled and well-known one, penned by song factory and ex-Argent guitarist Russ Ballard. The song had shown up on Ballard's album *Winning*, but most importantly had been turned into a beloved hit single in 1978 across America by Midwest rockers Head East. The song only got to #46 on Billboard for Head East, but their version went on to become a regular rotation staple on US classic rock radio.

"When we started up again with Rainbow, I kind of assumed it would go pretty much in the same direction," says Roger, looking back. "Then Bruce Payne, Rainbow's manager, played me 'Since You Been Gone' and he said, 'What do you think of this?' And I said, 'What am I supposed to think of it?' And he said, 'Well, is it a hit?' And I said, 'Yeah, sounds like a hit.' And he said, 'For Rainbow.' And I said, 'Never in a million years! You'll never get Ritchie to play that.' And he said, 'Oh really.' I'm still thinking of 'Stargazer' and the heaviness, and there's this bit of flippant stuff. And I'm thinking no, no, no. And he said, 'Well Ritchie really wants to do it.' 'You're kidding me!' 'No, he really, really wants to do it.'"

"And of course, it's a strange dichotomy. See, Ritchie, to me, kind of invented wild, screaming, really heavy guitar, and yet his heroes were Abba and he loved to play structured music. Even in Purple, he'd want structure. And I thought, God, just be loose, man, just let it rip; you're great. But he wouldn't want to do that. He does want to know where he was going. And 'Since You Been Gone'… of course, no one in the band wanted to do it either. God knows the problems just trying to get Cozy Powell to record it, and the rest of the band too, because they all thought it was trite rubbish."

"Anyway, as a producer, I managed to convince Cozy to just lay down the track, which he did, and then we did a salvage job. It was kind of pretty awful. And I went in the studio and just threw everything on it, handclaps, tambourines, harmonies, the lot, the works. And of course, it turned out to be really commercial and was a huge hit and in fact, turned Rainbow's career right around. As good as 'Stargazer' was, and as good as those early albums were, they didn't sell. They didn't sell enough to justify the band's existence."

Adds Ritchie, "A friend of ours mentioned that it would be a good song so I looked at it. And in those days, we were looking at any way to get on the radio and getting heard in general. Because our music was never radio-friendly. And 'Since You Been Gone' was perfect for us. I was all for 'Since You Been Gone' but Cozy hated it and I think he played drums on it once, on tape, and he said, 'That's it. I'm not playing anymore.' Because he thought the song was too poppy. And yeah, it was a bit of a pop song, but that's what you have to do when you're playing for the radio. But I liked the song personally. I like commercial songs. I like people like Abba. I love that band; I'm not ashamed to say that. I get more annoyed when I hear some of these jazz people, these purists who looked down their nose at nearly anything that plays commercially. But there are some good things. In the old days there was, anyway."

"The good part of Cozy," continues Ritchie, adding flesh to the "Since You Been Gone" saga, "was that he would bring the house down with his solo; he's a very flashy drummer. He had a brilliant solo, that every night, the thing the audience appreciated the most was his drum solo, playing along with the '1812.' On the negative side, I suppose, like for instance, when we did 'Since You Been Gone,' I remember him saying, 'I'm only going to play this but once.' He hated the song; he thought it was too commercial and too corny. And I remember Roger saying, 'Oh, come on, Cozy, just have another go around. There's a few more things we can put in here.' 'Nope. I've done it but once and that's it. I don't like the song.' And of course, it became our #1 in England. And then I remember hearing Cozy going around telling people, oh, that's his record, and great record, blah blah blah. It was interesting to see how he changed once it became a hit."

"To my mind Rainbow is a very heavy rock band and there should be no compromises," Cozy told Geoff Barton back in 1979. "Ritchie feels that we should compromise to a certain extent and therefore this album has a couple of commercial numbers on it. Of course there's the usual heavy stuff as well. There's one epic track that's a slight nick from 'Mars' in Holst's 'Planets' suite—we'll probably be opening our new show with it—but like I say it does contain these two commercial tracks. Ritchie and I have argued about their inclusion. Well, we have a lot of arguments anyway, as you can well imagine. When we don't agree over certain things he usually wins because it's his band. He started it all in the first place, so I'm not going to knock that. But I will make my opinions heard."

Hard not to pick out which song Cozy is referring to there as being a nick. If there's any doubt, "Mars" was the provisional title for "Eyes of the World," which, yes, shares the same classical music inspiration as "Black Sabbath" by Black Sabbath, as proudly admitted to by Geezer Butler.

"I'll say what I think to Ritchie and he respects me for it," continued Powell. "I think the only reason that I'm still a member of Rainbow is that Ritchie knows that I'll beat him up if he fires me. So we have differences of opinion—in fact it nearly came to fisticuffs at one point in Geneva—but at the end of the day it's usually okay. We have a few drinks and make up. But it's good all the same; it's healthy. We're men enough to know that united we stand, divided we don't necessarily fall, but it's not going to be so easy. So if we stick together we could end up conquering the world. Which'd be nice, wouldn't it?"

It is indeed true: for whatever reason, Cozy eventually came around to liking 'Since You Been Gone,' and indeed, who can resist a hummable chord sequence like that? Dozens and dozens of hits consisted of the chords to "Louie Louie" rearranged and this was merely another one in a long line. Then there were the complicated backing vocals, the modulation, and really, the song's got quite a sophisticated verse. And then there's the stop/start passage, which offers Ritchie a brief moment to play classical. What more could you want?

Candice Night, Ritchie's love mate and co-leader in Blackmore's Night (we'll hear more from her later), had this to say about the mercurial, now deceased drummer who resisted. "You know, the ironic thing about Cozy was that even though he was known for being such a hard rock kind of guy… the last time we saw him was at a festival in Sweden. We had just put out *Shadow of the Moon*, and he ran over to us and he told us that he was actually burning copies of *Shadow of the Moon* and giving them to all his friends because he loved it so much. So I guess he had a soft spot to him too."

"He had a very soft side to him," agrees Ritchie. "We had a love/hate relationship. He was a chocolate fanatic. He had a whole wardrobe—and I mean, a wardrobe—full of chocolates, in England. Even in France... you know, when we were speaking to each other and being the best of friends, he would say to me, 'Come on in and have some Ovaltine or Horlicks. Pick out some chocolate—what do you want?' 'Well, what have you got?' And he goes, 'Okay, top shelf I've got Kit Kats, bottom shelf would be Mars bars and middle shelf is Crunchies, chocolate cream...' And I went, I've never seen so much chocolate in my life. It was like a shop. So he had that other side to him, which is very calm. He was like a little granny."

"We used to play 'Renaissance Faire' (Blackmore's Night song), the riff, with Rainbow, before I got into recording it. And it was kind of... I used to make him play it, this little waltz, and I said to him, when I last saw him, 'Do you remember that tune?' He says, 'Yeah. I remember that tune. Can I ever forget that tune?' Like it was a joke. We would often play tricks on each other. Cozy was the ultimate trickster. You know, I used to be heavily into trickery and practical jokes. But he used to always go one more than me. So we used to have a truce, that we wouldn't play tricks on each other, because I would never know what the hell he was going to retaliate with."

"There's lots of stories," continues Blackmore. "For instance, one day he played a joke on one of our roadies, at one of the hotels, in Germany. He's actually... we used to call him Spiderman. He would scale walls and roofs and things. He had no fear of heights. So this one night, he has a few drinks, gets out on the balcony with the fire extinguisher, gets up on the next balcony. Now, this is like a hundred-foot drop, and he gets this fire extinguisher and lets it off through this window that was open, so that the roadie who is sleeping in there is covered in fire extinguisher foam. Now, of course, the trouble with a fire extinguisher is that it takes the oxygen out of the air. And he got into the wrong room, into a businessman's room. And the next day, this businessman… well, that night, the man managed to crawl out of bed and get to hospital and was in the ward in the hospital half dying, from asphyxiation. And Cozy had no clue that it was the wrong room."

"So the next day at breakfast, the management said, 'Guess what happened last night?' Cozy's saying, 'Oh, what?' 'Someone got in with a fire extinguisher and this businessman has been rushed to hospital.' And I was having breakfast with Cozy and his face went white as a ghost. It was like, 'What?! The guy is dying in hospital?!' It was not supposed to be like that. It was supposed to be a joke. It nearly backfired on him. He rushed to the hospital and apologized to the guy, and the guy took it as a joke. The businessman was okay. He could have really done a number on him."

"I think he was on some kind of medication at the time," laughs Jimmy Bain, recalling the same prank. "And he had gotten the floors mixed up. He was supposed to be letting it off in Ian Broad's room, Ritchie's roadie at the time, but he misjudged and let it off in the German salesman's room."

"I like the whole album, but I never listen to my own albums," reflects Graham, who goes on to offer his own take on the inclusion of "Since You Been Gone" on the record. "'Eyes of the World' is one of my favourites, 'Lost in Hollywood,' 'Love's No Friend,' plus 'Bad Girl,' which wasn't on the album but was a B-side. 'All Night Long'—I like that, because of my involvement on the melody side."

"Well, 'Since You Been Gone,' of course, because that was a kind of the hit (laughs). You've got to like that one. In fact, that almost didn't happen anyway. We had a recording of it by a band called Clout, a girl band (note: from South Africa). But we heard this, and Bruce Payne, the manager of Rainbow at the time, who is now the Deep Purple manager, said you've got to have something that will get you into the charts. And of course, being a heavy metal band, all the guys in the band said, 'Oh, we're not doing that fucking thing.' It was like the last track ever recorded, the last thing they wanted to put down, because it was a cover, and it didn't really represent Rainbow, as such. Anyway, we did it, and we tried to change it a little bit and it turned out good for the band, I think. It was definitely too poppy for Cozy (laughs). I remember, when we were recording, Cozy was like, 'Oh, we're not going to do that now. Record that later.' I think everybody was kind of hoping that Bruce Payne would drop the idea. The longer we put it off, it would be forgotten, you know what I mean?"

Bonnet goes on to recount what it was like recording at the French chateau with these serious metal minds. "Well, the cotton on the windows, being pulled open at night, for other people, not for me. I didn't get all this. But Ritchie was out there with cotton and pulling windows open all night when everybody was asleep, to kind of make that there were ghosts around. Creaks and groans and stuff like that. But I was never involved in that; I just heard about it afterwards. But being in that chateau, it didn't last too long. I was only in there about a week or so and then we moved to Syosset on Long Island, to finish off all the vocals."

And the reason being, laughs Graham, is that, "I think Ritchie wanted to go home as well. We all had had enough of the... 'castle' (laughs), the dungeons and whatever, the gloominess. There was nothing to do! You're in the middle of farm country out there and it's like, what do you do? When you're not recording. Just sit and look at each other? It got very boring. You know, Cozy used to go home as soon as he could, after recording. He'd get in his car, get on a plane and go back to England every now and then. He would get into his Mercedes in France, drive to the airport, leave it there and then fly home, and then pick another car up at the airport, drive home and then do the same whenever he had to come back and do some more tracks. That's the kind of guy he was. And then he had the chocolate—Mars bars and whatever else—because one of the bad habits he always had was that he was always craving chocolate, or something to eat, let's say that (laughs). But that's how it got; it was like being in prison, a little bit. So the vocals and most of the guitar solos were done kind of in the States."

In actual fact, proceedings at the castle were more desperate than Graham lets on. Bonnet nearly threw in the towel a few times, claiming illness, claiming dislike of the castle, claiming he just couldn't do his job, the band attempting novel locales (within the novel locale), having Graham try execute his parts set up in the dining room of the place. As alluded to, the move to Kingdom Sound was the clincher, Bonnet recording all his vocal parts there, at an infinitely swifter pace than was evident at the French sessions.

Also of note, recording in France, Ritchie was up to his usual hijinks, freaking out Don Airey with recorded sound effects, eventually ending the ruse by flipping Don the tape one day, indicating that he'd like him to learn the material on the cassette. Cozy got into the games as well, dressing up like a monk and spooking Airey from behind a curtain.

"It's all true what they say about him, and much worse," chuckles Airey, concerning Blackmore. "No, he's great, he's a genius. When we were staying at the Château in France, they were playing jokes on me. I was staying in a room called The Chapel, a spooky room. And they had a tape recorder they triggered, with ghostly noises on it, which was freaking me out. I could hear these things, and I heard a noise, and I pulled the curtains back, and there was a monk standing there. Very frightening. Turned out it was Cozy Powell. But I kind of ran out and said there's something behind the curtain. And they came, 'No, there's nothing there.' Of course Cozy was still there. The next day Ritchie told me what they'd been doing. He was just playing a tape. And I just went, 'Oh, game, set and match' (laughs)."

As for the band's lead singer, Airey says, "Graham is just so talented. He can just run rings around people, which he tends to do if he gets the chance. He can just make up lyrics on the spot. He can think up another song. He's got an amazing gift, but he's one of these guys who doesn't know quite what to do with it, and he'll often do the wrong thing. But I must say, he and Cozy were just the dearest, like my two other brothers. Graham is the dearest man on earth for me. And Cozy, I borrowed his car once, and I thought he had at least five children, all the sweetie wrappers in it."

"I know Ritchie very well," continues Graham, painting a profile of the boss. "As soon as I met him, I got on very well with him. I argued very well with him and we had lots of fights, which was very good. It was a good bonding situation, I think (laughs). And his girlfriend at the time would go, 'Now, you two aren't fighting again, are you?!' I think we were the only two that ever fought, for a little while, when I first joined the band. It was about silly things. Well, my hair, for a start. I had short hair, and it was one of those things that bugged him (laughs). Just stupid things. Of course it was confusing for the fans when all the other guys had long hair, black clothes and everything and I had short hair and my own very different style to them. But actually fans accepted me very well when they heard me singing and I never had real problems with that."

"But it was friendly arguments," continues Bonnet, "never anything that was really serious, coming to blows or anything. It was silly things like that. 'Well, you've kind of got to look like a rock kind of guy.' 'Well, you know… why?!' You had to wear a uniform. Why shouldn't I be a little bit different? Things like that. But he got on with me very well and I found him to be basically a very shy person, who kind of kept himself to himself if he could. He would often go off and wander with his girlfriend wherever, and keep himself pretty much just with her. That's how he felt comfortable. He didn't like hanging around with the band so much, I don't think. He didn't want to be on the bus, for instance, if we were traveling quite a ways. He would go on the plane, rather than be on the bus. Things like that. He very much kept to himself."

And what of Don Airey? Airey, forever in the orbit of Deep Purple (and now in the '00s, fully ensconced as a band member), was, as discussed, also new to the band. Along with Roger Glover. Along with Graham.

"Don is still one of my best friends, and I see him all the time," says Graham, on the new keyboardist who would stick around for two Rainbow records. "I played with Don a couple of times in England and Don was also with us before he joined Deep Purple. He went out with me and Dario Mollo and we went and did a Bonnet Airey Band kind of thing, playing Rainbow stuff."

"Don is a very typical down-to-earth Englishmen. He's very, very grounded. He lives in a village in England, very much a normal guy, so to speak, and he's very much the businessman. He knows when things are good and he knows when things are bad.

He's great at spotting great musicians and musicians that are kind of pretending to be great musicians. I'm going, 'Wow, that guitar player is great!' And he'd go, 'No, no, no, he might widdly widdly all over the place but he's not that great. Listen, let me tell you something...' And he'll sit down and explain to me why he ain't that good or whatever. He's very much a musician's musician. As I say, he's one of my best friends. I speak to him on the phone all the time. He calls me when he's out on the road with Deep Purple. We've been friends ever since Rainbow."

"Roger and I were never really close," continues Bonnet. "When I was in the band, he was going through a bad time in his life with his wife and things. He was another one that kept to himself very much. So Roger would wander off on his own a lot of the time and not really mix with the other guys. At the time, he was writing words and things, and melodies for this album, at the beginning, anyway. And he was very quiet. I never really got to be friends with him, and I found out later that he kind of put me down in a lot of interviews he did about me and said bad things about me. And I could never really understand why. It's just one of those things."

"Because he lost one of his best friends," continues Graham, suddenly offering a theory. "I got along with Ritchie better than he did, in the band situation. He never hung out with Ritchie, whereas I did. And suddenly his Deep Purple mate was hanging out with this shorthaired guy (laughs), who was an intruder to his world. And I think he was a little bit pissed about it, that me and Ritchie could talk before a show. Whereas no one would go into the dressing room... everybody had a separate dressing room; that was another thing. And Ritchie would often ask me over to his dressing room to talk about what we were going to do, what we were going to say, probably make a joke about something in the show or whatever. And no one else was invited but me. Things like that kind of pushed him away from Ritchie. They had been friends for a long time. And as I said, at the time, he was going through a bad situation with his marriage and he was not very outgoing, a lot of the time."

"I thought he wrote great lyrics. They always sounded good. Because you can write great lyrics but they sound wrong when you sing them. There are too many syllables, or the sound of the word on the actual note sounds weird, and sometimes you have to change them. But Roger had the right idea; I think he has a really good handle on that. But it was all done like on the day."

Back to the resulting record, the sweet power chords of "Since You Been Gone" quickly give way to a black and blue bruiser called "Love's No Friend." Essentially a trudging and doomy blues ballad, the song is actually pretty heavy. The 2011 reissue of the album includes an alternate version with completely different lyrics called "Ain't a Lot of Love in the Heart of Me," generating another comparison with Whitesnake and their signature cover of "Ain't No Love in the Heart of the City."

Things pick up for "Danger Zone," which is as passionately gothic yet modern of architecture as its co-masterwerk "Eyes of the World." Arguably, these two songs find the band triumphant over all other Rainbow eras and compositions with respect to this idea of gothic, symphonic rock for a mature, adult audience. Musically they are tight, intelligent and most importantly, above cliché, and both lyrically and vocally, there's a sense of worldliness about them.

Down to Earth closes with a ripper of a track called "Lost in Hollywood." Fast, melodic and metallic—suitably, the song's working title was "The Steamer"—this was an incendiary, explosive way to end the record. And Ritchie's solo cuts like an axe, even more stunning given that it is placed over an arrangement that had, thus far in the song, not come up. "Lost in Hollywood" is the author's favourite Rainbow track of all time and a big reason why the wider album, an anomaly, is his (my, whatever!) favourite full album of the catalogue.

The song is a master class in transition between sections and everybody is on fire, including Cozy, who exhibits a sense of groove and pocket that we usually have to go to the posthumous live albums to locate. Not the biggest Cozy fan, I've gained new appreciation for the man over the years through the manic Led Zeppelin-esque playing he and the band got up to when blowing up Rainbow songs live. At the vocal end, Ritchie asked Graham to sing it the way Little Richard would. It's a curious comment, because it's hard to see the connection—if there's anything Penniman-like from Graham on the album, it's "No Time to Lose."

"I was surprised that Ritchie did his solos as quickly as he did," says Graham, when asked about the most remarkable thing he could remember from the *Down to Earth* sessions. "That was one thing that we did at Syosset, back on Long Island. I'd never seen that process happen before. And also, to me, it was backwards. The arrangement was done before the song was written, if you know what I mean. And you kind of put the song into the arrangement, which I'd always done the other way around. I'd play the guitar, and I had the melody in my head and the guitar was just part of the melody."

"But this writing songs with a rock band… it's like, the band comes first and the vocal comes last and it has to fit in where certain arrangements happen. And then the guitar solo, of course! (laughs). So you get out of the way of that. It was all kind of new to me. That was one thing I found unusual. Because like I said, now I write the complete song, the words, the melody, in one go. And then put the arrangement to it later, if I just want to fiddle around with it and change little bits here and there."

"Anyway, Ritchie would come in and he would play three or four solos straight off, on whatever track it was, and then he'd just put the guitar down and say, 'All right, Rog, can you piece that together?' And then the solos would be mixed, put together, Frankenstein'ed, a bit of this one, a bit of that one, and then he would use that as a template to play live. That was one thing. But no ritual or method or anything. He might have had a glass of wine or beer or something. But I remember, Ritchie would just come in, sit on the couch and just play in front of the board and that's it (laughs); nothing unusual."

As for the other musicians, "Cozy did everything very quickly. He wanted to get his job over and go. He was always very fast and he knew exactly what to do. He told everybody where to stop, start or whatever and he was done very quickly, done before anybody. And Don was very much like that too; he's a very quick worker. He has ideas in his head and he's ready to go before he goes into the studio. And I guess everybody did, really. They all had their parts worked out in their head, if not actually physically played before. It was only really me that didn't know where he was going (laughs). I was the one who was guessing and feeling my way, with Roger—melodies and things. Ritchie, being the guitar player, would sit at home and have these ideas, and as I said, he would play different ways. But Don was pretty much… he had this one idea and it would usually be the right one straight off, and Roger with his bass parts too."

There was at least one properly finished track left over, "Bad Girl." "That was done at the same time we did the album and it was just like a spare track, which turned out in the end, actually. I had forgotten about that song, and we put it back into the set a couple years ago when I was with Don and Dario. They said, 'What about "Bad Girl?"' 'What the hell is that? How does it go? Oh yeah!' I had forgotten about it. So that went back into the set and I still do it now. But yes, same situation—Roger wrote the lyric."

Down to Earth marked a revival for the band, based around the hit status of "Since You Been Gone," which rose to #6 in the UK charts (in America, the single only saw #57, the album, #66). Top of the Pops played the video of the song and suddenly Rainbow was part of the mainstream, resulting in "Since You Been Gone" staying in the charts for ten weeks. "All Night Long" did even better, hitting #5 in the UK. The album also reached #6 on the UK charts (having entered at #11) and sold gold, designated for sales of over 100,000 copies. Up into the streaming realities of the present day, on Spotify, "Since You Been Gone" enjoys triple the amount of plays of any other Rainbow song.

One must bear in mind that *Down to Earth*, which, as I've argued, was actually quite heavy metal in composite, was issued in the summer of '79, essentially just as the New Wave of British Heavy Metal was kicking off. This pronounced, definable rock movement, which is bracketed roughly by the years 1979 to 1983, saw throngs of UK rock fans finding solace after punk's fizzle in a new, faster, more technical and quite simply heavier-rocking army of groups. For the first time in rock history, bands clung to the tirelessly denigrated and accursed heavy metal tag proudly, most deigning it unnecessary and even "naff" to put ballads on their albums. If they even made full albums—the NWOBHM was marked by an exciting profusion of singles-only bands scurrying about below bigger names such as Motörhead, Saxon, Iron Maiden, Def Leppard, Venom, Diamond Head and Tygers of Pan Tang.

In this light, I would argue that the success of the album (remember, we're talking relative and still modest success here) had less to do with the dastardly and endlessly-debated duo of "All Night Long" and "Since You Been Gone," and rather to its launching at this fortuitous, almost giddy time for hard rock. It wasn't that Rainbow had succeeded in finding themselves a whole new audience (presumably added onto the old one, without too, too much defection), it was that hard rock had added throngs of fence-sitters to its ranks as a whole, in tandem with it becoming an accepted, very buzzy, and, in circular, self-fulfilling fashion, very active and creative corner of the music industry.

Rainbow just happened to be along for the ride, as did Priest, as did Sabbath, as did Uriah Heep, as did Budgie. And, as I've argued many a' time before, the record Rainbow was wedging into the door jamb of the NWOBHM was every bit as heavy as its predecessor ("L.A. Connection?" "Rainbow Eyes?") to be sure, slightly less so than *Rising* (that album had its own "All Night Long," called "Do You Close Your Eyes"), and leaps and bounds more malevolent than the Elf-ish debut. As I've sworn countless times to anybody who might listen, *Down to Earth*, outside of "Since You Been Gone," "Makin' Love" and only half of "All Night Long" (the verses), is a ripper of a classic heavy metal album.

"I know it sold a lot, quite a lot," says Bonnet, on the record's success. "Gold albums. In fact, Joe Lynn Turner's got one of my gold albums, the bastard (laughs). He picked it up for me after I had left the band, another gold album from whatever country it was; I can't remember now. But it went gold over the place."

The *Down to Earth* tour was an exhaustive, exhausting rounding of the bases, typical for this hard-working band. Graham was rightfully nervous: he'd not done a gig in two years and had only done a handful ever. And let's not forget that Rainbow had only had one singer before him, and Ronnie was a man of peerless reputation. September and October '79 were spent solidly blanketing America, in support of Blue Öyster Cult, which took some of the pressure off. A (mostly) German tour was cancelled in order that the band continue trying to solidify US success. With that in mind, November and December were spent beginning in the west and moving east. Along as backup were Randy Hansen, Gamma, Scorpions and a plucky up-and-comer by the name of John Cougar.

"We played everywhere," says Graham. "We went coast-to-coast in the States, which was however many weeks. We played just about every damn city there is. Then over to England. All told, we were on the road about six months. When we first went out, we were opening up for Blue Öyster Cult and it wasn't really a very good match. They were too kind of soft, I guess. We were pretty loud and noisy and more obnoxious, I guess (laughs). It just wasn't a very good teaming-up, I don't think. They were too sweet. And I think they realized that. After we had been on, people started to drift in the audience, even though they were fans of theirs. It was a bit like that. And then we were out on our own, and at one point we had John Cougar Mellencamp, which was kind of strange. How things change! Suddenly things turn around. These guys are suddenly stars and now you're the bum. 'Oh fuck. What happened?!' (laughs)."

When asked for a memorable road tale or two, Graham says, "Most of those things I've probably forgotten because we were probably all drunk as skunks (laughs). Maybe, back then, anyway. But there was nothing really eventful like you always hear about, these manic things happening on the road with people. They never seemed to happen, because everybody would just do their job and go to their room, and 'I'll see you in the morning' (laughs). Kind of like that. The only thing that happened is we would hang out in the bar until it closed; that would be about it. No interesting incidents. I guess it was also because we didn't really know each other that well. It was like a new team of guys. It was kind of like, 'Okay, I've done the job now; I'll see you later.' It was a bit nine-to-five."

Graham says that for the most part he steered cleared of Ritchie's occult dealings. "I mostly just heard about it. One night we had a go in the chateau, just messing around. And of course nothing happened. We were doing the Ouija board thing. But I like all that kind of stuff too. It's nice to think that you actually live after you die, or whatever. Goblins and all the rest of it, UFOs. Anything that has nothing to do with the real world (laughs), it's a nice diversion. I mean, I'm still into that. I like to hear about haunted London, this, that and the other. And I think he's still like that. It's like fairytale land, isn't it? When you're a kid, you like fairy tales that scare you, but at the same time they're exciting."

Presenting the band on stage, Ritchie was concerned that Graham Bonnet's short-haired look and good-time rock 'n' rollsy stage presence would cause problems with those accustomed to the serious heavy metal godliness of Ronnie James Dio. Bonnet also had a predilection for white suit jackets, sunglasses, red pants and loud Hawaiian shirts, one of which saw its end in a prank ritual burning at the hands of Ritchie. Indeed, Graham's short hair was almost offensively so at times. With a fresh haircut, and in those togs, accompanied with stage moves that occasionally seemed to "take the piss," Graham could look like a snobby art rock new waver parachuted in amongst grave cavemen.

Muses Graham, "People think about the image before they think about the music sometimes and it's totally wrong. But I remember the first time I went onstage with Rainbow, people were going, 'What the hell is this? Who is this geek?' (laughs). Until we started playing, and then they said, 'Oh, okay. That's all right.'"

The look was a tribute to James Dean. "Oh, of course it was! It happened over the years. I was just always into 1950s music and that era; I always loved that era, the doo-wop stuff, The Platters, Fats Domino, Little Richard. I grew up with that and I still love it."

Indeed, Graham, as regards Rainbow's sartorial sense, proved merely to be ahead of his time. Roger would start dressing up a bit as time went on, adding a white hat and sports jackets to his look, and Don Airey wasn't against similar fashion sense. Even Cozy could be spotted in white dress shirts pure as the driven snow. And then when Joe Lynn Turner joined, well, all bets were off. The odd wristband couldn't hide the new upscale look.

Addressing the issue of the band's set list, Graham recalls that, "We did 'Man on the Silver Mountain,' which is pretty cool, 'Catch the Rainbow,' which I liked. I think we did 'Mistreated' as well, at that point anyway. Oh yes, and 'Long Live Rock 'n' Roll,' which I didn't really like (laughs)." *Down to Earth* tracks that made the grade included "Since You Been Gone" (oddly, a bit of a wobbler live), "All Night Long," "Eyes of the World," "Love's No Friend" and "Lost in Hollywood," which housed much of the band's noodling this time 'round, including traces of Beethoven's "Ninth." Other surprises included casual runs at Deep Purple's "Lazy," the band's own blues called "Blues" and "Kill the King" as an instrumental.

Adds Graham, "The cover we did was 'Will You Still Love Me Tomorrow;' that's about the only one we did, by The Shirelles. It was a song Ritchie liked that I had done in the past on one of my albums, before I joined Rainbow. He liked that track and he kept playing it at his house. He'd say, 'Listen to this.' He said, 'One day, we should play it live.' And so that's what we did."

"It was theatres and arenas; big crowds," notes Bonnet on the business the band could do. "We could actually fill arenas. And when we went to Japan, we did all the big venues there, Budokan and what have you. The audiences were bloody wild. I couldn't believe it. I mean, just being out in the street, kids running at us and everything; it was nuts. I didn't expect that at all. I was expecting something completely oriental, sedate, laid-back, very polite, but it was the damn opposite. You know, Cozy said me, 'We're going to go to Japan in a few weeks.' And I said, 'Well, so what?' And he said, 'You fucking wait' (laughs)."

"And he was right. It was just like we were the Beatles or something. They're fanatics—where the word 'fan' comes from; they're the ultimate fans, and their loyalty through all the years is incredible. Since I'd been with Rainbow and onwards, they say, 'When is the next album out and when are you coming over to play again?' I haven't been there for a couple of years though. In the shows, they used to have to sit down. That was the law, I seem to remember, at one time. But now they're allowed to move around and jump and throw stuff around; things have changed. They're very Americanized now."

The apex of the *Down to Earth* tour was the band's headlining appearance, August 16th, 1980, at the inaugural edition of a huge new metal festival called Monsters of Rock, at Castle Donington, which came to be known as the must-see heavy metal event of the season in the UK—and pretty much the world—for quite a few years. But emotions were mixed, due to the knowledge that Cozy Powell, disillusioned with the band's poppier direction, would be leaving the ranks. Graham's sartorial choices for the big event must have really pushed Ritchie's buttons: Bonnet wore red pants and a red shirt, along with white boots and a white suit jacket. Blackmore wore black but both Roger and Don split the difference, with a mix of red, white and back, more casual than Graham in total but still fairly stylish. Even Cozy, thundering away, had on a collared shirt.

"I know my parents were very proud of the Donington thing," recalls Graham, who I spoke to near the time of the death of his father. "I'm glad my dad saw all that. Yeah, he would have been 92 this month; he was an old man. I'm going to miss talking to him every week. So yeah, I'm proud of that era. That show was an experience of a lifetime. I can't remember who we played with, but lots of bands. Every band in the world was on, and we were headlining. Scorpions—yeah, oh God!—and Touch. I forgot all about Touch! (note: the baby band on the bill, thanks to management by Bruce Payne, also Rainbow's manager; rounding out the list: April Wine, Saxon and Riot). I remember they used to put creases in their Levis. A nice crease down... what the hell is that all about? There were loads of people."

"We didn't see them all though, because we were back at the hotel, being the headliner and everything—it was so posh (laughs). We were the main draw; it was an incredible night. But for the rest of the tour, sometimes we would take up local bands. And I think one night in England we played with The Troggs (laughs). Now how's that for a match? They opened up for us when we played Wembley, in London."

The Troggs were a '60s band known for their anthem "Wild Thing." They played the second of Rainbow's two Wembley gigs, at the expressed request of Ritchie. Predictably it did not go well for them.

The first of the two Wembley gigs, February 29th, 1980, resulted in a riot by the fans, enraged when Blackmore refused to do an encore after the band's already stingy 70-minute set, something he had done many times over the years, usually based on his perception of fan reaction throughout the brunt of the show. It was said that Ian Gillan had been slated to guest-sing during this cancelled Wembley encore, but he had not been spotted in the venue. Support on the quite extensive UK leg came from Samson, Saxon and an obscure one-single Manchester act called The Katchies, who were also on board for numerous mainland European dates.

The previous month, Rainbow nipped into Sweet Silence studio in Copenhagen to record a Bach-themed instrumental B-side called "Weiss Heim," (meaning "white home," the track having been inspired by Ritchie's house on Long Island). This was used on the single release of "All Night Long," which also received proper production video treatment, which, granted, was mostly live performance mimicry, similar to the "Since You Been Gone" clip.

"It was fantastic," continues Graham, back on the subject of Donington, at which the band were flanked by a huge graphic of the debut album cover stage right, the cover of *Rising* stage left. "I don't know about the planning and everything else, but I think that was pretty good too. It was the time of my life. I think for all of us it was a fucking great day, but I said 'day' at the same time, because Cozy left the band that very day. All our families were there, my mom and dad, my brother, nephews, aunts and uncles; it was one of those deals. And the crowd was huge. It was amazing. I'll never forget it. Ever. I've got it on tape. I've seen the thing a million times, different versions, some good quality, some bad quality. It was probably the best thing I've ever done. It was exciting and we played very good, I think."

"But, that was kind of it—Cozy left that day. That was the big finale. I remember we sat up 'til about six in the morning saying goodbye to him. We tried to convince him to stay, but he had another thing offered him and he'd had enough of Rainbow, I guess. He just didn't want to do it anymore. He wanted to do something different. And he had a good wage packet coming on (laughs). I imagine that would be it more than anything. He just got fed-up with the Rainbow thing. I don't really know in-depth what it would be. But I think he just got cheesed-off with the whole thing. But we knew ahead of time it was going to come, and we tried to convince him to stay way before then."

In fact, perhaps fuelling his decision, back at the beginning of 1980, Cozy had seen unexpected success with his (surprisingly stodgy) *Over the Top* solo album, especially in Japan, where it went gold. Concurrent with the album's issuance, Rainbow were making good on their German dates, also playing Sweden, Belgium and The Netherlands. Of note, the Donington gig resulted in an album documenting the event, Rainbow represented with versions on the day of "Stargazer" and "All Night Long," dreary crowd participation portion included.

In 1981, Cozy would issue a second solo album called *Tilt*, but his main claim to fame just into the new decade would be his work with the Michael Schenker Group, on the band's second studio album plus the live *One Night in Budokan*. Then came a brief appearance as part of Whitesnake, and later in the decade, a considerable period with Black Sabbath.

Final word goes to Roger, who succinctly sums up his Rainbow experience, specifically the effect of the *Down to Earth* album on the band's demanding fan base. "Well, it was Ritchie's band. It was like Purple; I didn't have much of a say. I was a paid member like the rest of the band were. Ritchie was lord to himself. When Graham left (more on that next chapter), Joe Lynn Turner got the gig because he's actually a very good singer. He had a great voice, natural timber to the voice, and he's a great entertainer. Now unfortunately again, he's not hard rock. But of course it's all very well looking back. We thought we could mould him. But my favourite era of Rainbow in fact is Rainbow *Rising*, with things like 'Stargazer'—it's wonderful. But with the advent of pop success, which is what *Down to Earth* brought us, we lost a lot of the older fans. And we had reached a plateau which we would never get beyond."

Chapter 7

Difficult to Cure

**"We used to call him Judy now and again,
as in Judy Garland."**

Rainbow can most definitely be split into two main era, with the Bonnet album and the way off context Doogie White album (more on that later) serving as high-relief anomalies to the two dynasties at three records apiece. *Difficult to Cure*, issued in February 1981, marked the first of the three Joe Lynn Turner albums and, along with a marked shift in sound, the band also picked up a new drummer in Bobby Rondinelli. Ergo, a couple Americans replaced a couple of Brits (it could have been just one— there were rumours Bruce Dickinson was bandied about). The record went that way as well, Rainbow emerging with a sound that was primed for radio across the pond to the promised land, the band constructing a record that arguably caved to '80s-styled label pressure to try a little harder to come up with some hits, pressure also applied by the fact, says Roger, that it was costing $50,000 a week to keep Rainbow on the road.

As events would transpire, *Difficult to Cure* was started at Sweet Silence Studios in Copenhagen, Denmark and then finished up with a repeat trip to Kingdom Sound on Long Island in New York. Graham Bonnet was still supposed to be Rainbow's vocalist.

"I was only in the band with Graham for about two weeks," recalls new drummer Bobby Rondinelli, starting the significant part of his career right here but going on to so much more, including Blue Öyster Cult and Black Sabbath.

"And he seemed okay. I was there from the beginning, on that record. But I literally worked with him two weeks, so what I remember was, he was okay, a good guy, good singer. Then him and Ritchie had some differences, a falling-out over musical ideas or whatever and he was sent home. I enjoyed it; I like Copenhagen and I like Denmark. Sweet Silence was... we were like the first big band to record there, I believe. And the engineer we worked with, Fleming Rasmussen, went on to work with Metallica. It was a good studio, good room."

"The saddest thing about it was when we were recording that record, John Bonham died. I'll never forget it. Because when we were getting drum sounds, we would always start talking about Led Zeppelin and John Bonham and his drum sound and preparing. And one of the guys who worked with the band, who was a practical joker, while we were talking about Bonham, he comes in the room and says, 'Bonzo's dead.' We thought he was kidding at first, but he wasn't. So we took the day off."

"All the basic tracks were done there; all the music was done there. Graham Bonnet left the band a couple of weeks into the recording—I think we had only done about two or three songs with him. So we finished writing that album without even knowing who was going to be the singer. We didn't even know if the songs were in the right key or what."

Here's how Bonnet recalls his last days with the band. "Oh, I did one tune, the Russ Ballard tune, 'I Surrender.' I started to do that. I did some backup vocals on that, and I was going to start to do the lead vocal, and I went back to Los Angeles for something. For some reason, I don't know; I can't remember what it was. But I just got there, and I thought, I've had enough of this (laughs). And I kind of changed my mind about the whole thing, which, I think, now was the wrong thing to have done. But at the time I just thought it wasn't fun anymore. We were looking for a new drummer and stuff like that. I don't know… all the joy went out of it."

"And Don was miserable, I remember, and I thought he was going to leave. And I thought, well, if Don is going to leave, I'll go home and think about it for a bit. So I came back home here and I decided to quit. We were rehearsing in Copenhagen, and we got a new drummer, Bobby Rondinelli, and he came in, and rehearsals were just terrible. I mean, nothing happened at rehearsals. It was just like hanging around and waiting for everybody to turn up. It was all very casual. 'You're here, then? Oh, okay.' And we would stay there, and Ritchie sometimes would just turn his guitar up and play to himself and nothing was produced. And so we had the song by Russ Ballard come along, which was completed. So we started with that, obviously, because it was the only song we had. So I went down and started doing the vocals and, I don't know, nothing was happening. And I thought, 'What am I sitting here for, in this damn hotel, waiting for the band to get together?' And everybody was thinking the same thing. So I went home, and as I said, decided to say, 'Oh, I've had enough' (laughs). I don't know why. I just felt that I could do something on my own at that point."

So to reiterate, nobody had done any writing. "Yes, well, we started. I remember we had started on the thing that eventually turned out to be called 'Spotlight Kid.' I started on the melody of that, and when I heard it later, I thought, wait a minute, that's my tune there; that's my tune! I recognized it and I thought, bloody 'ell! They nicked it; they stole it! Because we used to just put a cassette recorder in the corner and just jam away a bit. So that was it, yeah."

Surreal as it is, there was a chance that Graham might have landed within the ranks of Black Sabbath. "Yeah, I actually got a call from their management and I kind of went, 'Huh?' I was never a big Black Sabbath fan and I thought, well, I don't know, it just didn't seem right. Then Dio joined them and they had three pretty good albums; Ronnie made that band better, I think. I was never a Black Sabbath fan, sorry. So I turned it down which was probably a mistake because I had nothing else lined up and it probably would have been a good idea for me to give it a chance. I just didn't like their music very much. But when Ronnie did it, they changed, and I liked their music more."

"I thought he was a great drummer and everything," continues Graham, on the subject of Bobby. "Again, it was just the change of personnel. It was another new personality; it just wasn't family anymore. I was still just getting used to the other guys. With a new guy in, it was like, oh no. And he wasn't Cozy. I'll just leave it at that (laughs)."

Indeed, many fans grumbled that "he wasn't Cozy." It must be remembered that Cozy had lasted through three very, very good Rainbow albums—and after four more records to close out the band's history, we were about to appreciate how very good they were. Cozy was also the drummer on the one official live album from the band, and live is where Cozy really shone, Powell being a rare showman at the skins position, rare at least, for that era.

But even on the studio records, the drumming had a certain character, a heavy metal character, and all that a term like that encompasses. Powell's choices come fill time, as Spinal Tap is wont to muse, rode the fine line between cleverness and stupidity. And Rondinelli? First off, he was new. Second, he was American. And although he had some of Cozy's hard-hitting habits, he was somewhat of a new hotshot breed. He wasn't a character. Or at least, it was going to take a bunch of records—and some character—to earn that title. Amusingly, as heavy metal history got strange, Cozy would take verbal shots at Bobby, for sort of aping his every move, first following him into Rainbow, and then doing the same with Black Sabbath.

I asked Bobby if he was there that fateful day when Joe Lynn Turner was brought in to sing.

"Me and Ritchie went to see him at some school or college somewhere in New Jersey or Connecticut, and we saw him there. I don't think I was there the first day he sang with the band. I think Ritchie was there with Roger, at Kingdom Sound Studios in New York. I don't think I was there. All my parts were done, you know?"

So yes, enter 29-year-old Hackensack, New Jersey native Joe Lynn Turner.

"My parts for *Difficult to Cure* were actually done right here in Long Island at Syosset," explains Joe, who proceeds to add the story of his hiring. "They did their parts in Denmark. In other words, that album was pretty much recorded. Graham Bonnet's parts were being put on and they came back to the States, got a place called Kingdom Sound in Syosset, Long Island—it's no longer there—and that's when I got the phone call."

"I was living in New York. Kind of an interesting story. I'm done with Fandango, who was a band on RCA, the recording cemetery of America, right? Four records, unsuccessful, minor pockets of popularity. So anyway, we lost all our equipment, stolen at the Chicago Fest; it's a long story, but it took the wind out of our sails and we broke up. I was living down in the West Village, with a guitar strapped to my back, sleeping on a mattress, just in a studio apartment with a couple other guys, just looking for work."

"And I get a phone call from this guy named Barry Ambrosio, not Ritchie, but Ritchie's personal, who was asking me all these questions. And I'm like, 'Who the fuck are you? What are you, the IRS? What's going on here? What's all this nonsense about Deep Purple?' And he goes, 'Well I'm sitting next to Ritchie Blackmore and he wants to talk to you.' And I'm going, 'Yeah, sure you are.' And he goes, 'No, really I am.' And he puts him on and he's like, 'Hello mate,' and I'm like, 'This is Ritchie Blackmore?' And he goes yeah, and I go, 'Are you fucking with me?' All this kind of stuff, and he's like, 'No, this is really Ritchie, and I like your stuff. I'm a fan of yours, and I think you sing great.' And I go, 'Well, I'm a fan of yours,' (laughs) you know, like floored. And he says, 'I've got an opportunity for you if you'd like to come out and audition at Syosset.'"

"So he gives me an address and I got on a train out of Grand Central, and I zip out to Long Island. I was there in a couple hours and I'm like, this could be heaven or it could be hell. There was very little small talk at first; they were very business-like about it. I got on the mic and started singing this song called 'I Surrender' and actually started to rewrite the song lyrically, because certain things fit better than others. I mean, that sounds very arrogant, but I just wanted it to be more melodic, so I started to sing it a bit more my way, and they really liked it. But of course Russ Ballard never gave us any credit. He just said, 'Screw you guys; it's going to come out the way it comes out.'"

"So Ritchie kind of loved it and the next thing you know, I was doing all kinds of backgrounds and I started to realize, something's going on here. I was there like four or five hours. And all of a sudden Ritchie comes walking in. There's all this talk going on; they're outside and I'm in this goldfish bowl on the mic looking in going, 'Oh Christ, what are they talking about?' And he comes out with a couple Heinekens and hands me one and says, 'Do you want to be in the band?' And I went yeah, of course, and that's how I got in the band."

"And I realized that we were wiping Graham Bonnet's tracks. Because every time I would do a harmony or something they would wipe another track. And when I started to peek through and listen, there was Graham doing the tracks. So he had already put them down but they were getting rid of them. So that's the story of my entrance. Boom, there I was. And I never went home from that moment. They put me up in a hotel, bought me some clothes, because all my clothes were at the apartment, and I just stayed out there for weeks on end, and we just wrote the rest of the songs on the album, Roger and I."

"I think they were convinced on mic," says Joe, elaborating on his initiation into the band. "We broke for dinner; I guess they saw that I wasn't a bad guy. I was a bit naive maybe. Ritchie always said that I wasn't evil; I was just a troublemaker, but naively. Whatever it was I was doing, I didn't realize I was doing it fucked-up. I think they thought that I had the voice, and then I pulled out my writing bag, which Ritchie always called my magic bag, so they saw that I had some lyrics. I didn't look half bad so away we went."

"I was always in bands," adds Joe, charting his formative years. "I'll skip playing the accordion at seven years old and my dad bringing the Beatles albums out and me learning how to play the guitar. There was this girl I liked in school who like fainted over me, so I thought that's it—this is what I want to do. So anyway the Vietnam War is on and I'm #94 in the draft, so my ass is going. A couple of my friends came back in body bags unfortunately. I said to myself that wasn't going to happen to me 'cause I didn't believe in that war; it was an unjust war as most wars are. I was just out of high school and I was doing real well with my band and all of a sudden this war pops up and I was like, 'Fuck them, this is bullshit.'"

"So one of the ways to get out of this, and honour my father who was in two wars, was to go to school. I was going to continue my education anyway. I went to state college here in Patterson and during orientation one of the most perfect mistakes of my life happened. A woman from the college asked me what I wanted to do and what courses I wanted to take and I told her, 'I'm a musician but all you've got is classical guitar courses; I wanna play jazz guitar, rock guitar.' They didn't have a good music department, so she asked me what my second choice was. I was into psychology big time; I loved philosophy as well. She said, 'You're not going to get much out there in the real world; I know what would be good for you, English literature.' I said, 'English literature?' She said, 'All of life is contained in English literature.' So I said 'Okay, sign me up.'"

"I went into it with Shakespeare as my major and little did I know that all the tools of the trade, like rhyming for verse, meter and storyline and such, these are the tools you need for writing. It opened a whole other world for me. I got my degree in English lit, but I had to work my ass off because they would draft you right out of college. I really enjoyed it; to this day I still read three or four books at a time. It's true: everything is contained in literature. Whether it's in the mind, body or soul, it's in literature."

After a band called Ezra, named for poet Ezra Pound, Joe has his run with Fandango, putting out four records of funky easy listening country pop rock (!), a dizzying pastiche which Joe fully admits was the problem—no definable direction. Fandango's lineup included a guitarist, oddly enough, by the name of Ricky Blakemore.

"Ricky died in a tragic car accident that was not his fault," says Joe. "I miss him deeply to this day. I still thank him on every album. He was the big brother I never had; he was the most amazing guitar player/writer and person that I have ever met. I miss him greatly. He taught me the angles, how to reach in and grab a lyric, pull something out of it and how to write it. He taught me how to play guitar phrases properly, things like that. He was a mentor really. One thing I took from my experience in that band was how to forgive. The other guys were just too bitter. I don't hold a grudge. I don't forget, but I do forgive. You're not going to fuck me twice. I'll let it go the first time and just never work with you again, you know?"

Back to Rainbow, I asked Joe for an impression of *Down to Earth*, the album preceding his first for the band. Prompted by my estimation of it as "a barnstormer," Joe volunteered that, "Yeah, it is.

I was like, why are you doing this? However that record was a lot more commercial, but a different commercial than our commerciality. Like different from 'Street of Dreams' and 'Stone Cold,' which I think was an attempt of theirs at commerciality, Russ Ballard writing a bunch of songs. 'All Night Long'… but a great album, and well-produced I thought—sounds great."

"That's why I was really surprised that they were getting rid of Graham. But hey, his loss was my gain. I didn't know Graham. I don't think I've even crossed paths with Graham once, literally. I don't think I've ever had the honour of shaking his hand. I think Graham's got a phenomenal voice, very stylized voice, but phenomenal nonetheless. I think his work with Rainbow, with Malmsteen... and I love *Night Games*. I thought his solo album was great! So, all I can say is I've never had the pleasure to meet him, but my hat's off to him."

"I don't know if I'm equipped to do that," ventures Rainbow bassist, producer and key writer Roger Glover, when asked to provide a psychological profile of this cocksure new Rainbow singer.

"He'll turn in a great performance. He's a real pro in that respect. I think what Joe lacks—maybe I shouldn't say this—it's original thought. If you play... if you give him something no one has ever done before, he's got no way of knowing whether it's any good or not. He will respond to something that sounds like someone else. So if you play him a song that sounds like Bryan Adams, he'll go, 'Yeah, yeah, that's great.' Whereas if you play him something that is totally original, he won't have a frame of reference in which to put it. So he tends to be a bit predictable. He's a bit of blotting paper. He can take the best of someone else, or various people, and kind of turn it into a mix of them. He does that very eloquently, but it's not an original voice. That's my feeling on it. He certainly had the ability to turn people off because he's got a larger-than-life personality. You know, he's an Italian from New Jersey, and a performer, and a huge ego and a killer voice. People with huge egos actually do tend to be kind of insecure, and Joe is actually a really nice guy."

"There's a big showbiz side to Joe," reflects Ritchie, when asked particularly about whether Joe shared in his dealings in mysticism, "and sometimes I think it might be a bit hard for him to turn that off. I think he was serious about it as much as he can be serious about that stuff."

Getting Bobby into the game, I had him sum up his thoughts on both Roger and Ritchie: "Roger's a good guy, easygoing, great producer, good bass player, yeah. Nobody does it like Roger. Roger writes a lot. Roger and Joe were responsible for virtually all the words and the melodies, and Roger is a great guy. Roger was the guy who sat in the studio for hours after we were done and made it work, you know? And Ritchie, well, Ritchie gave me my first break, so he'll always have a nice place in my heart. Ritchie was Ritchie, you know? He either liked things or he didn't like things; there was no in-between. That was his rep and he was true to it—that was him. He was a brilliant musician. Could he be difficult at times? You know, a lot of people are difficult at times. And a lot of people aren't as good as him. He can be difficult, yeah. But he was also either the nicest guy in the world, or stay out of his way. There's really no in-between."

Rainbow's fifth studio album hit the shelves February 3rd, 1981. With respect to the striking *Difficult to Cure* cover art, featuring an intimidating team of doctors seemingly armed with bad news, Turner says that the band wasn't around for the choice.

"I had just joined the band," chuckles Joe, "and Hipgnosis, which was the cover art company out of London, England, a real reputable company... I mean, they're all dressed up in the doctor suits. There's not one of us that is on the cover. None of us were there. It's their actual staff. We would be somewhere in the world and they would just send us a package and say, 'Okay, here's the cover,' and we'd go, 'Okay, fine,' and just throw the package in the wastebasket." One trivia note, it is rumoured that this particular doctor photo had been around the company for awhile, and that it almost made its debut as the wrapper for Black Sabbath's *Never Say Die*. Storm and Aubrey from Hipgnosis did this all the time. If they had an idea they liked, they'd keep pressing it upon bands until one gave it the nod of approval.

As regards the title of the album, Joe says that it was "a statement. We were difficult to cure; everybody in this business was, you know? It was almost like we had this disease and really couldn't get around it. Yeah, that's the way I remember it." Conversely Roger says it came from a dirty joke, nothing more nothing less— incidentally, he claims that the motivation to call the previous album *Down to Earth* refers to the idea that the band was coming down from the ethereal topics of Ronnie onto this plane. *Difficult to Cure* is even more so boy/girl stuff, not a wizard in sight.

"I liked *Difficult to Cure*, the title," adds Ritchie, with a third explanation. "It just summed up all these thoughts about 'What the hell were we talking about?' And I saw it in a music magazine, Melody Maker, and it was regarding something completely off the wall. And I said to the management, that would be a good title. So that went down as the title. And then we said, well, wait a minute, what kind of cover are we going to have for that? And I think the management came up with, well, what do you think about doctors? And they showed me... I think what happened was there was this particular agency that does covers, who were involved, and I'd forgotten what they were called. But they were doing a lot of bands. So it's more than likely that that cover went around to these other bands. But I've never heard that about *Never Say Die*."

The first record of the Joe Lynn Turner era opens with the aforementioned "I Surrender," a poppy hard rocker written by the songwriter and hard rock solo artist Russ Ballard. Joe elaborates on the above comment with respect to Rainbow's treatment of this track. "They tried on *Down to Earth*, 'Since You Been Gone,' another Russ Ballard tune and it was really a big success. 'All Night Long' struck a chord with a lot of people as well. When we took off with 'I Surrender,' I mean the inside scoop on that one is, yeah Russ wrote it, but we modified it. We asked for a writing credit but he wouldn't give it to us, so we said fuck it, we're putting it out our way. If you heard the original you'd say yeah it's the same chorus but that's about it. I had just walked into Rainbow at that point and they said your voice can do this type of material; your writing style is more down to earth. You know, it wasn't dungeons and dragons stuff like with Ronnie."

"There were times when Bruce (Payne, manager) was actively pursuing great songs," recalls Joe, on the subject of Rainbow and covers in general. "I mean, Russ Ballard is just one of the greatest songwriters alive, so he's always got tons of stuff. But later on, we really wanted to take this thing in our direction, and we decided that once we saw the capabilities between Ritchie and Roger and myself to actually write this stuff, and we were pretty prolific about it, then we were doing a great job. We had commercial stuff but yet we were still hard rock. I mean, we were sort of like the harder end of Foreigner or Journey, the harder end. We were never a metal band and neither was Purple. It's hard rock and it's melodic."

"So what I'm say is, yeah, after the first album, we were able to do it ourselves, so Bruce felt very confident that we didn't need anything. Unless it was a bona fide out-and-out perfect-style hit for us, we probably wouldn't have done it. Because I heard a few things come through the pipe back then. But we all looked at each other and said, 'Oh, we can do that ourselves.' There were a couple of Bob Halligan songs, and a bunch of people sent stuff in. There were a lot of writers writing for a multitude of bands."

Adds Ritchie, "'I Surrender' was a great song, by Russ Ballard, and that used to go down well. That was a great vehicle for improvisation on stage. The chord structure was a classical chord structure, more of a Bach structure or a Handel. But the rest of the songs, they were just music."

"I Surrender" worked a charm for the band, just like "Since You Been Gone" did one record earlier. The spiffy, compact, pert new single, backed with "Vielleicht Das Nachste Mal (Maybe Next Time)," hit #3 on the UK charts, as did the attendant full-length album, pushing the record to gold status for sales of over 100,000 copies. In the US, the single got to #19 on the sub-chart Mainstream Rock with the album stalling at #50.

Next up on the record is speed metal rocker and concert-opener "Spotlight Kid," not one of the band's best in this fast class of Rainbow songs. Perhaps it's the timid production values, or the overt melodies, but the end effect is somehow powerless despite its briskness. Live, however, the song took on a marked ferocity, due to Bobby Rondinelli and his thundering double bass drums.

"I like Bobby because he's very relaxed," mused Ritchie, in a wide-ranging conversation with Steve Gett at the time. "He's a very strong technical drummer and in fact he's spent a lot of time teaching drums at a special clinic back in the States. I think he's possibly more patient than Cozy was. Bobby's a solid drummer and he plays on the beat, not before it, in a very similar fashion to John Bonham. He's also a very hard hitter and he always hits the drums in the same place every time—no rim shots or anything like that. He likes Zeppelin a lot and Bonzo was his favourite drummer. He's very strongly influenced by Led Zeppelin and I suppose I am in a way. I never go out and buy their albums but they're one of my favourite bands."

"'Spotlight Kid' was just fantastic," offers Joe, "and Roger told me it was about me. He said he had written it so it could be about anyone, but the last couple of... when he finally refined the verses, he said he saw my attitude. And that was sort of a way to pinpoint the last part of the direction. And even to this day, in Japan, they've made a cartoon called Spotlight Kid in Burrn! magazine, and the character looked like me. It was really flattering and at the same time almost pathetic (laughs), because there I was being this silly-minded rock star. I mean, I got a lot of mileage out of that, so I don't really care. But 'Spotlight Kid' is such a classic. I still play it today; it's a cornerstone of my set. Even when we do Hughes Turner Project, it's like 'Burn.' We have to do 'Burn' and we have to do 'Spotlight Kid;' these are songs you have to do. What can you say? It's a typical rock star song. It's about a young kid going out there and all of a sudden, boom! Lights, camera, action, you're in the thick of it. All of a sudden you're thrown into this world."

In the same conversation with Steve Gett, Ritchie offers profiles of both Joe and Roger and their roles in the band. "Joe's 28 and he's been playing around for a long time. He's been playing the guitar since he was 11, so he's a very good guitarist as well. That means we'll be able to do some of the quieter songs and things like 'Weiss Heim' on stage with a second guitar. The last time I worked with another guitarist on stage was with the Outlaws back in 1963. In fact Joe is an extremely competent all-round musician. He can sing a Hendrix-style phrasing or a commercial song in a much straighter vein. I saw him playing in New Jersey after a friend of mine recommended him. He was in a group called Fandango and I heard their album first and was quite impressed."

"I'd had it in my mind to look for a new singer in the last six months because I wasn't completely happy with the way things had been going. Suddenly I realised that something was wrong but I couldn't figure out what it was. For a while I thought that it was me. Things weren't gelling and I must admit I had grave doubts about Donington with so many people coming. There seemed to be no sense of direction. Fortunately Donington turned out to be a lot better than some of the other gigs we'd played at the time—maybe I was just a lot more drunk than usual. Afterwards I came to the conclusion that there was no rapport between Graham and myself and that Rainbow was simply five professionals out there going down well and being accepted for that reason."

As for his old Deep Purple co-conspirator, Ritchie said that, "Roger and I get on extremely well together. Sometimes he and I violently disagree about certain matters but he knows why we disagree. Most people assume that I'm just throwing another moody but he really understands our differences of opinion. That's why we always reconcile and make up ten minutes later. He always understands me which doesn't necessarily mean he agrees."

"A lot of people don't understand. I'm a moody person and I won't deny the fact. But Roger has known me for so long that he can determine when the mood is right and when not to even acknowledge me in a lift. I can't blame a lot of people for not understanding me because the fault must lie with me. But I can't change myself—that's the way I am. I guess it's a weak sense of discipline. I can't really explain it. I find I can get into a mood very easily if I'm pressured by responsibilities or commitments. They're the things that seem to bother me most of all. That's why touring often gets to me because sometimes after two weeks on the road I just want to pack it in but I can't since I'm committed through contracts. Maybe I'm simply very unorganized. I think one should always be totally behind what you're doing rather than doing something just for the sake of it and that's what happens to me a lot of the time. If I'm not into something, then I do become moody about it."

"He thrives on pressure but I hate it," continues Ritchie, back to Roger. "Sometimes I think he's a masochist. Someone said to me the other night, 'How can you go out to nightclubs and leave Roger working so hard in the studio?' And I answered that I could do it very easily. My work begins when his finishes. Now I'll go home and start writing ideas for the next LP. I deal with the early stages and

Roger comes in towards the end. He also helps a lot in the middle obviously. We'll get together, I'll pass on the message for a song and he takes it from there."

"No Release" follows, announced by a classic Zeppelin-esque intro from Ritchie, who acknowledges the Led Zep influence while also citing Jimi Hendrix's "Gypsy Eyes" as an inspiration. A rumbling heavy metal rhythm emerges with Joe turning in an appropriately grinding, passionate vocal. Cool track, very under-rated and seductively catchy come chorus time, when Ritchie's intro riff returns.

Next up is "Magic," a pure pop rocker with just a hint of the mysterious, Don Airey heard loud and clear in a variety of roles, the track credited to Brian Moran. Laughs Joe, "Don, as a keyboardist, has played with you name it. I don't think there's anybody left that Don hasn't played with. He gets around; he's quite a keyboard player. And as a personality, Don is a very stable, dry, witty, funny person who always has a different slant on life, and was refreshing to be around. Now he's in Purple and that was inevitable, I think. It really was inevitable, because Jon wasn't doing so well; he just had to slow down."

Jon Lord has passed on since this interview but yes, it bears reminding that he was still alive when Don took over the reigns, bringing to Purple the same chops he exhibited with Rainbow, including the same comedic licks when it was his time to solo.

Closing side two of the original vinyl was a grand, surging, classical-steeped instrumental, the aforementioned "Vielleicht Das Nachste Mal (Maybe Next Time)," where Ritchie shows his tone amongst more than a few ripping sections still wholly musical and appropriate to the relaxed pace of the song. The use of German language for the title is a nod to Ritchie's love of all things German. Including the women—Ritchie's first marriage was in 1964, to Margit Volkmar. Not only did they live in Hamburg in the late '60s, but they named their son Jurgen, Jurgen now being an accomplished guitarist himself. Ritchie's second wife, Barbel, was also German, their nuptials taking place in 1969. There was a third marriage and divorce in Ritchie's life as well, before he met Candice. This was to Amy Rotman, who he married in 1981 and divorced in 1983.

"It's a very sad piece that was inspired by the idea of a girl being left high and dry and miserable," Blackmore explained to Gett. "It's a very depressing tune and everyone seems on the verge of bursting into tears when they hear it. But I think that the world needs all types of emotion and that's why I've included it. At this stage I'm very pleased with the way this album has worked out and I think it's definitely our strongest effort to date."

Side two of *Difficult to Cure* opens with what might be the album's best track, "Can't Happen Here" beginning like an innocent blues and then gathering a head of steam upon a dependable riff.

"We didn't realize, I think, the power of video," opines Joe, when asked about this one's low budget but memorable pastiche of politics and playing. "Maybe we did, but we didn't give a shit. We thought that medium was an actor's medium. And all these bands were making these videos with enormous hair, clothing and all this crap. We thought that wasn't about the music at all. So we had a weird taste in our mouths about videos, yet we had to make them. So here we are in a position. Now, if you notice, a lot of the Rainbow videos, we're not even in them (laughs). 'Can't Happen Here' was animation mostly. Yeah, 'Stone Cold,' you know, has me walking around in front of the mirrors—I'm still trying to live that down (laughs). Although, a lot of chicks dug it, so that's cool (laughs). But you know what? As soon as we hit 'Street of Dreams' and all that... we weren't really in our videos. We were in for like two seconds and popped out. Because we were too busy on tour and too busy working. We'd be led to an hour shoot in a basement someplace and we'd go, 'That's it! That's enough! Get what you have to out of that.' So we weren't real video hogs. We were more concerned with the actual music."

"But we actually won the gold medal for the 'Can't Happen Here' video at Cannes," adds a bemused Joe. "And the story is actually really quite funny, because there I am backstage after one of the performances. I got a call backstage and I'm sweating and wiping myself down with a towel. And I pick up the phone and it's like, I don't know, somebody calling from Cannes or someplace going, we've won the gold medal. And I turn around to the band all sweaty, and say, 'Okay, we've won the gold medal for "Can't Happen Here,"' and they all went, 'Oh, fuck off!'"

"And it was like… I just looked at the phone and I got on the phone and I went 'Fuck off!' And I hung up the phone (laughs). Taking it as, I don't know, a joke or something. Nobody cared. Nobody cared about all those accolades. When we were nominated for a Grammy, I hung the nomination in my bathroom. It's still there, in this house, now. I digress. But that song, look, I mean, Roger, first of all, give credit to Glover, he's a wonderful man, great lyricist, great bass player, and he wrote the lyrics to that and I just thought it was so poignant about what was happening in the world. And if you listen to that song today, there's not much difference. Have we learned anything—hello?!—in 20 years?! So it's really, really profound."

Joe's right—this was a great lyric, Roger offering in smartly poetic fashion, a laundry list of environmental horrors mixed with world-beating examples of corruption. His thoughts are compact and insightful, and there are a lot of them.

"Can't Happen Here" is followed by another fairly heavy track, with "Freedom Fighter" rocking out for everything but the verse and pre-chorus, evoking similar complaints to those that plagued "All Night Long." In other words it's a nose-wrinkling mix of heavy metal butted up against, come verse time, a type of "pomp rock."

Says Joe of the lyric, "There was always, at that point, you know, the world never seems to be not at war, for whatever reason. Hello?! We're so evolved as human beings. I can't really place what political incident was going on, but freedom fighters were a big thing at that point, Sandinistas and stuff like that. And Roger and I just went, 'Hey, we've got to write this right now.'"

"'Midtown Tunnel Vision' is basically about New York City," says Joe of the album's second to last track, a pure old school heavy blues akin to Cream, Mountain or Jimi Hendrix. "And me, being so familiar, being a New York boy, living in New York at the time, I think I brought a lot of metaphor to the lyric. I mean, we just knew we had something going at that point." Joe stylizes a fair bit like Paul Rodgers on this one, and Ritchie turns in a solo that is not so much bluesy, but closer to his classicist metal roots.

Closing the record is "Difficult to Cure (Beethoven's Ninth)," a rousing hard rock classical romp (celebrating the closing "Ode to Joy" segment of Beethoven's "Ninth") which Bobby Rondinelli considers one of his favourite drum performances on a Rainbow album, even if he had problems with the track's shuffle premise, eventually recording his tracks last—the reverse of the usual. Indeed the tune had been used as intro music on past Rainbow tours. At the rollicking climax of the track, a chortled laugh sampled from Laurel and Hardy's *Way Out West* from 1937 enters and fades, perhaps signalling that the joke was on us.

No one would go so far as to say the entire record was a joke though. True, many were appalled at the new lighter direction, although the pumps were primed with some of those similar oft-lamented moments from *Down to Earth*, which, in total is still a pretty damn heavy album.

"It was the one album that most people who are Rainbow fans don't like," says Joe of *Down to Earth*. "It's the album with 'Since You've Been Gone' on it. I follow it up with 'I Surrender' and 'Stone Cold' which are both great rock songs, not pop songs. We sold millions of albums. Einstein said, 'I don't know which is greater, the infinite universe or the infinite stupidity of mankind.' I think it is the latter. Our thing was its own thing. It was done very well and millions of people agreed with us. For every fan we lost, we picked up five. Ritchie certainly went all the way to the bank with it."

And yet there was a tentativeness about *Difficult to Cure*, a vague dissatisfaction that the band was grasping at straws... a couple covers, a couple more instrumentals, a blues, some blatant pop and then some other... stuff. For sure, the reedy, lifeless production didn't aid the cause, but these songs wouldn't have done much better with enough bass and treble. I suppose we didn't really have a "band" here yet, and the fragile cohesion between members was being echoed by the lack of cohesion between the songs. Indeed, Roger has said that he was quite nervous about the album, not quite liking it, wishing he could go in and re-mix it. He seemed to sense something the fan base would soon figure out as well, that this was a Rainbow muzzled.

Amusingly, out on tour, it turned out that Joe was a bit too theatrical, shall we say, for Ritchie's tastes. "Well, we had many talks about that," says Joe, good-naturedly as always. "In the beginning, I was a young kid coming out of New York and I was American. So what happened with that is that I didn't have this 'stand up there, pose like a rock star' kind of mentality. I was very... let's put it this way, I wasn't really conscious of trying to put on some kind of air. I just did what came to me and I had a lot of energy and a lot of physicality at that time. So I was just running and jumping and in the audience's face."

"And that was okay for Rod Stewart, as Ritchie put it. He goes, 'That's like Rod Stewart, leaping about and doing all this.' And he kind of told me, 'Look, you've kind of got to have some grace and form, and you've got to stand there and wrap your leg around the mic and sing with power, which you can,' and all this. And I think he brought me into a... you know, he grew me up a lot. I owe a lot to Ritchie for that. Because he gave me a lot of words of wisdom and guidance because I think he believed in me and saw the spark. And I took it. I took the advice, and to this day I'm thankful. And now I do a little bit of both. Because I still like to get in the audience's face, like an American. As opposed to the English pompous Coverdale twirling mic stand routine."

"That's right, I felt sometimes that he was a little bit effeminate with his projection onstage," explains Ritchie. "Most of the singers we had in the band were more hard-edged. And Joe had this way of skipping across the stage, and laying on speakers. We used to call him Judy now and again, as in Judy Garland. We'd tell him, don't do that, because it looks a little bit Liberace-ish, you know? I much preferred him in the studio, when he just sang there. And at rehearsals he was great, because he would just get to the mic and sing. I wasn't too keen on Joe's movements onstage, when he started acting and running around."

As to whether Ritchie was able to stamp it out of him in the end, he chuckles, "Sometimes, but it would always come back. In the end, we just kind of let it go."

It wasn't only Ritchie that couldn't relate. UK and mainland European crowds heckled Joe relentlessly, but with

Ritchie's combination of support and admonishment, along with Joe's thick skin as a seasoned entertainer, his position as Rainbow's front man solidified.

"The first time we went out, we had the big Rainbow *Rising* thing, didn't we?" muses Joe, asked about stage props. "Behind us, with the hand gripping the rainbow, the Ronnie thing. As I recall, it was a leftover. And then we went all white; I remember that. We had a white stage floor. They'd come in and roll out this white sort of rubbery carpet, this half-inch sponge or hard rubber, so we wouldn't slip and everything, and then all the amps were white and the drums were white, and I wore white and Ritchie of course wore black. And it was just great, really crazy. It was the white tour (laughs). And we had bombs and explosions over time and God knows what else. But that Rainbow thing was just a behemoth, a bitch to carry around and set up, and you had to have a crew of 20 extra guys and shit, so it was very expensive. That's still someplace in storage, I think. Can you believe it?"

Joe adds further musings on the "white" tour, the most notable featuring being the black and white amplifiers, with the white accenting the round black cones. "The stage people, they had to keep it clean. Because it showed everything. I remember them cleaning it before we put the equipment on, then after, putting tarps down so the roadies could walk over it. It was more of a pain in the ass, but it looked great. But Ritchie and wearing black… that was really yes and no. He had a white outfit; I remember that. But you know Ritchie, of course—he wore what he wanted. And of course he wanted to always be singling himself out, to be the odd man out, in a black suit. But yeah, there was a point where we started to say, well, you know, if we're all in white it gets a bit too Moody Blues, when they did sort of a white thing or whatever it was. What happened was we started to wear dashes of colour here and there and both black and white. Really, we didn't make too much out of it. I think everybody else made more of it than we did."

Also on the theatrical side was Ritchie's famous guitar-smashing routine, which, as Joe explains didn't happen all that often, much less than the old days, when it was almost expected.

"He did it occasionally. I must have seen it about three or four times on my trip. He'd have to be in a certain mood. He'd have to be in a certain place, in a certain mood, and that's the only time he felt it was warranted, really. What I mean by that is that it would be a certain show. We would even know... he would set his mood. 'I'm gonna smash one up.' Because Roger would always say, 'Are we gonna do smash-up tonight?' You know, that was the word, smash-up. And he'd be like, 'Nah, I don't think so.' Then he'd surprise us another night, when he said he wasn't and then he would. Because that's the way Ritchie is. He likes to keep you on your toes. But it wasn't all that much. I think it was enough to be effective, and I think the crowd wanted it more than anything. And of course, when the crowd wanted something, Blackmore won't do it. He loved to piss people off. That's him."

And piss them off he did, still sometimes blowing off shows, cutting them short, or at least skipping the encores. "Quite a few times. Yeah, one of the worst situations we ever had was on this Danish island. It's part of Denmark but it's an island off the mainland, small island. And we were in Germany. I'll never forget flying from Germany to Copenhagen, to do the surrounding area there. I think we were going to set up shop in Copenhagen. Because we always used Copenhagen as a hub, and we'd fly out and into different places in Europe. And we'd always stay in one place. This way you had your suitcase open and you had a place you actually lived in instead of hotel to hotel."

"Anyway, we were in Germany, and I remember this vividly. I don't know why, but I do. We had to be on a certain flight to get to this island. Of course there aren't that many flights going there, right? And we had to be there at a certain time to get this show together. And Ritchie decided, screw that, that the flight's delayed one hour, and that it was five o'clock, and five o'clock every night, he ate dinner. Okay. So now, he's pulling a moody and saying, 'Fuck that, I ain't getting on the flight.' So Bruce Payne stayed with him and, I guess it was Amy at the time, one of his wives, and the rest of us took off."

"So now we're all on this island, the rest of the band. We're all settled, showered, ready and going to the hall, and Ritchie's not there. And we found out through the grapevine, well, through

Colin, our tour manager, that he had to take a later flight and his flight wouldn't be arriving until like ten or 11 at night. Now, you can picture 5000 people on this island. I mean, it wasn't a big island but it was big enough to have that many kids that were in the audience, and they were drinking all night."

"So now they're drinking and it's getting like ten, 10:30 and they're starting to get rowdy. So what happens is, he finally shows up, Ritchie, late, and now we go on, but the audience is absolutely legless piss drunk. I mean, you can literally see it, you know, that they were just there too damn long. And Ritchie decided to fuck off, to not... he was in a terrible mood for a couple of days. And we played the show, and he wouldn't come back on for an encore. And they were tearing the house down literally, because they were climbing up the lighting trusses, to the point where enough of them got up onto the top and pulled the weight down upon the audience."

"So now you've got people rushing on to the hospital, ambulances and all this kind of mayhem going on. And we're out in the back, with all this dynamic tension going on. 'Fucking Ritchie wouldn't go on and look what's happening now' and everything else. And I remember that they had to sneak us out in a van, at different intervals, just to get out of that area. Otherwise this crowd was going to kill us. Later on that night, Bobby Rondinelli and I, we were in the hotel and we were all sitting around in the bar, really concerned what was happening to these kids and stuff and we were getting reports from the hospital on how bad the injuries were."

"And Bobby just said, 'I can't take this anymore,' and he said, 'Let's go out, onto the main drag and go to a bar,' just try to loosen up. So we did, and when we got to the bar and everything, we were trying to be sort of nonchalant about it and undercover about it, keeping to ourselves a little bit. But some girl came up to me and said, 'I know who you are' and she slapped me right across the face! And I was like, 'What the hell is that for?!' And then they went off on the fact of what was happening. So we went back to the hotel, just totally embarrassed and humiliated."

So they got a full show but no encore. "Yeah, well, it might have been cut short a little bit too. Ritchie was really pulling a fucking mood."

Ritchie walked out on an outdoor show in Missouri as well. "Yeah, and he flipped me his guitar (laughs). He flipped me the guitar and said, 'Yeah, you play it.' And I remember playing the lead to 'Smoke on the Water' (laughs). Yeah, he got into a mood. When he got into a mood, we called it moodies. When he got in a mood, it was a mood. Who ever really knew what it was about? His philosophy was, whatever I want to do, I'm gonna do. It didn't matter. Did not matter. I mean, he saw all these kids there and he would turn around to me, and you know, I thought we played a great show and maybe the audience had been quiet earlier in the evening. And when I say quiet, they were very attentive but not as responsive? And then at the end of the show they went hog-wild. And Ritchie wouldn't go on and do an encore at this particular place either, and I was going, 'What the hell is the matter with you?!' And he goes, 'They don't deserve it. They should have been more responsive in the beginning.' And I said, 'Well, really, what's the difference? They're there in the end' blah blah blah. He said, 'They don't deserve it, and you'll understand that one day.'"

Adds Joe on the subject of tour mates, "We had Pat Travers tour over here with *Crash and Burn*; that was fun, here in America. I would have to say that sometimes we had two or three bands on tour, and then another band would jump off and another band would jump on. It got quite interesting."

Indeed North America was first, commencing in February '81, with the mercurial Canuck guitarist sometimes headlining sometimes not. North American dates into April included Swiss AC/DC-lovers Krokus as part of the bill as well. The European leg began in Gothenburg, Sweden, June 3rd, 1981, with Def Leppard as support.

With respect to blowing off steam on the road, there was always soccer. "Yeah, that was the thing," recalls Joe. "I mean, I sucked when I first started and Ritchie always tried to put me on the opposing team, whether it was Def Leppard or anybody. In fact, that was the game, exciting moment, where I was back on the Rainbow team. Because I was an American. I grew up with track and baseball. I was too small to play football. I was pretty fast and agile, so I was a good runner, but I didn't know how to ball-handle. So he always tried to sell me to the opposite team. So one time I was playing with

Def Leppard and I think it was Rick Savage who passed to me, and I kicked the ball and miraculously scored a goal, from midfield. And Ritchie was just like, awestruck, gob-smacked or whatever it is they say. And he just said, 'You're a secret weapon!' And I go, 'I guess so.' And from then on, I was on the Rainbow team. Oh yeah, we blew off steam. We played everybody, Iron Maiden (note: a year later), Rod Stewart, you name 'em, we played 'em. When we were on the road, we would play everybody. And we had the charity events. I can remember one time down in Florida, we raised all kinds of money for kids, playing against some semi-pro teams."

"We'd play soccer, even in the snow," continues Joe. "We would rent a gym at a high school, anywhere, whatever we had to do, so we had a chance to play, so that we would keep in shape, keep the blood moving. Ritchie was really big about that, and I thank him to this day about that, because I still have a treadmill here at my house and I still go out and play and kick the ball around; it's great. In terms of the other stuff, séances and stuff, those guys, no, not really. Roger, a little bit but not really. It was really Ritchie and I. We both see eye to eye on that kind of stuff. We both believe… not only believe, but we know. And that really was unto us. Bobby was like, 'It's a load of crap' and that kind of stuff, so we never pushed it on anybody. It's like religion. You can't push it on somebody."

Both Joe and Bobby verify that soccer games were played against the Pat Travers Band as well, Bobby commenting that, "we did quite a bit of it. I didn't play soccer much in Brooklyn when I was a kid going up. I loved sports, but soccer wasn't my sport. So I didn't play that well. I don't think Joe was very good either. We used to play against Maiden and we played radio stations, whatever."

Oddities in the on-stage track selection included, on occasion, "Smoke on the Water" plus bits of "Fire" and "Hey Joe," while the Bonnet-era "Love's No Friend" found Joe in fine fettle. In fact, besides expected tracks from the new album ("Spotlight Kid," "I Surrender" and a sped-up "Can't Happen Here"), a good dose of the excellent *Down to Earth* album was on offer, including "Since You Been Gone," "All Night Long" and the storming "Lost in Hollywood." The Dio-era material got comparatively short shrift, with the likes of "Catch the Rainbow," "Man on the Silver Mountain" and "Long Live Rock 'n' Roll" making the grade.

This first tour of the JLT era also included the infamous bullring gigs in Spain with UFO, where hostilities between the two venerable acts were at a high, much to the bemusement of a youthful and innocent Def Leppard.

"Yeah, we were playing bullrings with those guys; quite hysterical," recalls Joe. "A lot of times we were up on the ramparts and stuff, screwing around with the bulls, I can remember. But one night, there was this huge fight that erupted, and I remember Ian Broad, who was Ritchie's personal at the time, who we later called The Drunken Hurricane... Because Ian would just booze it up and absolutely just be a wild man. And Ritchie loved all that stuff because he could get Ian to do just about anything. I mean, just ridiculous stuff. One time up in Canada—Edmonton I believe it was—we were staying at a place called the Chateau Lacombe, and it had one of these big huge double doors that opened up into this huge, very extravagant-looking lobby, with chandeliers—big, expensive. And he had Ian drive a white Jaguar right into the hotel lobby, and pulled up by the desk and said (in English accent), 'Have you got a room for Mr. Blackmore?'" Of note, this tale bears suspicious resemblance to a similar story from the Graham Bonnet years, the locale being France, for the recording of *Down to Earth*. However there indeed is a Chateau Lacombe in Edmonton.

Continues Joe, "It was insane stuff. But one night in the Spanish gigs, I don't know how they got into it, but Broady pushed Phil Mogg I guess, and, you know, Phil's a pugilist, a fighter, and he beat the shit out of Ian. And there was this big crowd around us watching this huge fistfight going on. Of course, Ian got his bell rung. We thought that was quite hysterical. But I mean, we used to play soccer before that, in the bullrings in the dust and dirt, because these things were just hot, dry, dusty old bullrings. So by the time you finished playing ball, you were just covered in red clay dust."

"We might have been bad, but UFO were a mess!" laughs Joe. "I mean, let me tell you. Those guys, we used to call them Nyquila, because they got into drinking Nyquil, that cough medicine? Like Godzilla? We called them Nyquila. Because they would come staggering onto the fucking stage, bottles of Nyquil all over the goddamn dressing room. Because that was their high; it was kind of an opiate and an alcohol-based medicine. So Nyquila. Yeah, you can put that in quotes. Nyquila, UFO (laughs)."

After the considerably detailed European jaunt for *Difficult to Cure*, Rainbow found themselves closing things out back in the UK with Australian AC/DC-ists Rose Tattoo in tow, followed by a final leg consisting of nine dates in Japan, winding things up end of August '81 without much of a break for seven gruelling months.

While on tour, "Can't Happen Here" was floated as a single, backed with the non-LP "Jealous Lover." It went to #20 in the UK and failed to chart in the US. Five months later, "Jealous Lover" (recorded April '81) showed up as an A-side, along with "Can't Happen Here," "I Surrender" and non-LP instrumental "Weiss Heim," to form an EP. Both studio rarities would show up later on posthumous compilation *Final Vinyl*.

"That was amazing," begins Joe on the chunky, tough but sweet and civilized rocker "Jealous Lover." "What happened was, we were in Minneapolis-St. Paul, and we were supposed to be doing R&R for a few days, three days off, right? Because we were on this whole extensive tour of the States at that point, and we had just come from Europe and Japan and everywhere else. We were kind of burned-out. So we were taking three days, and it was going to be Ritchie's birthday, during those three days. And we were also supposed to record a track or a B-side or whatever it was, and we rented the Orpheum Theatre. So it was a big theatre, we had set up on the stage, and I was writing to a track that Ritchie had given me a couple weeks earlier."

"Okay, so I'm all set with this track, right? We get to the Orpheum Theatre, and it's his birthday, so he's pulling a moody. You know, he's all... he doesn't want to get any older, he's pissed-off; I think he's 40 or something (note: more like 36), and that was a big turning point. So he's being difficult and whatnot, and all of a sudden he starts this track that I have no idea what he's doing (sings the "Jealous Lover" riff). I go, 'What the heck is this?' And I said, 'Well, I've written to this one.' And he says, 'Well, that's not what we're doing.' So I'm going, 'Well, what am I supposed to do?!'"

"And I went backstage and I got my pen out and I wrote the story about, I had a fight with my girlfriend, on the phone. And it was exactly that. I mean, shades of red, eyes of green, sees black-and-white, tell me no lies and all this crap, you're like every other jealous lover and I'm pissed-off at you and I really thought more of you and all this other crap. And it turned out to be one of the bigger songs we ever had. It was like a huge B-side. And to this day, I still play that song live, because it's seriously requested by everybody. You gotta play 'Jealous Lover.' So, in other words, it was really another magical accident, or as we say, a perfect mistake."

The "Jealous Lover" experience also saw the band hang with Eric Clapton. Explains Joe, "I don't know if it was in Minneapolis or St. Paul, because we were staying at the Radisson Hotel and Clapton was there convalescing. And Patti Boyd/Clapton whatever, his wife… I remember, in a spandex leopard suit—whoa, was that heavy—doing mandies at the bar fucked-up as all get out! She was high as a kite. I can remember Clapton being in a wheelchair and Patti pushing him around. And because it was Ritchie's birthday, all of us were in the hallway, with candles and balloons and presents and stuff and Blackmore was so morose at the fact that he was turning 40. I remember him answering the door of the hotel suite, and he was just like, 'Fuck off.' And there we are with Clapton. But he just didn't want to turn 40 (laughs). He was pissed-off that he was having a birthday and he got like that a lot. But yeah, Eric was there, but he wasn't at the actual recording. Because, again, he was mostly in a wheelchair. He was at the hotel and at the parties and everything else and we were hanging out for three or four days."

Of note, once the *Difficult to Cure* tour had wound down, Don Airey would be leaving the band, fulfilling Graham Bonnet's intuition that his old friend's remaining time in Rainbow wouldn't be long. Airey's last show was in Hawaii, August 5th, 1981, on the way back from Japan. Due to equipment problems with Ritchie's amps, Don was left to improvise 25 minutes worth of soloing—the band had given up the ghost and gone back to the hotel. Airey was not amused. As well, Airey had voiced the same concerns brought up by Bonnet, that there were just too many personnel changes, and that the band had become too "transatlantic," and that playing this material night after night had most definitely lost its lustre.

Dutch "All Night Long" single, left to right: Ritchie Blackmore, Cozy Powell, Graham Bonnet, Don Airey, Roger Glover.

The Man in Black, in black.
© Rich Galbraith.

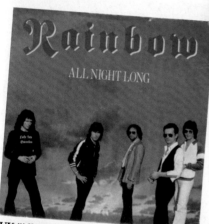

UK "All Night Long" single

Front cover of the UK *Monsters of Rock* live LP.

Joe executing his novel stage miking technique, Maple Leaf Gardens, Toronto. © Martin Popoff.

Difficult to Cure T-shirt design.

Full page two-colour ad for *Difficult to Cure*, Melody Maker.

UK "Can't Happen Here"/"Jealous Lover" picture sleeve.

Japanese "Freedom Fighter" single.

Roger, amused. © Rich Galbraith.

Picture sleeve art used for "Stone Cold" single in most territories.

Roger Glover fired up in Toronto. © Martin Popoff.

Ritchie Blackmore and Bobby Rondinelli.
© Martin Popoff.

. Dutch "Death Alley Driver"/"Tite Squeeze" single.

Ritchie and his distinctive white Fender Stratocaster. © Martin Popoff.

Japanese "Can't Let You Go" sleeve showing black-and-white stage design.

Joe and Roger looking kind of southern rock. © Rich Galbraith.

White Strat as archery bow; Circus ad for *Straight Between the Eyes*.

David Rosenthal, Roger Glover, Joe Lynn Turner. © Martin Popoff.

Joe and Ritchie loving their work. © Rich Galbraith.

Lead singer Doogie White, shown in Japanese ad for *Stranger in Us All*.

Ad for *Stranger in Us All* and attendant German tour dates.

Rainbow rising again, 2017.

UK Stranger in Us All ad.

Chapter 8

Straight Between the Eyes

"I knocked the cymbal over and it hit a gravestone."

The second album of the Joe Lynn Turner era, *Straight Between the Eyes*, is often cited as a fan favourite. Certainly it is the heaviest—yet perhaps only by a shade or two—over either of its bookends. Still, that shade is amplified by the fact that Roger (who had actually quit the band and been cajoled back by Bruce Payne!) knob-twiddles his way to a rich and heavy production job that is a pronounced improvement over the mealy, timid tones of *Difficult to Cure*, and maybe the equal of *Bent Out of Shape*, which would most definitely be less of a Deep Purple-ish rock album than *Straight Between the Eyes*.

"You know, I've kind of forgotten what the hell is on *Straight Between the Eyes*," opines Ritchie, focusing from another time and space given his current immersion in all things Blackmore's Night. "Those albums are kind of fuzzy memories. I just know that listening back, I find that most of them are a bit... good ideas, but they weren't loose enough. I think we spent so much time tightening up and making sure that there were no mistakes, that to me, it lacked a lot of improvisation qualities, personally. So that's my criticism of those records."

To be sure. I mean, we are back at the remarkable dichotomy between making records and playing live that Ritchie represented and celebrated so well. Again, go listen to the documentation of the band live—on official records, on Youtube—and you will soon realize that the albums were a stepping-off point, a brief missive, a suggestion, a calling card, after which the artist took flight. And by artist, of course, I'm referring mostly to Ritchie, but also to Cozy. And Don. And even Ronnie in the old days and Joe now. All of them, but mostly Ritchie. Blackmore is a performer, not a recorder. Nonetheless, Ritchie has some fond memories of all three Foreigner-challenging records with Joe, including some of the music on this one, as we shall shortly see. But first we have to get past that title—*Straight Between the Eyes*—and the attendant ghoulish, garish—and frankly plain bad—cover art.

Says Joe, "*Straight Between the Eyes*, to the best of my knowledge, and I'm pretty sure I'm accurate on this, Ritchie was talking about Jimi Hendrix, who was one of my favourites, because I'm a guitarist as well. Ritchie was saying, 'You know, his music hits me straight between the eyes,' and it's just that simple, as far as I can remember. He just went, 'Yeah, that's it, *Straight Between the Eyes*.' Graphically, Ritchie had the idea, and not that we had to agree to it, but it was a great idea with this Strat coming through this forehead, straight between the eyes and all that. And we wanted it to be like a cartoon, and not some sort of superimposed image."

Of note, it has been said that the "straight between the eyes" assessment of Hendrix came from Jeff Beck. As the story goes, back in 1967, Ritchie was in a bar and Beck had sauntered in, having just witnessed Hendrix live. Blackmore asked Beck what Jimi was like, and Jeff said that he comes at you straight between the eyes.

Examining the context of making the record, Joe comments that, "It was a brilliant time, because I was new to the band when *Difficult to Cure* came out and we had a tremendous response to 'I Surrender' and all those other songs, and the album itself. But it was kind of done in several different studios and I really didn't like the sound. We expressed that, and I think that's what kicked us into going up to Saint-Sauveur and Morin Heights. So it was kind of like we had full guns drawn and we were going into a great studio, where The Police were coming out of, with *Ghost in the Machine*; in fact, they were there a couple of days while we were changing over and stuff, nice guys—we got to check out some of their tracks. And we got into a great environment up there and I just thought the juices were turned on, as far as creativity goes. We set up camp for like two months, skiing, hockey, drinking, womanizing. But that's where this thicker, bolder sound came out—'Stone Cold' and all that stuff. I think that was the start of a much better sound."

This particular studio was recommended by Nazareth, the connection with Rainbow being that Roger had produced that band's most universally revered albums, *Razamanaz*, *Loud 'N' Proud* and *Rampant*—only *Hair of the Dog* from that most fertile period was not a Roger Glover production. The band worked there in December of '81, with new keyboardist David Rosenthal, the album not emerging until June 10th of the following year. Adds Joe, "The environment was also notable, with a beautiful 'band house' on the property... maids, fine amenities, beautiful surroundings including a frozen lake where the band enjoyed scenic inspiration and played hockey."

"Wow, that was a long time ago, before I was married," adds Bobby on the Montreal experience, "so... we made friends! (laughs). Yeah, we would go out to clubs a couple of nights a week, socialize. We had a cool house there, and sometimes we'd have little parties there; it was fun, and beautiful."

Continues Joe, on a comical tale he likes to tell from those days, "That lake was manmade, I believe. And it was irrigated and aerated, with these pipes underground. But at the same time, the surface would freeze over, so you could play hockey. I still have my hockey skates from those days. And we'd go out there and exercise a bit and play hockey, slap the puck around. One night—it was a little bit of a warmer night I suppose—me and Roger decided to walk across the lake to get to the studio. Because from the house you could see the studio's lights, straight directly across."

"And as we got about to the middle, that's when we started playing the survivalist (laughs). We laid down and crawled back because all we heard was 'crack! crack!' and we were going to go under. And man, to get there, we jumped in the Jeep and just said, 'Fuck this!' That was harrowing, and that's when I sung 'Stone Cold.' Because later on a blizzard picked up, which is weird. A front came in, and the next thing you know, it was just freezing, icy, wind, really a major storm. The weather fronts can come in there pretty quick, especially in the mountains; it's crazy. So all of a sudden, it was this beautiful night, with the snow and the ice cracking, and the next thing you know, two hours later, there's this huge blizzard."

"I still think we came up with one of the better Rainbow albums there ever were," pronounces Joe. "To me, we were on a high, we also felt the new blood, and Ritchie was very, very into it at that point because it was working. It's always nice when you pick a plan and it works. So everybody was feeling super positive, super energetic, and it was just like full-blown... we were going for it."

And does "Death Alley Driver," opening salvo on *Straight Between the Eyes*, ever go for it. Skulking into view through some dinosaur noises from Ritchie and his tortured axe, the song explodes on the back of Bobby Rondinelli's exquisitely tuned and boldly recorded drums. The band then enters "Highway Star"-style and it's off to the races.

"'Death Alley Driver' was my lyric about a drug run," laughs Joe. "Honest to God. It was really sort of about a parallel to people's lives. There used to be this guy that dealt all kinds of drugs down here in Jersey. And it's the same highway that Bruce Springsteen talks about, Highway 9. Well, Highway 9 runs all the way from northern Jersey down through South Jersey, and that's on *Born to Run*. And on Highway 9, what happens is, that's the main thoroughfare and it's mainly what we call a truck route, because it's traveled very heavily by the industrial big rigs. But when you want to get to Jersey City and all these places—Union, Newark and stuff—you take Highway 9."

"So this guy would make this run, this Death Alley run, where routes 1 and 9 join up, and he was just dealing pounds of coke and heroin, and I just thought it was just this incredible way to live, you know; I mean, not good. I meant, this is going to fucking kill you, man. Because I remember stories about Uzis coming out and guns to the head and all this kind of stuff. You're dealing with some heavy people here and they were doing the chemical tests to see if the stuff was pure and how pure it was, 90%, 85%. And if it wasn't measuring up, his people were pulling guns, their people were pulling guns."

In later tellings of the tale, Joe intimates that he was there for all this. As he explained to Jeb Wright, "That song, I wrote about going on a drug run on Highway 9. I was with a friend, who I found out I really didn't know that well. I ended up in this place where there were all these machine guns. This guy was a doctor that was brought in to analyze the cocaine that was coming in from Columbia. There were pounds of it. I stood there and I was thinking, 'What did you get me into to?' He was all coked-out and I was like, 'Get me outta here.' I was sweating bullets. I wrote the song about that. Highway 9 is a crap highway. It's a two-lane highway about as wide as an alley but it was the run where you went to get the Columbian blow, which was the best blow around."

"And it just hit me, with this incredible beat we had going. And Ritchie said, 'What do you got in your bag on this one?' And I said, 'I've got this story I think might fit here.' And he said, 'Well, what is it?' And I said, 'It's called "Death Alley Driver" and it's about this guy,' and he said, 'Let's try it,' and it came out to be one of the best pieces we ever did. I mean, to this day, it's so classic. But yes, the song is about drug dealing or those who abuse drugs, living life dangerously, killing themselves without seeing the warning signs."

Classic in many ways already, the song becomes superlative come solo time, at which point (just over two minutes in) Ritchie executes a slow and steady scale, underscored with eventual harmony accompaniment, that goes straight to the memory banks, Blackmore then branching off root for a typically manic yet musical romp. New 21-year-old keyboardist David Rosenthal even gets to solo, ripping off a sequence that recalls the great synths of Tony Carey and the *Rising* album. With respect to a bit of history on Rosenthal, Ritchie hired the fresh-faced Berklee College Of Music grad from New Jersey based on his impressive demo tape on which he blew through a piece by classical composer Franz Lizt.

"The band seems more cohesive ever since Dave joined," commented Turner, speaking with Richard Hogan from Circus in the spring of '82. "Of course, nobody can expect to be with Rainbow forever and ever, including me. But I'm going to give it all I can for now. The attitude that no one will last hurt Don. He thought Ritchie was breaking up the band, that he was grasping at straws, not knowing what he was doing."

"I'm not so crazy," added Ritchie, "that I'd change a member of the group to make it worse. Don didn't see the point that certain people were becoming passengers who rested on their laurels, and that they'd rather be racing drivers. Don was Cozy's best friend. He didn't know that I had got Bobby Rondinelli to replace Cozy, and when he found out, he was fuming. I know Don's a good keyboard player; he's a musician's musician. But Don and I never spoke. It was a very tense situation. I can't blame him for taking that position about Rainbow; Don's not used to temperamental people like me. But it got to the point where I wanted Don out of the band."

Turning to the stage, Ritchie says that, "Unfortunately for Don, and for Dave, too, I'm a guitarist who likes to take a lot of leads and introductions. At the same time, I won't put up with someone who's second rate on organ. That's why I go through so many band members. I have to have the best players available, ones who will sit back and listen to me play!"

"Though I hate to record, I enjoy performing live," continues Ritchie. "I'm usually very drunk when I play. Part of me is shy, and I have to drink a lot to come out of myself. I do stay in control; I just like to have a good time playing. But I don't like to glamorize everything. I don't even like to do too many theatrics. Of course, it wouldn't work for us to go out with lutes and play Elizabethan melodies, as much as we might be tempted to. We have to put on a show. But all I do on the guitar is to emulate classical violin, which takes from 16th and 17th century organ music. The organ is so commanding, as opposed to guitar, just whimpering along."

A curious comment there, to be sure—we've all heard about Ritchie's insecurities, and how the huge ego is a sort of armour against them. But here he's also pointing out an inferiority he feels between his very instrument of choice and the majesty of a honking loud organ. As well, Ritchie's always had a reputation for being a heavy drinker, lighter in the studio, just to loosen up, but a little more laissez faire live. But this comment, which he's made repeatedly throughout his interviewing record, makes sense in the spirit of what the band has always been like in performance, which is unpredictable, rife with extended versions and always fiery and occasionally goofy. The stage really is the place where Ritchie explores creativity. In that sense, he's a jazzer who loves heavy metal, an explorer and regular and ready soloist who is comfortable exploring the collision of heavy rock and classical music, white-knuckled, no safety net required. But then the records are made to sound sober, maybe a little too sober, by Martin Birch, by Roger Glover.

Rosenthal turned out to be the butt of one of Ritchie's most notorious pranks. Says Bobby, "He's always playing practical jokes on somebody. One night it was snowing and really cold, and after going out to the bar, Dave Rosenthal got back and his whole room was set up outside. He was shivering for days. Ritchie is always trying something. We just went to bed and let David sort it out. He's putting all his stuff back in the room. And his stuff is all cold, his bed is cold—I felt that afterwards. He was just the new guy. It was just like an initiation."

Not entirely all of it, the complete story is fleshed out by Joe. "We had written 'Miss Mistreated' for *Straight Between the Eyes*, which I thought was a really good track. We said, 'David, you can have writing credits for the theme, but you can't have writing credits for the song.' So David sends a letter from the lawyer to Ritchie. Ritchie had told me two hours earlier that he was going to pull something on David, and that he would give me the nod, and it happened that night at dinner. At one end of the table, there was a view of the lake, and you have to remember it was winter now, so the lake was frozen. We were sitting there and the snow was coming down and everything."

"Ritchie said, 'David, I got your letter from the lawyer.' David went, 'Oh, you did?' Now he was scared because Ritchie was annoyed. Ritchie kind of told him, 'That wasn't right; I really don't respect it. We told you that this was not writing the song, and clearly it's not, and this was really bullshit.' David was like, 'Well, I feel this and that.' And Ritchie said, 'Well, you're dead wrong and it's just not right.' And then he said to his roadie, 'Charlie, turn on the lights.' Charlie went okay and Rich put down his fork and knife. Charlie flipped the switch for the outside, and all of a sudden, outside, David's complete bedroom is set up in the snow. David saw that and got completely humiliated and never mentioned it again. That's how Ritchie would get you. He would just do something with a statement."

"I mean, he dropped 10,000 ping-pong balls on me in Lisbon at the end of the tour in Portugal," continues Turner. "Ritchie would always get the roadies to do your room. He would remove everything, put it in the bathroom, put the mattress in last, and then he'd be down at the bar, getting you drunk. You'd come up to locate your room, and he would have put glue in your lock. You finally get into your room, a little drunk, you'd look around and there's nothing in your room and you'd have to sleep on the floor."

"We would pull jokes back on him, except that Ritchie wasn't as good at taking the jokes. When we pulled jokes on him, he'd get upset and pull bigger, more hurtful ones on us, so we just stopped joking him. Finally he stopped joking with me as well because I tricked him. One time he tried to do something to my room… it's a long story, but anyway, I got my room changed and was already down the hall in a room, and he was waiting for me to find out that all my luggage was gone or something like that, and he sees me going over to another room. He says, 'No, your room is down there.' I said, 'No, my room is here—goodnight' and I blew his trick."

Relates Bobby further on Ritchie's pranks, "One night he threw all the contents of a hotel room… anything he could fit, he threw out the window. And it was landing out the window, right near where people were having dinner. The hotel got mad at Ritchie and he said he'd pay for it all, no problem, and then they weren't that mad."

Joe's got the details on this one as well. "Copenhagen, Denmark. I was brand new to the band. I came home from after going around to the bars, with a couple of girls and a couple bottles of wine. I'm doing my thing and there's a knock on the door. It's his drunken roadie Ian Broad, who we called The Drunken Hurricane, and he's like, 'Joe, give me my passport.' I say, 'Ian, I don't have your passport.' And this is all through the door. Ian says, 'Joe, it's in your black jacket.' I go, 'I don't know Ian; it's not in my jacket. I would never lend you my jacket and that's because you're a beast. I would never lend you anything, so just go away.' Ian went, 'No, I'm pissed, I'm going to break it down.' I went, 'Ian, what's your problem?'"

"So I opened the door, took the chain off, Ian pushes through the door and in comes Ritchie in his bathrobe or something and a couple of wonderful Danish girls behind him and Bobby Rondinelli in his bathrobe with a couple of bottles of wine. Ritchie is playing guitar and he goes completely berserk. He starts throwing everything out the window, not personal belongings, but like the whole room. And I'm freaking out. I'm running over to my road manager going, 'I'm taking pictures of it. I'm not paying for this. I can't believe you're doing this!' He says, 'Fuck off, I'm not working at 9:00 in the morning.' I'm getting all upset and everything, and they take everything out of my room—everything is out the window. Whatever they couldn't get out the window, they dragged to the elevator, pushed the button and sent it down. They dragged me on a mattress, they pulled me across a long hallway at the hotel. I ran back to my room and locked the door."

"The sun's coming up, I go down to the desk the next day and very sheepishly, drunk and with a hangover, spoke to the manager saying, 'You'll have to excuse me. Please come and see this; something's happened to my room.' The manager was very friendly and said, 'What could possibly have happened to your room, Mr. Turner?' I went, 'You come and see this; I don't think I can explain it.' And the guy just smiled and said, 'Whatever it is, let's go see.' Now I'm shitting bricks, he gets upstairs, opens the door, looks around and goes, 'Oh, this should only take a couple of months to fix, some fresh paint, new furniture.' My mouth is open and I'm like, 'What?!' And he goes, 'It's already been paid for by Mr. Blackmore, and by the way, welcome to the band.'"

"The video was a little wild for that, because we did it in a real graveyard," says Bobby of the "Death Alley Driver" clip, which featured a chase scenario and Ritchie tarted up as the Grim Reaper.

"Oh, it was terrible! Because I'm the only one making noise. You know, I've got to really play the drums to make it look right. And the first hit of the cymbal, I knocked the cymbal over and it hit a gravestone and the cymbal splits in half, you know, just put a big split in the cymbal. And I'm like, 'God's trying to tell me something here. I don't really want to be doing this' (laughs). But you know, it was a real graveyard in the middle of Connecticut, a real graveyard. I just thought it was a bit weird to be playing drums on somebody's grave. Hopefully I don't have to do that anymore. And it took a while, and it was like winter. It was kind of cold; we were there for a couple of hours."

"Yeah, up in Connecticut; that's where we were," adds Joe. "There were some really old New England-type graveyards and roads. It was fall so the trees were starting to bare. And I remember we got banned on MTV for that video, because they said that this was just evil and all these other things. I mean, nowadays it would be nothing; it's come so far. 'Death Alley Driver' was actually my idea, and I don't mind taking credit for it, good, bad or indifferent, but I just said, 'Let's follow the story line.' Ritchie is Death in the back seat of the limousine, and I'm the rider on the bike, and then we would shoot to the graveyard."

"And of course, we got a lot of publicity because it was banned on MTV. But you know, I couldn't understand half of that stuff. Because Skid Row could come out and have a shootout at high noon and kill each other. Sure, we were in that graveyard; we brought the drums and amps and everything to the graveyard. But what gets me—granted this is years later—is that something like Skid Row '18 and Life,' there were people shooting each other and our video got banned on MTV. Murder is okay but do not go into a graveyard! I think there really were a lot of dark forces chasing us around—I really do. But murder was okay, you know what I mean? It just shows you the typical American mentality. But yeah, sitting in the graveyard and all, and we had the fog machines going. It was cool to us. We were like, yeah, this is exactly where we're at. Back in those days, especially Ritchie and I, we were heavily into the occult and things like that. For us, this was fodder for our enjoyment."

It's actually a really cool video. Ritchie sits grinning in the back of an antique black limo tailing very closely Joe on a motorcycle through the Lovecraft-ian woods. Blackmore's dressed formally, but he clutches his axe, almost like a cane. Interspersed is faux-live footage, where, granted, Joe postures like a girly pretty boy, undermining the menace of the narrative and the aggressive musical soundtrack.

Song #2 on the album, "Stone Cold," would be the hit single prequel to the record's issue, emerging in the UK as both a blue vinyl 7" and 12" one month before the full-length's debut June 10th of 1982. Actually, the track (backed with "Rock Fever") didn't do all that well, rising only to #40 in the US (albeit #1 on the sub-chart Mainstream Rock) and #34 in the UK, precipitating the cancelling of a second single, purported to have been "Death Alley Driver." In Canada, the song got to #28, partially favourably affected by the album being recorded in Quebec.

In tandem, the album rose to #17 on Canada's RPM 50 chart. The best placement however was in the UK, where *Straight Between the Eyes* enjoyed a #5 posting, arguably due to that country's fleeting predilection for all things AOR, which in Rainbow was embodied shamelessly by Joe Lynn Turner.

"'Stone Cold' was interesting," reflects Ritchie, "because I'd put that together just as a riff. I had no idea how the melody would go, but then Joe put the melody to it and it really worked. It's always very nice when people help you out, not just for a chord or a note, but they actually put in a substantial amount of creativity, as Joe did on 'Stone Cold.' I think on 'Street of Dreams,' the melody was more mapped out for him. But on 'Stone Cold,' he came up with that on his own. I just gave him basically a chord structure, with no top line."

Roger Glover is credited on this one as well, but when asked about collaboration with Roger in general, Ritchie says "not particularly. I would write more with Joe. Roger would get involved, but more as an overseer, really."

"'Stone Cold'... again, these things are magical," says a typical ebullient Joe. "To me, life is magical and if you don't look for it, you'll never find it. Every day, every moment, there's a miracle happening someplace. And what happened with that was Roger had just broken up with his wife, or she broke up with him, actually. And he was absolutely dejected and felt terrible as you would, and he said something like, 'She left me stone cold.' And I went, wow, there's a title there. So I ran back to my room (laughs) and started writing the song."

"And I went to Ritchie and everything, and before we knew it, Roger was like, 'My God, there's a whole song here.' Except he put in that middle eight part, which was 'Standing in the darkness, reaching for the door' and all that. And I just said, 'We've got something here!' And really, I think it was a breakthrough. Because that particular performance... it was sort of a hard rock band with a very soulful vocalist. I mean, that vocal is not a heavy metal vocal. It's really just a soulful vocal coming straight from the heart, and it was influenced by the snowy environment—as I've said, there was a blizzard going on when I recorded that vocal. At one point I looked outside and sang 'You put me in the deep freeze.' But yeah, that marriage, I think, took people by surprise, in a good way, and actually they responded to it and it became one of the Top Ten hits here in the States. It's a real crowd-pleaser and works well acoustically or electrically. So yeah, that was the start of our direction."

The production video for "Stone Cold" was directed by Edd Griles, who went on to produce the MTV Video Music Awards, the ESPYs and all sorts of beauty pageants. The clips for "I Surrender," "Can't Happen Here" and "Death Alley Driver" were also directed by Griles, his other big clients of the day being Cyndi Lauper, Sheena Easton and Huey Lewis.

Next up was "Bring on the Night (Dream Chaser)" which expertly melds hard rock, heavy metal and the Middle Eastern tonalities pioneered by Jimmy Page, Uli Jon Roth, but most prevalently Mr. Ritchie Blackmore, a little bit in Purple but a lot more in Rainbow. Through this tripartite function, the track is one that glues the record together, refines its purpose.

As Joe explains, "'Dream Chaser,' or 'Bring on the Night,' the reason why that has two titles is that Roger was writing 'Dream Chaser' and I was writing 'Bring on the Night,' and we put our lyrics together (laughs). And the next thing you know, we came out with this really different type of song, you know, with a great chorus and everything else. Ritchie wrote the music and Roger had a part during the B section. That was basically about the phenomenon of dream state vs. waking state. And, I mean, Roger was a philosopher—I called him The Philosopher—and I kind of had that sort of mind myself (of note, Joe was nicknamed The Reverend), so we really got on, on that level. So that was one of our more quote unquote spiritual tunes."

For a demonstration of recurring themes in Blackmore's music, compare the closing chords of this one's chorus to the closing chords of the chorus to "Gates of Babylon." Indeed, even the "take you away" lyric matches up quite well.

On the subject of all this melody found throughout the Joe Lynn Turner years, well, Ritchie has always said he was a song guy, adding at times that he really, really liked Abba. With a guy like Ritchie, you never knew whether he was being serious, possibly exaggerating on a kernel of truth, or just having a go.

Joe attests to the fact that Ritchie wasn't kidding: "Seriously into Abba. Seriously into Abba. In fact, he would write songs with Abba in mind (laughs). He would go, 'Well this is Abba, but I'll disguise it in a hard rock way.' Yeah, deeply into Abba. I mean, honestly, truly. And I can understand why. Abba was just a huge melodic type of band. Ritchie's a really melodic player; he's got a melodic ear. So again, it's not surprising. In fact, he turned me onto Abba. I was like, 'Abba? Isn't that like some disco band or something?' And he would play me the Abba songs and I would go, 'You know, these guys are absolutely fantastic!' Then we got to meet them, and that was fantastic, in Sweden and we also used their lighting trusses at one point. So there became an association there. Yeah, he loves them."

"That's very true. I was listening to a lot of Abba," confirms Ritchie. "Abba was a big influence for me. I really felt that the songwriting of Abba was excellent, so it did kind of wash off on me a bit. So I did kind of go that way, more commercial, simplified, away from the heavy rock stuff."

And being a song guy during this time, Ritchie has said that soloing took a bit of a back seat. Joe indeed saw this side of the Man in Black as well. "Yeah, he was struggling with the concept. I don't know why, because I always thought that he was brilliant in his approach. Okay, some nights he'd fall apart because he'd be his own worst enemy. So are we all, at one point or another. But I don't understand that torture. Because I just thought he was really onto something and he was brilliant and that he really didn't need to suffer that much about it. But there must have been something personally inside of him that he knew he wanted to bring out, that he wasn't. That's a man's private situation, a private issue. But I saw him struggling. And I'd tell him many times, 'Man, you're fuckin' brilliant; just go out there and play. You don't have to think about it. Thinking will drive you crazy.' We all have great nights, we all have bad nights, and there's just no way, being human, that you can escape that. But to struggle about a gift that he had, it was just so obvious, at least to me. All he had to do was put his fingers there and play."

Bobby wasn't aware of Ritchie's admission of struggling with solos during this era. "Well, Ritchie is known as one of the best guitar players in the world. He writes great riffs and he plays great solos. So I don't know if he struggles with them, but he sure knows how to play them. I mean, maybe struggling for someone like Ritchie means doing it a couple of times, you know what I mean? But he gets it done and he plays amazing."

Underscoring the commercial aspect of Rainbow at this juncture, Ritchie told Andy Seeker of the Asbury Park Press, "Unquestionably, we've turned in a more accessible direction on the last few albums. A few years ago I would have insisted that selling records means nothing. I realize now that a statement like that is made only by someone who isn't selling many records. I imagine that seeing a sickening band like the Bee Gees sell millions of records helped me form that philosophy. Every artist wants people to buy their product, and even though I'm certainly not happy with the more commercial aspects of rock 'n' roll, I am happy that our albums are doing well."

"This is an album that should appeal to everyone," added Roger. "What we've done on this album is strike a balance between the accessibility of the last few albums and the progressivism of the earlier ones. This is unquestionably the most diverse album that Rainbow's ever done, and I believe it's the best as well. It's the type of music that we've been trying to make for a long time."

"Tite Squeeze," a Roger Glover favourite, follows with a heavy and funky blues vibe that would not have been out of place on *Burn*, *Stormbringer* or *Come Taste the Band*. "Obviously a very sexual song," volunteers Joe. "I mean, it's pretty blatant. And it's got a real sleaze groove, and back in those days I was Jumping Jack

Flash, so I was having my share of that kind of stuff. And it really was about any woman. It wasn't about any one particular woman, that particular song, anyway, not that I can remember. Maybe I had somebody in mind, but it's usually the person you're with at the time. So anyway, that went down."

Closing side one of the original vinyl is "Tearin' Out My Heart," a brooding and bluesy but dark ballad typical of the spooky JLT years approach to such compositional matter. Ritchie's solo contains some sublime melodic passages but for the most part, this is a Turner showcase. The track, when presented on stage, bulged into a jam, of course with an extended Ritchie solo spot.

Offers Joe, "'Tearin' Out My Heart' was all about this Canadian girl I was in love with, and actually she was with me when I wrote it, with the candlelight and the whole thing, and we were breaking up and it was just awful, and it came out to be... I think when I sang it I had every feeling in the world about this thing happening, and that's why it came out so real and people related to it—because it was real life. It actually happened and I transferred it to the microphone. Some people have told me that it's their favourite song on the album. I always give license to people's opinion. The song went over great in concert; it had a lot of drama."

Offering a glimpse into his methodology as a vocalist, Joe explains that, "if I don't have it by three takes, then I don't know the song or it's the wrong day or something. So what we do is probably go back to the first take, take maybe a little bit from the second or third. I know guys who really work on their vocals. Lou Gramm from Foreigner goes over every syllable. I've never done that; I just go for it and try to capture the moment. That's what's important to me."

"I'm an incredibly varied singer. I just grew up that way. I'm lucky and I'm fortunate that I have this gift. I'm not a one-sided singer. I grew up around all kinds of music, thanks to my father. I love the blues; I love hard rock and heavy metal, love country music as well. I listened to everything and just soaked it up; jazz and Etta James—I love that shit. I listen to sax players for vocal phrasings, just like guitarists do."

"So getting back to the varied vocalist thing, it's a gift and a curse as well, because sometimes you're too over-qualified for some things. Some times people are surprised that I can sing R&B. I mean I grew up in a gospel church, in a black Baptist church. I'm a black man in a white man's body—it's unbelievable. If I really turn it on and go to the R&B side, it would just be too black. Glenn Hughes used to do that and do it real well, but he got killed for it. They used to say he's too funky, he's too black. You know what? He's too gifted, so fuck you!"

And in later years, this versatility actually led Joe into the world of singing for commercials! "You're assuming a character; it's a challenge really," says Joe of this sometimes secretive type of gig for a singer. "You can make a whole lot of money doing it which certainly isn't a sin anymore, when you've got everyone from Led Zeppelin to The Who doing it. In the States it's all classic rock jingles. Michael Bolton got me into jingles; he's an old friend of mine—I sung on his record. He told me to check it out; he was about to hit the big time around then. I told him, 'I don't do fuckin' jingles man,' he said, 'You have no idea.' So he took me to this Miller Lite commercial and we were partying in the China Club. He said, 'Get on the mic and sing this one,' so I got up and sung this kinda bluesy number. I nailed the song and ended up winning the account."

"About two weeks later I get a check and I couldn't believe the money that was involved. I sung for ten minutes and made all that money. I liked it because it was something to fall back on. There's such a wide variety of things to sing on and it's fun as shit. I did Sudafed, and I just did one for Folgers to the tune of 'Feels Like the First Time' by Foreigner; that's me and Mick Jones from Foreigner—we redid the tune. I was actually in Foreigner for a couple of weeks, just around *Say You Will*, 1987. I told their manger to go fuck himself and Mick and the boys were agreeing with me saying, 'Fuck these ballads; let's rock.' So their manager got all pissed-off at me and he's still pissed-off at me to this day."

One thing that always bothered Turner in doing vocal work however—and it's something he fixed on latter years solo albums—is this idea of being rushed. It's a logical occurrence, given that vocals are usually one of the last things to get done.

"That pressure… not that I can't handle the pressure. I'm a pretty clutch player, but at the same time, what happened was, as we would do the whole album, then I'd have like ten minutes to do ten vocals. I think we let a lot of things go in the past. I think we said, 'My worst is somebody's best' and kind of had that philosophy."

"But that's not enough in my opinion. I always felt short-changed on the vocals. Let's put it this way. I'm not standing in there fixing every word or doing anything like that. I mean, I sing the songs pretty much straight through. I do three passes, we comp one good one, see what needs fixing, and that's usually the keeper. Sometimes we don't comp any at all and the vocals come straight through. I would have to say that Ritchie had a certain idea, and I would do something and they would do something, and they would say 'Okay, that's fabulous.'"

"And what I realized is that personally, you know you can do quote unquote better. But most people think that what you're doing is great. So, if they think what you're doing is great, and they're like, 'No, no, no, that's great, that sounds great.' 'But I've got one more in me!' And they're like, 'No, that's great, this is it.' And I would say, 'Okay, if that's it, then that's it.' Roger Glover was producing, and occasionally I would get the opportunity to squeak out and just say, 'Roger, let me just do it one more time and show you.' And then he'd be like, 'Well, yeah, but I like the other one better.' For who knows what personal reasons, control, whatever."

"Let's see, 'Power'… just personal stuff," reflects Joe, back on planet *Straight Between the Eyes*, discussing the stomping, straight-eight, yet irresistibly melodic side two opener.

"I was going through a transition myself, sort of a personal resurrection. And I just realized all the personal power you have. You know, there's an old adage that says people only have the power over you that you give them. This stuck in my head. And I started to realize, you have to take your power back, as a person. You have to make a stand as a man. You can promote things. So this kind of stuff is always very indicative of my lyrics. I just take personal experiences and relate them; everybody has these experiences. So 'Power' turned out to be a really big song because I think everybody got what I was saying. You know, you hold the key to yourself and you hold the key to your own transformation and your development and whatever. And I think everybody got that. Plus, it's a real strong rock tune. So it just worked out well. I mean, we were making magic; that's what it really was; that's what it really comes down to. That magic is the music and the music and the lyrics just connected to people in the way they should; it was a marriage."

"We got ripped on that song because everyone said it was too commercial," continues Turner. "That song was *the* concert favourite. Everyone was up off their seats and screaming 'Power!' I knew it would be that way when I wrote it. But yes, it's an autobiographical song. I was indulging myself to myself."

"Miss Mistreated" is very much in the mould of "Stone Cold," as well as future classics like "Street of Dreams" and "Can't Let You Go." On this one, Joe brings together the worlds of Deep Purple and Foreigner to dramatic yet still radio-friendly effect.

Says Joe, "Purple had 'Mistreated,' and I said to Ritchie (laughs), we were talking about some girl or something that he was interested in, and I said, 'Oh, she sounds like Miss Mistreated.' And he looked at me and he went, 'Write that!' And I said, 'Write it? What do you mean?' And he said 'That's a song!' 'It is?!' 'Yeah.' And he came up with this track, and I said, 'This sounds like this "Miss Mistreated" track.' And he said, 'Good, let's shove it up Purple's ass.' Because they had 'Mistreated,' but this was 'Miss Mistreated.' And he said, 'I know I'm going to get a lot of flack from it, but it's such a good song.' And really, it's a relationship song, but from the end of positive strength. It revolves around the question of, in a break-up, who really has hurt who? And it's really a true story. It's more like who's mistreating who? But Ritchie loved it and he said, 'That's great. Let them suck on that for a while.'"

Somewhat awkwardly, the band telegraphed the comparison by presenting the song on the back cover—and even in the lyrics—as "MISS Mistreated," while on the titling on the inner sleeve, the "MISS" shouts even louder by being bolded. And then it's a distinction lost on the record label where all the songs were presented in all capitals.

"Rock Fever" is classic Blackmore, Ritchie weaving one of his patented circular note-dense riffs (think "Lady Double Dealer," Sensitive to Light," "No Time to Lose" and "Hard Lovin' Woman") around an old-school rocker, even if the verse gets a little too sweet and melodic for "rock fever" standards.

"With 'Rock Fever,' I was looking for an anthem," proffers Joe. "And at that point, you know, being a much younger man, I mean, I actually had rock fever. I just loved rock 'n' roll; I still do. It's like a disease that won't go away. So that's basically where that came from. Again, difficult to cure, aren't we? So it's like, you have this disease and I just put it out there and that became an anthem, with fists raised in the air and everything else. It was really written for the stage. It was another concert favourite, another Blackmore/Turner song. Ritchie would write these riffs and I would take over and tell him, 'We've got to be more mainstream, Ritchie. We can't just keep writing about dragons.' We wrote about spiritual things like ghosts but we started writing about things that people on the street could relate too. It went over huge in concert. We were designing these songs for the live performance. It should have been a hit but in those days there was a lot of pay for play going on. There still is."

It's interesting that Joe says "another Blackmore/Turner song," demonstrating his cognisance after years and years that in fact only two songs on the record are credited that way, this one and "Death Alley Driver." Rosenthal is in on "Miss Mistreated" and Bobby gets the nod on "Eyes of Fire," while the rest are all assigned to Ritchie, Joe and Roger.

Fairly brisk, the song still grooves hotly, due to Rondinelli's predilection for playing "behind the beat." Offers Bobby, "Behind the beat means, if you have a tempo and you have a metronome clicking away, you can play right on the beat, or you can play a bit ahead of the beat, which makes things sound a little more urgent, or you can play behind the beat, which makes it feel a little more relaxed. I do tend to play behind the beat. I'm even more like that now though, I think, versus when I was with Rainbow. But I guess I was like that back then too somewhat. I'm pretty critical with myself though."

Closing the album is "Eyes of Fire," the album's epic, kicked off with a gong bang and then a seductive and snaky guitar sequence while the band gradually builds to full volume, driven by a distinctive, very Middle Eastern bass line and guitar lick combination. Perhaps a bit forced as a nod to "Gates of Babylon," the song is nonetheless a bold addition to what is an album mostly lacking in such overt gothic metal gravitas. Also along for the ride is a prominent string arrangement that constantly dovetails with Ritchie's Egyptian musings. "Eyes of Fire" contains the only Rondinelli writing credit on the album, Bobby explaining that, "That's because when Ritchie wrote the riff, me and him were working on it together."

"I was trying to get some R&R one night in the bar, as usual," laughs Joe on the track's lyrical spark. "I think we were all there pretty much. Ritchie was somewhere else in the bar chatting up a circle of friends. And I went to the bar to get a drink and as you know, most bars had the big mirrors behind them, to show off the liquor and things. And I caught a girl's glance, from all the way to the other side of the bar, through the mirror, and her eyes were just incredible—she had that bewitching siren look. This is absolutely true. I mean, it sounds kind of sappy, but it's really not; it's what dreams are made of."

"And her name was Erica Varga; I'll never forget this girl. She was just stunning, platinum blond hair, and these incredible green eyes that would turn colours, almost like red to green to brown. It was very strange; I've never seen a person like this before. I mean, you've obviously seen people with strange eyes, violet eyes. But she had this particular attribute."

"And I couldn't help myself, so I got my drink, and sent one over to her and she kind of nodded, and this was all done through the mirror, which was really strange. I think it's mentioned in the song somewhere. So anyway, I had to meet her and I walked over and introduced myself and she ended up being an incredibly intelligent fashion designer from Montreal, and a very cultured, cute girl. And we talked politics, religion and things like that, all night, and there was no hanky panky going on or anything, although I would have jumped at the chance (laughs)."

"But it wasn't like that. It was just an incredible capture. I was absolutely captured by her eyes. And I called them eyes of fire, because they would glow a little bit. It was so strange. I've never seen anything like this and I asked her about them, and she said her mother had this genetic trait and she passed it down. So the next thing I know, I developed it into this incredibly mystical person. So it started in reality I think, and it ended up quite a bit in fantasy. But yeah, that is one of my wife's all-time favourite songs. Like I say, through this mirror it really looked like this woman's eyes were glowing. Okay, maybe I had a couple of beers but it was really weird. I've always wondered if she even knows she was the inspiration for that song."

When all was said and done, *Straight Between the Eyes* rose to #30 in the US charts and, as mentioned, a bold #5 back in the UK. Out on the tour trail, that considerably ugly album cover continued to keep watch over the band… "On the tour, the eyes would be above the stage, draped off with the curtains, and they would just come down over my head and move around and shoot beams out and change colours," explains Rondinelli.

"The eyes were amazing!" adds Joe. "And with the eyes, there was one point of contention, because in the middle between the two eyes was like a carriage or a bucket, and not really noticeable to the audience from that point of view. But anyway, you could sit and ride in the bucket. And originally I was in the bucket and I would come up out of the eyes, and as soon as the crowd went crazy and stuff and I'm singing from up there, Ritchie just kind of looked at me one night and said, 'All right, that's it, he's out the bucket' (laughs). A little jealousy or something happened there and he went, 'No, no, I'm the guy. Joe's off the bucket. You're down here on the stage, on the floor with us.' (laughs). But the eyes were phenomenal because they were lasers and they had pulsating bloodshot red lines in them, and they could move anywhere they wanted in the audience; it was quite overwhelming."

Support for the tour, which saw the band gallivanting around North America through the spring and summer of '82, and then into Japan and Europe to close out the year, was varied, including the likes of Iron Maiden, UFO, Riot, Scorpions, Krokus, 38 Special (co-headliner), Saxon and eventually Girlschool. For touring purposes, the band included a pair of female backup singers, Dee Beale and Lin Robinson from Purple Records recording artists Reflections.

"They were there before I got there," cautions Joe. "I had heard that they were on the *Down to Earth* tour. Dee and Lin; they were actually Benny Hill girls. At one point they were on the TV show with Benny Hill. And I think Bruce Payne took a fancy to the dark-haired one, Lin, and they were having an affair. But I thought it was fantastic that a hard rock band could have these... it was kind of like the Crüe-ettes or something, when Motley Crüe did it. But they were there before I got there. The unfortunate thing was, a lot of times they were put under the stage. But there was a tour... was it here in the States? I think it was here in the States because it was probably more acceptable, to have the girls here, than in Europe, where all the hardcore guys are. And they actually were on the stage, up on a platform, I think, behind Ritchie."

And then at one point, there was apparently just one of them. "Yes, I think Lin stayed on a bit, and I think that's all because of Bruce, really. I think the affair... you know, the tangled web. The tangled web! It was crazy."

In terms of non-JLT era material, "All Night Long" was retained from *Down to Earth*, while "Smoke on the Water," "Long Live Rock 'n' Roll" and "Catch the Rainbow" were also included. An officially issued video called *Live Between the Eyes* was issued from this tour, filmed at the band's San Antonio stop on August 18th, 1982.

Asked whether he or anybody in the band ever found themselves on stage jamming with any of these bands, Joe says that, "I remember Ritchie once telling me that I shouldn't go out on stage, because we were headlining, and I shouldn't go out on stage beforehand. And he was absolutely right. But I got on stage, I think it was with Klaus or somebody, Scorpions. And he just felt that that would ruin the mystique. And to a point, he's right."

Bobby also fostered a Scorpions connection through touring with the blowing-up Germans. "Yeah, I was good friends with The Scorpions, all of them, but Rudolf Schenker in particular. And I'm still very friendly with them. I spoke to them about three weeks ago when I was in Germany, and was inviting them to our Lizards show; Rudy was in the States at the time. I ended up drumming on *Love at First Sting* and that's Jimmy Bain on bass. We were there the whole time, doing the whole record. Jimmy was over there for a couple weeks before I was, and they called me in and I was there for two weeks. We had a good time. Jimmy's a great guy; I love Jimmy to death."

"Lots of reasons, lots of reasons," sighs Bobby, on why he would no longer be Rainbow's drummer after the *Straight Between the Eyes* tour. "It was time to move on and I was maybe doing a few things that I shouldn't have been doing chemical-wise. You live and learn, you know what I mean? (laughs). But I can listen to both of those albums and like them. People still hold them up; they're both good records. I don't think I have a favourite; I like them both. I think they could've both been mixed a little heavier, but they're both good records. They actually brought Rainbow to a different level commercially in the US."

"Did Bobby Rondinelli tell you that? Okay, then I admire his honesty," says Joe, when asked about Bobby leaving the band. "What happened was yeah, Bobby was doing a lot chemicals and at the same time he was shagging a lot. So his legs were gone; he was partying. He was living it up. It was sex, drugs and rock 'n' roll, and believe me, sex, drugs *and* rock 'n' roll. So the sex and the chemicals were weakening him, as far as we remembered, because he would start at sound check, with the meters, hitting the snare and so on, and they would be at a great level, and then two, three songs into it, he'd be huffing and puffing and the meters would go down, the sound levels, and his time would drop, and Ritchie would just get fucking pissed!"

"So, saying that, you had to keep your stamina up and yourself in good shape. Especially the drummer and the singer. Because those, in my opinion, are the two roughest jobs in the whole band. You know, because they're so personal and so physically powerful. I mean, look, I play guitar, and I could be drunk every night playing guitar. You know, you stand there and play some strings and some notes and stuff and have some fun. But the energy you have to exert playing drums, especially the double kit, and singing, was very difficult. I remember I had to temper myself and pull back because I wasn't going to make it if I didn't. In those days of course, we were running wild. So yeah, Bobby was very honest about that and I've got to admire his candid approach to that."

Even Roger was on the outs—for a time. "Oh, well, Ritchie had told him to fuck off and that he was a lousy producer. You know, those two had hundreds of years behind them. You know how it is sometimes with old friends. There was a little resentment and I don't know what you call it, tension of course. But they had a falling out. That's the best way really to put it. And they kind of repaired it, of course, and then *Bent Out of Shape* came out, and in my opinion, it was a great album."

Roger's replacement was to be Jack Green. I asked Joe if he actually played with the band at any point. "Ah, he was hanging around, you know? Nice guy and all. Because Ritchie, at that point was dissatisfied with the teenage eighth note type of bass playing. I mean look, Roger almost developed that old style, that thumpy dum-dum-dum type of stuff, which we called teenage eighth note (laughs). And he played it better than anybody else. You know, he had a great feel. And I thought Roger was an invaluable team player in that respect, that he could do many things. He's a good lyricist and writer and producer and bass player, all-around. But Ritchie and him were just at it. I mean, they had just had enough of each other at that point and then of course they came back together."

New commercial levels or not, after the *Straight Between the Eyes* tour, machinations were already in place to get some version of Deep Purple back together, so much so that the band was, for a space, given their walking papers. David Coverdale was offered the Purple gig but turned it down. Ian Gillan then took the bait, but before long it was Ritchie who threw ice on the idea, opting instead to record another album with his long (and temptingly) bubbling-under Rainbow franchise.

"We pretty much knew what was going on," says Joe, "because we had to, obviously. You know, there was some covert stuff going on there where Bruce Payne was really trying to keep it on the hush, but we knew; the rest of the guys knew. There's not much you can keep from people who are living and breathing the same air. So we knew about it, but I wasn't rattled about it. In fact, I was happy about it. And I was happy about it when it actually happened, because the way it was supposed to go down, was that there were going to be one or two Purple albums, and then Rainbow was going to reform, that same lineup, which we thought was a successful lineup, and then unfortunately it never happened."

David Coverdale? Ian Gillan? "You know, those are all speculations," sighs Joe. "Probably, yes, no, maybe so. You know, who knew? There were even rumours really just within the band. Rumours are rumours and they'll never die. But when it was either David Coverdale or Ian Gillan, we all just said, you know what? It doesn't affect us either way. We still have to go on and do what we have to do. As I recall, there was a well-deserved break and we weren't quite sure what was going to happen at that point. So all of us were lining up different things, of course, as we always do, because we like to keep working. But when we got the call and it was, 'No, no, we're going to go through with the third Rainbow album,' everybody was ready, like we didn't even miss a beat."

Chapter 9

Bent Out of Shape

"I could just disappear into thin air."

Not counting the watery *Stranger in Us All* "reunion" album (and, in some respects, it shouldn't be counted), *Bent Out of Shape* was Rainbow's last record, Ritchie breaking up the band to rejoin Deep Purple for the solid, successful *Perfect Strangers* album in 1984. The third of the poppy Joe Lynn Turner years, *Bent Out of Shape* was nevertheless the most sophisticated, cohesive, elegantly gloomy… basically, it worked. Sure, there's an enduring passion for the Dio years, in fact, a certain timelessness to records like *Rising* and *Long Live Rock 'n' Roll* that has passed the Turner turners by, but *Bent Out of Shape*… its seductions runs deep.

Speaking to Hit Parader's Andy Secher in late 1983, Ritchie had acknowledged as much, saying "I've come to realize that playing music people can enjoy isn't a sin. When I first left Deep Purple and started Rainbow in 1974, I was committed to making music I viewed as challenging. Regrettably, that style didn't sell too many records. Over the last few albums, we've added more commercial elements to our music and become much more successful. That was true on *Straight Between the Eyes* and it's true on the new one as well."

Roger Glover seconded that emotion. "Joe worked with Ritchie on almost all of the songs. In the past, I had done quite a bit of the writing, but Joe's a great songwriter, and since he's the singer, it makes it easier for him to write the words as well. The new album has a great mix of traditional Rainbow hard rockers and more commercial things. Some of the band's long-time fans got a bit upset about our more accessible sound, but I always remember what Jimi Hendrix once said: 'There's nothing wrong with walking into a bar and hearing your song on the jukebox.' That's the philosophy that we've adopted even though we're rocking as hard as ever."

"We approached this album in a slightly different way than the last few. Before going over to the studio, we all went up to Vermont and took a skiing chalet for a couple weeks. We set up all the gear in the living room and just rehearsed material over and over again. It proved to be an incredibly prolific time for us, and for the first time in our history, we actually had an over-abundance of material. Usually we have to scrape the bottom of the barrel just to complete an album. Now we have enough tracks left over to put new songs on B-sides of singles. It's a great feeling to have some extra material left in the can."

Joe and Ritchie were writing most of the record alone also in part because Roger was directing his writing toward what would become his Peter Gabriel-ish solo album *Mask*, eventually issued in May of 1984.

Of the Vermont diversion for the record's writing session, Joe recalls, "That was the kind of place where Ritchie actually liked to do albums and rehearsals and things. We would go to Vermont, Killington or a place like that, outside of a ski resort area and get a big huge band house with a huge fireplace, where you can walk into the fireplace. Set up the equipment in the living room or what have you. Of course, these chalets would have to be big enough, and we'd have these rooms because they were ski chalets and they would accommodate a lot of people, and we got a lot of work done that way, because we were right there, on the spot, in the house, got a big fire going, and we would jam and play, right through the night and whatever."

Joe indicates that some actual skiing took place as well. "Oh yeah! Ritchie never skied, really, but Roger was a big skier, and Rosenthal I know skied. And I was lousy, snowplowing down the hill. I actually got up to a black diamond run one time with Roger (laughs), when we were actually doing the previous album *Straight Between the Eyes*, outside of Montreal. Because a similar situation happened: there was this great skiing up there. So Roger took me up to this black diamond run, and that's when I had more guts than brains because I couldn't ski down a black diamond run (laughs). And I kept falling and he kept picking me up and I landed in snowdrifts and almost hit trees. I'll never forget it, I was up to my neck one time and they had to throw a ski pole out to me to hang onto and then yank me out—a couple of guys—because I was so buried (laughs)."

"We had some trouble making that album," explains Turner, examining the assembly of the record, which was to take place at Le Studio again, but couldn't, due to it being booked solid. "We started out in Denmark at Freddie Hansson's studio, Sweet Silence, which John McLaughlin actually named, as part of his meditation. It's an interesting story. He used to say 'Stop and listen to the sweet silence.' And Freddie said, 'Yeah, I'm going to name the studio Sweet Silence.' In those Copenhagen days, I remember Phil Lynott, God rest his soul, he was just fabulous—this guy was a real inspiration to me. I got friendly with Phil for a while, and he would come up once in a while. Because we were there for six months."

Relations with Phil extended to the band attending a Thin Lizzy concert; other recreational activities included yet more soccer, this time with Iron Maiden's crew. As well, certain Deep Purple members were skulking about, speaking furtively with Ritchie about things that might transpire some day.

Continues Joe, picking up the tale, "We're sitting there and we had this drummer that Ritchie had picked from Long Island or something, obviously someone who had played in a local band and we really weren't getting very far with this guy; he wasn't cutting the mustard. He shall remain nameless to protect himself. Obviously Ritchie had made the wrong decision and he was hard-pressed to admit it. I was getting completely frustrated because we had six or seven master reels of tape and no keepers. None of the track were really good enough to keep and build on. So we were running into time restrictions, money, and I was getting really frustrated. I just looked at Rich and said, 'He's ruining all the great songs we've written. We can't have that.' I said, 'I know my seniority in the band isn't all that long, but you know what? The writing is on the wall here; the truth is easy to see.'"

"So with that, he said, 'Do you have any suggestions?' And I said 'Yeah. There's a guy back home called Chuck Burgi and he'll just come out here and nail this.' So I called up Bruce Payne, the manager and said, 'Look, we can't go along with this. Something has to happen here. I have a friend of mine who is an amazing drummer; he'll come in and knock it right off.' So that's how Chuck Burgi came in. He flew in with a bunch of trap cases and whatnot, set up and bam! We started to knock it off. So in that respect it was a little difficult at first. But Chuck had been in everything from Brand X, Meat Loaf... I mean, this guy had chops up the ying yang. He was playing fusion, rock and he's an incredibly professional person. He just laid it down, and I think he's always been one of Ritchie's favourite drummers."

"But they're both great drummers," adds Joe, contrasting Bobby Rondinelli and the newly acquired Burgi (Tico Torres, soon to find fame with Bon Jovi, was briefly courted as well). "Bobby plays a little behind the beat and Chuck plays a little on top of the beat. I mean, that's musical talk, but they're great guys, both of them. Completely different personalities. Bobby's one of the funniest men on earth, I think. He's hilarious as a personality. Chuck, I have to say, is sort of my paranormal brother. He got me into a lot of the supernatural stuff, all of that, in the beginning. Now I'm getting him into stuff (laughs)."

"Bobby left the group a few months ago," said Roger, interviewing at the time. "He worked with Scorpions for awhile. Whether he'll stay in that band or not, I'm not sure. He's a great guy and we're still close friends, but we're very pleased with the work Chuck has done with us. He's not a traditional hard rock drummer. In fact, he's worked with Hall & Oates, but he can really be powerful when he wants to be. As the bassist, I work very closely with the drummer, and I've been able to develop a rapport with Chuck in a hurry. It is rather strange about how many personnel changes we've made. When I first joined the band a few years back, I told Ritchie that one of the first things I wanted to do was stop the ridiculous number of changes. I wanted to give the group a degree of stability. Rainbow will never lose its identity as long as Ritchie's there, but it's still important to keep the same musicians together. We should be able to do that now."

Countered Ritchie, "There's nothing wrong with change. It brings new blood into the group and keeps everybody awake. I can be difficult to work with and I understand those who choose not to deal with me after awhile. That will always be their choice."

"*Bent Out of Shape* was something that Cookie Crawford always used to say," explains Joe, with respect to the album title. "Cookie was Ritchie's personal at the time, and soccer buddy. And Cookie was a real funny character, and he was always using the expression, 'Don't get bent out of shape about it,' when anything came up. So we thought that was a cool title."

"The record company wasn't too thrilled with that idea," said Roger, about rumours that the band actually wanted to call the album *Don't Fuck Around with Love*. "They wanted something a little more conventional. That's when we came up with *Bent Out of Shape*, which is a term Ritchie heard one of the roadies use one day. I was a little worried about it; I thought it might have too much of a gay confrontation (laughs)."

Once past the moniker and wrap, the music enclosed turned out to embody a warmth as well as a chill, graphically evident when butted up against the heavier *Straight Between the Eyes* and the weak dissipation of *Difficult to Cure*. Warmer and colder: again, a seduction, upscale but uneasy.

"I think it was a little more refined," reflects Turner. "I don't know if that's good or bad, refinement for a rock band. I think it's an extremely fine album because of the material on it and the recording and the sound, everything… it's just probably one of our better efforts, although *Straight Between the Eyes*, in my opinion, has a magic that just cannot be duplicated; just that point in time, with 'Stone Cold' and all those kinds of songs. But then again *Bent Out of Shape* with 'Street of Dreams'… we had something going on there. And I really believe that we were headed toward becoming a melodic, heavy Foreigner or heavy Journey. I think with one more record we really would have broken through into the commercial market. Because we still had legions of fans, and we were heavy enough and obscure enough to keep them. But at the same time we were picking up new fans. Here in America we were in the Top Ten and things like that; we were on MTV and it was just working. We were on the verge of something greater but unfortunately it broke up right at that time (laughs)."

One important part of making this album special was Roger Glover's production, which again addressed a dichotomy, this idea of sounding plush and hi-fi yet with sparse componentry.

"Roger was extremely important," emphasizes Turner, "more important than what Ritchie every gave him credit for, I'll tell you that. Because there was always a tension between the two. But I always thought that Roger shaped the thing, took the clay and shaped it. There's no doubt that he was the producer, but we all had input as well. Sometimes it can be a disaster without the band members having input. But I think with us, it was well-selected input. Roger would listen to what we had to say, and if he agreed, we would go that way; if not, he would stick to his guns. But he always made sure that the sound was good and that it had a nice finished quality. Because when I listen back to these things occasionally, I have to say that they stand the test of time. I have to take my hat off to Roger and say I think he did a very good job. Also he was a great lyricist in my opinion. He showed me how to write cryptically, where you can write a lyric where nobody actually knows what the hell you're talking about (laughs), with a deep meaning there somehow, a lyric that could exist on different levels. So he was a master of all that as well."

"Philosophy, the way it should go," continues Turner, asked what Ritchie and Roger would butt heads over. "Roger would be sitting in the studio 24 hours a day, and Ritchie would drop in, when he wasn't needed for his parts or anything, just to listen. And sometimes he would really give it the nod and sometimes he would go, 'That's fucking awful,' and Roger's face would just drop and he would go, 'Well, what's awful about it?' And Ritchie would say, 'I don't like the way this is, and the way you've got this and what you think should go here.'"

"And one time he really insulted him by telling him he couldn't produce and all this. You know, familiarity breeds contempt. They've been together for so many years that you've got to take that with a large grain of salt. They were just at each other's throats a little bit because they were the veterans, they were the ones from Purple; there was some competition there. And I always thought Roger was very popular in Rainbow. He was like a cornerstone of Rainbow. But he didn't feel as popular, I guess. Because when I came in I kind of pushed him to the side; not personally, but he just felt pushed to the side. Here comes this kid and the girls like him and all this stuff and now I've got to contend with that. Now I'm third on the rung of the ladder. Now it's Ritchie and Joe and then me. But I mean, that's normal band shit. People go through that all the time. There are egos and personalities and you have to deal with it."

But there was also fun and typical rock frivolity. "Yeah, there was always a lot of that," laughs Joe. "I can remember, I think the roadies put a huge… at the time cocaine was pretty popular. Ritchie never did any of those drugs; he always did downers. He never did coke or anything like that. He didn't like to go up. He liked to go down. Drinking and downers. But the rest of us would all indulge, so I think what they did is they got this huge piece of Styrofoam and they covered it with tinfoil and then they got more Styrofoam and they crumpled it up and glued it to the tinfoil and had this huge tube; it looked like a McDonald's straw. And there was this huge straw on what looked like a mirror and this huge line of coke. And it had to be ten by ten feet. You know, it was just nuts."

"And there were other things like this little raccoon hanging in the studio. We called him Midi because in those days Midi was a big thing. We would Midi up everything through the keyboards, and you would trigger drums and trigger things, and we would always say, 'So the question today, Midi, is…' and this little raccoon would be rolled down on the string and he'd have a little sign, 'Well, how would you Midi this particular interface with this other thing?' And that was the question of the day, all kinds of silly things."

"And then another time there were so many speakers in the studio that Roger had brought in because he had all kinds of… 'I want to check it out through here, check it out through the Tannoys, the Yamahas,' that the roadies started tagging it with price tags, like Crazy Uncle Rog, like Crazy Eddie's, all this audio equipment, all over the studio. So they started tagging it with prices. And of course, when Ritchie did his parts, it was always filled with candles and incense and the spirits would have to come through and things like that. So you had a lot of different colours going on (laughs)."

"News to me," says Roger, casting a veil of suspicion over the above tale. "I don't know what he's talking about. I don't know anything about a raccoon. Raccoon, in the studio?!" What about the cocaine mirror made out of tinfoil and Styrofoam? "No, you know, maybe Joe noted things I didn't (laughs). None of those things ring a bell with me. I'm sorry to say that. It sounds like a good story. And who am I to ruin a good story?"

Recorded May through June of 1983 and issued on August 24th, *Bent Out of Shape* opens with considerable enigmatic presence, Turner delivering the hushed verse lyric to "Stranded," beginning a mere nine seconds into the track and album, the song then developing fullness, substance and volume as it progresses. It's quintessential spooky Rainbow but it's also reminiscent of "urgent," Foreigner, Lou and Mick at their most tension-filled.

Turner sets the scene. "'Stranded' came about from being in Copenhagen, Denmark, looking out my window from the hotel on a particularly dreary day, just having those lost emotions. I remember very clearly thinking I could just disappear into thin air here and not be heard from again. I guess it's a feeling everyone goes through at some point but I had a feeling of estrangement and being literally stranded. It's a true lyric."

Track two is actually quite similar in wispy tone, "Can't Let You Go" featuring some extremely tasty guitar textures from Ritchie. "'Can't Let You Go' is one of my absolute favourite passionate songs," notes Joe. "That song's magic. It just came alive. True story again, just about my relationship, anybody's relationship really. Again, written in Denmark."

Ritchie affirms that "The best Joe ever sang was on 'Can't Let You Go.'" "Well, yeah, I have to agree with that one," says Turner, when confronted with that quote. "I mean, we just had a magic going on at that point. And you know, some days you get lucky and you just hit it right. So I have to agree with that. 'Can't Let You Go' is definitely spine-tingling when you hear it; it's got a lot of emotion and power."

"Ritchie had this idea to put this piece in front of the song by a German composer," explains Joe, concerning the song's classical church organ-style keyboard intro. "One day we just knocked it out. We just had a moment. It was really a well put-together and perfect type of song. We had chills when we listened back to it. We knew we had a classic song when we heard the tape. The video (directed by Dominic Orlando) was based on the movie *The Cabinet of Dr. Caligari*. Ritchie played the doctor in the video; he wore that top hat. It was kind of like Dr. Jeckyl and Mr. Hyde. By day, he was a doctor but by night he would go out into the night, find women and bring them back to the lab and boom! It was scary and gross. I was the alter ego of the doctor. I was a zombie. He created me but the zombie had him inside of him. We loved it. At the time we were into very dark and heavy things like Aleister Crowley, which we will not repeat again. We knew the entire story would be our little secret, as we knew no one would ever research it and see it was based on this movie from 1920."

"'Fool for the Night,' that's me, totally about me, very autobiographical," explains Turner on the album's melancholic third track, a quick but poppy rocker with a sinister, gothic chorus. "I was really sort of self-deprecating, looking at myself saying, you know, you're just so hung up for the lights and you're so addicted to all of this, all the trappings of this world that I was living in, that I had become a fool for the night. I was living by night and sleeping by day."

"Fire Dance" is one of the album's three heavier metal rockers, this one featuring a typical Blackmore widdle riff circa "Burn" or "A Light in the Black." Yet still it hums along with a smooth pop disposition, especially during the verse. David Rosenthal is prominent in the mix, even turning in a synth solo. Indeed he's louder than Ritchie on the riff, really signalling that the band was trying to sweeten their sound. The highlight of the entire record, inn this writer's opinion, is the short break taken after the synth solo. The second most magical moment on the album is what comes next, namely Ritchie's solo, followed by a return of the ripping break riff.

"That's about our side of the occult that we used to dabble in, sometimes more greatly than others," reveals Joe. "I was basically literally possessed to write about it because it is one of my favourite subjects, even today on this album. I'm into all of that kind of stuff. I'm into all kinds of occultisms, conspiracies, Illuminati, you name it. I am a David Icke freak. This guy will open up a whole new world. Do yourself a favour and get yourself a book called *The Biggest Secret*. Icke will rock your world. He will give you information that you will never have thought of in your life and document it… bibliographies, footnotes, other books you can refer to, cross-referencing."

I asked Joe if Ritchie was into the occult with the same enthusiasm he was.

"*Was*, I believe. I don't *believe* he was, I *know* he was; I don't think he is so much anymore though. Neither am I. In fact, I burned a lot of books and altars that I had. We were into Wicca and a lot of things, Aleister Crowley, 'Thy will shall be the whole of the law,' all this stuff. We used to do séances with Jimmy Page, all kinds of shit like that. Early on we were into it a lot deeper than we were later on. Because I really found that it works and it's a dangerous place to go if you don't know how to handle it. And obviously I was somewhere in the middle. So it overtook me, and like an addiction, I had to give it up. Because there are a few incidents that would probably raise your eyebrows if I told you about them. You'd say, 'Wow, that's some really freaky shit that happened,' and yeah, all kinds of really strange stuff, poltergeists and witches and my finger almost being cut off. So I realized I was messing around with the wrong powers and I said that's it, I'm out of it, I'm walking back into the light and I'm staying there. It's really a very heavy spiritual transition."

Turner recalls the lyric to "Fire Dance" as an example where Roger's sense of wordplay helped Joe unlock the key to the song.

"Yes, 'Fire Dance' is a good example of that, yeah, because most of the other ones were my titles and lyrics. You see, sometimes I would lead the lyric and sometimes Roger would lead the lyric. But on 'Fire Dance,' he actually had the chorus lyric and then I went and put this whole story to it and followed his lead on that—'The wrong begin the rite,' rite, the fire dance, this whole ritualistic thing. But he would always come up with a spark of genius and that would ignite me. As I've said before, 'Stone Cold' was like that. He walked in the room and he was going through a divorce and he said, 'She left me stone cold' and I wrote it down and I made a song out of it (laughs). So that was basically about his, or anyone's breakup, but it was essentially his and his mood. So I just wrote down this whole moody dreamy sequence and it works. So we were always jumping off each other, igniting each other. And there was tension sometimes. There's a statement I'll never forget that says, 'Out of the fire comes steel.' And that's kind of what happened with us. There was a lot of fire and sometimes you need that. Out of chaos comes order. So we had a lot of fire and chaos but we always came up with the steel or the order."

Closing side two was a drafty, icy, brief instrumental called "Anybody There," again Ritchie and Roger collaborating on a guitar sound that is pure precious alchemy.

"'Anybody There' was an instrumental that Ritchie wrote," begins Joe. 'You see, the first three words of any séance are 'Is anybody there?' That's what that's about. You say that, and you get people coming through, spirits coming through, entities coming through, what have you, if you're lucky. If not, you have a dead night. But that's what 'Anybody There' is about and that was always one of my favourite instrumental tracks."

"That's a misprint on the sleeve," Ritchie told Garry Bushell, in the fall of '83. "It should be 'Anybody There' with a question mark, as in the way you open a séance. The song's based on Bach's 'Prelude in C.' It's got no middle eight and no chorus. The chord structure goes for 28 bars and then repeats so it's very unlike the usual rock song. There's no catch line, just nonstop continuity; 300 years ago they would have accepted that. Now bands only go 12 or 14 bars before they get into the hook. I initially called it 'Doomed.'"

"Desperate Heart" was another track that was a reinforcing glue, fitting nicely between "Stranded" and "Street of Dreams," underscoring the record as a pomp rocker with a hidden black disposition, again like a bunch of the most aggressive Foreigner songs lined up in a row, or a similar collection from the Brian Howe version of Bad Company.

"'Desperate Heart' was done back here in the States, the vocal anyway," explains Turner. "We were up in New York, at Bear

Tracks, which was Spyra Gyra's studio. They were a jazz band that was pretty big at the time and they had a lot of money so they bought this beautiful studio, and we needed a place up and around the New York area. So we were at Bear Tracks and I remember finishing the lyric as I was singing the track, literally (laughs). It's pretty autobiographical. You know, I always feel that I'm just a transfer for Everyman. Everybody experiences these emotions and these feelings; it's just that somebody has to put them down, like any artist does, whether it's painting, lyrics, poetry. You jump inside that lyric and you find yourself. So that's basically for Everyman, but again, it starts in an autobiographical place. I mean, I was the desperate heart, obviously."

"I've got a good story about "Street of Dreams," explains Joe on the album's biggest hit, a song that is essentially "Stone Cold" Part II. "That came to me literally in a dream. See, I'm a reincarnationist; I believe in souls and that we have all been here and that there are a limited amount of souls and that we reincarnate and we come back to sort of clean up our past lives, and we suffer from all that. All the reincarnationist theories. Because I studied all kinds of contemporary religions and comparative theologians and things like that and was very deep into organized religion as a child. I was born Catholic and I went through all that, studied Latin for 15 years, wanted to be a priest, so I digress."

"What I'm trying to say is that this was always a major interest of mine. And 'Street of Dreams' really literally happened to me in a dream. And I jumped up—again in Copenhagen; we were doing the record in Denmark—and I jumped up and wrote the lyric down and went back to bed and when I awoke that morning it was there. And it was quite unusual because it was fitted to this track that I had put together with Ritchie, the intro, the verse, the chorus and it all fitted. So it was one of those magical moments that you just went 'Holy shit!' This is like transference. This is like something coming out of the ethers and just like channelling through you. So it reinforced all my beliefs, of course."

Turner delves deeper into the psychic darkness. "I don't think people can really believe in things like this unless they experience something that really happens to them time after time. When you're into it, it's just like exercise. The muscle comes up. If you don't exercise, it won't. That's just it. So if you exercise these belief systems and you exercise these incantations, things happen to you, that cosmically you can really go through. You go, 'Yup, okay, here it is,' a manifestation of it. It's like anything else: use it or lose it."

"So 'Street of Dreams,' I barely remember getting up and scratching some lyrics down. And then, we got into the studio, and this is really strange too. Ritchie was intimidated by the melodies and the lyrics because I guess I had done a pretty good performance, I have to say. I had a lot of emotion in my voice and I was singing it like I believed it. And he was just like, 'Fuck, how am I supposed to play a lead? This vocal is so strong.' And he was telling this to me privately. And we went over to the refrigerator in the studio in this little corner by the galley and took out some Heinekens and we were talking about it, and it was during a terrible storm. If you know, Copenhagen is on a grid pattern of weather that is incredibly electric. Electrical storms happen over there all the time; high-intensity energies. So yes, I had sung a very passionate vocal, and he looked at me and said, you know, 'Man, I've got to catch you on this one, with the solo; it's got to be right.' And we popped open the two Heinekens and said 'Cheers,' and I said, 'Look, just go in and play this melodic solo and put your heart and soul into it.'"

"So all of a sudden, we went into some talk about unearthly things and this crack came out of nowhere. And we both almost hit the floor. It was like, what the fuck was that?! It was like a gunshot. And what had happened is that a lightning bolt had hit the lightning rod on the top of the building. We had an incredible surge of lightning hit us, right above us, and knocked all the electrical out. It knocked all the guys that were watching the videos, the VCRs, knocked that out, knocked the studio out. It was just like bam! Like God threw down a hammer. And we were like, fuck!"

"So we got the candles out, of course, and the whole place was lit by candlelight. And of course, we were in downtime at that point because nothing was operating, and we just had this incredible discussion. And then when finally the power and everything came back, I said, 'You just go in there'—after they fixed all this—'and just play and sing your lead.' And that's what he did, and he came out with one of the most memorable guitar leads that I can, to this day, still sing. He went in and played a beautiful solo. So I don't know, I just remember that as a remarkable event, a real moment."

Ritchie calls "Street of Dreams," "one of the best commercial songs that I've been involved with, a personal favourite." The song was floated as the album's lead single (backed with "Anybody There"), preceding the full-length LP by a month, reaching a modest #52 in the UK charts and #60 in the US. It is said that part of the problem was that the video received scant airplay, due to fears over its hypnosis scene, which almost caused the clip to be banned from the airwaves.

"That was unfortunate," Joe told Jeb Wright, concerning the Storm Thorgerson-directed clip. "The band never wanted to do videos. We were on tour and they called us up and they found some basement that we had to go crawl around in. They took some video of that and then they had this professor hypnotize this girl and do that stuff. We had nothing to do with any of that; we were just crawling around a basement for about half a day and then we were back on tour. It was such a cheap shot. Ritchie hates videos. Video killed the radio star, right?"

"Again, we're in Copenhagen, and it's a wild town," recalls Turner on *Bent Out of Shape*'s rip snortin' death-warmed-over rocker "Drinking with the Devil." "A lot of beautiful women and clubs, so the roadies were out all night, fucked-up. Everybody would do that occasionally. But this one particular time, Charlie came into the studio and he was just so hung over and I was like, 'What's up, man? What were you doing? Out drinking with the Devil?' That just came out of my mouth, because I was totally into all of that at the time anyway. And he was like, 'Man, that motherfucker kept pouring one drink after another,' and it became this… and we're talking this animated, anthropomorphic thing, like he was actually out with some invisible sidekick, the Devil, getting fucked-up (laughs). So I just went, 'That's a great title.' So when I heard this really steaming track that they had, I just said, 'That's it! That's it! I'm writing this song.' 'All night till the sun comes up… I'm gonna explode… heading for an overload,' and then I get into this story where he sits me down, pours one more and says, 'I'm at your command.' So here we are, drinking with the Devil, man, face-to-face. And Charlie said, 'The last time I saw God, I threw up on his shoes' (laughs). We were cracking up."

Next up was another instrumental, lending a sense of balance to the original album's second side, the same way "Anybody There" tempered side one. Remarks Joe on this delicious interlude, "'Snowman' was nominated for a Grammy, which was a very proud moment for Ritchie, I'm sure. That was a song from a cartoon, that basically this old gentleman, Howard Blake, did. And Ritchie interpreted it, how shall we say, his way? Ritchie was so taken by this theme and this cartoon. I'm pretty sure it was black-and-white, and probably silent, just animation, about how a snowman lives and the kids play with him and how he eventually melts and disappears into this puddle. And it's so reflective about life in a way on different levels that Ritchie was really moved by this thing. And we all saw it, several times. Of course it was all part of… you know, he had it on the tour bus, and this snowman cartoon was becoming like our philosophy."

As Ritchie told Sounds, "It originally came from an animated cartoon I was watching about a snowman who picks a kid up and flies away with him. It's a great fantasy film. It took me back to my childhood dreams. I have an affinity towards snowmen, you see. Anyway, the excerpt on the video had about 16 bars of this tune which I took and elongated and added my own arrangement. The guy who wrote it, Howard Blake, is probably this 60-year-old pianist living in Brighton; he hadn't even heard of us. Originally he called it 'Walking in the Air.' To me it's one of the best tracks on the LP; it's the direction I'd like to go in. I love that sort of intense, majestic kind of rock. I'd love to have a whole backdrop of snowmen. We've changed it from a happy snowman into an abominable snowman incidentally—I have this effect on people."

"I'm still at that crisis point," continued Ritchie, reacting to Gary Bushell's reminder that on the previous record, he had told the magazine that the band was at a crossroads, "and I think I'll be there for the rest of my life. As John Cleese said, 'I think I'm stuck with it.' Musicians should always be at crisis point. One is never progressing unless one is at odds with one's self as to how to progress. I was very satisfied with the new album though I know it's not exactly the hard rock people want, and we'll probably lose a few fans by deviating, but that's the price you've gotta pay. It'd be so easy for us to do a really clichéd heavy album but that's not the point. A lot of people are very discontent in England at the moment but it would be dishonest of me to try and reflect that in my music. I can't raise my fist in the air and play moronic 12-bar blues and 12-bar progressions either. We all grow up. I'm just not interested in doing that kind of thing any more. Maybe we'll lose some people but I refuse to fall back on moronic albums to make a few more bob. I don't need it."

"I was nominated, I think," recalls Ritchie years later, speaking with the author, concerning "Snowman"'s surprise Grammy nomination. "I think Sting won it, because they felt sorry for Sting. This is the story I heard. They felt sorry for him because he didn't win in the vocal category. So they had to include him in something. So he got the instrumental category for something, which is really strange. Now, that's not a slight at Sting, but that's how the story came back to me. I'm not a big one for the glamour side of the business, the Grammys, going to Hollywood and having my feet or my hands put in whatever and being in the Rock and Roll Hall of Fame. They've asked me a few times to be in various halls of fame and I've always turned it down. I don't see any kind of prestige in that. I try and stay away from that stuff, you know? And being nominated for something, I have actually no interest in. I like to write a hit song, or have people like something, but I have no interest in that side of the business. I find that that side of the business is far too pretentious and full of people that... that whole Grammy thing is just people who are in the business. It's a very corrupt set-up. As you know, as people in the business can be. And they're just going to vote for the people... it's all political. It has nothing to do with a good song or bad song."

"I have it in my guest bathroom," chuckles Joe, referring to whatever it is you get for being nominated. "When you're taking a pee you can look up from the toilet and see our Grammy nomination. We were never into awards. The one good thing I can say about that band is that we were not full of ourselves. The egos were massive but we were not full of ourselves."

Closing *Bent Out of Shape* was another stomping riff rocker, again, like its two companions on the same album, quite sweet for the verse, nastier for the chorus. "'Make Your Move' was probably something that me and Roger were just saying. It's just a point in life where people have to do something different, and you just have to have the balls; you have to do it. And it was nothing more than a motivational song, like 'Power' was a motivational song. When you see that somebody is out there listening and it's motivating in their life, sending them in a certain direction, that's the reward. It's not the money and it's not the fame; it's really listening to these letters I used to get and still do. It's amazing; it brings tears to your eyes. Or if someone is in the hospital and they listen to your song constantly and it helps them heal. It's unbelievable."

"*Bent Out of Shape* is the best sounding record, sonically," says Roger Glover, summing up his run with the band. Significantly, as alluded to, Roger is all but left out of the writing credits on this record, showing up only on "Fire Dance." Perhaps that allowed him the dedication to craft the album's sound picture so perfectly. Each of the previous two albums with Joe seemed somehow scattered, not cohesive in terms of the productions. Here it's all of a piece, and what's more, the warm, high quality production matches the breathing and atmospheric arrangements of the songs, not to mention the mystery and drama of Joe's lyrics. Roger got some quality help along the way. His engineer in Denmark was Fleming Rasmussen, assisted by Thomas Breckling. Mixing at Bear Tracks, using the "SSL Computer and Sony Digital System" was Le Studio legend Nick Blagona.

Venturing a comparison, Glover figures, "*Difficult to Cure*, I don't know, I haven't listened to these for such a long time. *Straight Between the Eyes* was fun to make. I remember enjoying making that one in Morin Heights, in 40 below temperatures, which has a tendency to bring a band together for warmth. If I look back at my diaries, I know some of them were fraught with difficulty. *Difficult to Cure*, I know we had a hard time with it. It always seems to me when I look back that consecutive albums always seem to be easy or hard. You know, it seems to go easy, hard, easy, hard, easy, hard. I don't like to believe that too much because then I'm anticipating that our next Deep Purple album is going to be hard. I'm trying to figure out if the last one was easy or hard. If I could live my life again I probably would pay a bit more attention to songwriting. On those albums there was a certain amount of formulaic... you know, here's the riff, what's the verse? Bang out some words and Bob's your uncle!"

"This is the biggest tour we've ever done," said Roger enthusiastically, looking to Rainbow's bright future, in an interview with Andy Secher back in 1983. "We'd love to play China if we can get permission. Once that market opens up, it'll be incredible. Right now though, we're quite content with playing the rest of the world. We hadn't played England in two years, and since we sold out every gig, that was a lot of fun. And we're heading out to the west coast of the US to begin this leg of the tour. It's amazing. Rainbow has become as big as Deep Purple ever was. In fact, now when we ask promoters if they'd ever like to see a Deep Purple reunion, they say 'No thanks. We're quite satisfied with Rainbow.'"

Ironic words indeed.

As it turned out, China in fact did not make the dance card, Rainbow kicking things off with exhaustive coverage of the UK in the fall of '83, followed by a brief foray into Scandinavia. In late October, the band set their sights on America (no Canadian dates would be logged), with Aldo Nova in tow, finishing up the US leg in early December, the latter dates in support of Blue Öyster Cult. After a two-month break, three dates were played in Japan, with the March 14th, 1984 stop in that Rainbow-loving territory filmed for video release, highlight being "Difficult to Cure" being performed by the band with orchestra (more on that shortly)—the results can be heard on posthumous compilation *Finyl Vinyl*.

With many of the album's tracks making the live set, the band also offered "Stargazer" in medley form, along with the tenacious Bonnet-era pairing of "All Night Long" and "Since You Been Gone," plus the even more tenacious "Catch the Rainbow," "Long Live Rock 'n' Roll," "Kill the King" and "Smoke on the Water."

Ritchie was in pain for much of the proceedings, thinking he had injured his neck playing soccer. As it turned out, it was ascertained that Blackmore likely had, in and around his neck, mild arthritis, which he had been able to keep at bay through physiotherapy and stretching.

I asked Joe to keep it honest and try articulate how successful the band had been at this juncture. "I really don't know, maybe a couple hundred thousand," ventures Turner, quite sensibly. "I never did get a gold record for the States. I think we were at 450,000 (now he sounds high!) or something crazy like that, which was frustrating because they weren't really interested in chasing gold records. As I said, Ritchie was indignant about being popular."

Of course, Rainbow never got the chance to break big. According to Turner, nefarious backroom dealings around an ensuing Deep Purple reunion ultimately killed the band.

"We toured the album all over Europe, Japan, South America and then we came to the States and I think it was a limited tour on that particular record and I'm not entirely sure why. We headlined. But going back one, with *Straight Between the Eyes*, that was one of the pinnacle points in my career because that was the first time we ever played Madison Square Gardens, here in New York, which is like my hometown. So that was thrilling, we were headlining and Scorpions opened. That was a funny thing. Metallica used to open for us and look how huge they became, and Scorpions; look how huge they became. Def Leppard open for us and they became incredibly huge. And we at that point of course were broken up. But that's why I say, if we had stuck together and kept on the path, something like this would have happened because we were destined—we were going that way. And I guess a lot of personal things got in the way as well as business."

"What really happened was that the manager, Bruce Payne, got an opportunity to put Purple together. Only a couple years ago did I really find out the truth about this, and so did Ritchie, which is really surprising to both of us, that we were really played and duped. The manager told Ritchie, 'Well, Joe wants to do his solo album for Elektra Records and he doesn't want to do Rainbow anymore, so we have this opportunity to do Purple.' Then he came to me and said, 'Ritchie wants to do Purple and he doesn't want to do Rainbow. He'll come back to it at some point in time and you've got your solo career, so shuffle off and have a good time.'"

"And the band was never really communicative, so Ritchie and I never went up to each other and said, 'Hey, what's your fucking problem? How come you don't want to do another record with Rainbow?' Because I found out later that he was disappointed that I didn't want to continue with Rainbow. And I did! I would have easily put off the solo record for one more Rainbow album. We were duped. Because there was a lot of money involved in the reunion of Deep Purple, and they put out an absolutely fabulous album, *Perfect Strangers*. So I always felt like a part of that. It's like, 'Well, I helped, because I didn't get in the way.' I took a sidestep, and I helped to put this band back together. I always felt a little part of the reunion, and I think rightfully so. But at the same time, I really felt we were going to get back together at some point in time and continue this. But as we all know…"

In a separate interview years later, Joe summed up Bruce and the story of the break-up of the band this way. "I think Bruce was pretty amenable to us. I thought he was a great manager and he did what was best for the band at any given time. I look back and of course, you're always clashing at some point. There is just one thing that I still have a bit stuck in my throat, and that was the end of Rainbow and the beginning of Purple, what happened there. It's a story that basically he got what he wanted, and I suppose that's the way you do it politically. He wanted Deep Purple to reform. I was doing a solo album for Elektra, so I was on top of the world. You know, he told Ritchie that I was just more interested in solo recordings, and Ritchie got a bit upset, and Ritchie went and proceeded to do the Deep Purple thing. So the truth really is that he kind of played us both against each other, in a way. Because the real truth is Ritchie thought that we would do at least another album; that's what I figured. Bruce had promised me that Rainbow would get together and that we would do another album—it never really happened. So I guess he was just being a manager, and getting what he felt was best for himself and the band and everything else."

"I think Bruce is a fantastic manager if he's on your side," continues Joe. "I like him as a person, so there's nothing there. We always left as friends and everything else. But Bruce has to do what's right for the band, and what the majority of the guys want. There's no ill will or anything, and I always felt that Bruce was a splendid manager, a very smart and articulate person. So I've really got nothing bad to say about Bruce; he can be as ruthless as the rest when he has to be. You know, like I said, if he's on your side, you've got somebody in your corner. But if he's not, look out, because he'll rip you to shreds. But that's what you want; that's basically what any manager should be, in that role. Now, of course, Bruce is a fifth Beatle; he's a member of the band. He's not just the manager. He's so much part of that family and community, whether it was Rainbow or Purple. And I had great times with Bruce on the road, because we were both the Americans, with Bobby, and we would pal out, and just, you know, let the teabaggers do what they do (laughs)."

"I guess my thoughts on Ritchie haven't changed over the years," continues Joe, switching to the enigmatic six-stringer. "Everybody's got a really strange idea of Ritchie, I think. And he likes it that way; he wants it that way. I believe that that creates the mysterious air. But at the same time, I find Ritchie to be a very straight-up guy. We never had a problem with our relationship. I mean, any of the problems we did have were solved face-to-face, man-to-man kind of thing. And we went along. So, when all the shit hit the fan, with Purple especially, I was in the last incarnation (Joe is referring to being the lead singer of Deep Purple on 1990's *Slaves and Masters*), and he was still adamant about me being in the band. Of course, the other guys wanted Gillan. So what I'm trying to say is, history will show you the truth. I mean, they came out with an album (*The Battle Rages On..*, from 1993), good or bad as it might be, and they split. If you look back, you'll see what the attitudes were and what was really going on, for the fans and everything to look at and say, 'Well, this is obvious now, isn't it?' That he was very unhappy there. He just wanted out of that whole situation."

"Generally, I was pleased with the way things were going," mused Ritchie in the fall of 1984, asked by Geoff Barton about putting a pin in Rainbow. "Joe Lynn Turner was into ballads and I was going through a melodic phase. But the trouble was, every time I wanted to play a real hard rock song, Joe couldn't quite manage it. This didn't bother me too much at first. As I say, I was going through a kind of mellow period and I thought, 'Oh well, it doesn't matter; Joe handles the ballads well and that's just fine.' But then I started to miss the hard rock so much, and that's when things started to get a little weird.

"I felt responsible when I brought Joe over," continues Ritchie, reacting to Barton's assertion that the British fans never took to Turner. "I remember taking him to one side and saying, 'Now look, over in Britain they don't like all that cabaret stuff; just keep it hard and aggressive.' And of course he'd listen to me and for one gig he would be alright—and then he'd start prancing around again. I remember pulling him up one time backstage at Leeds. I had been playing an instrumental and he hadn't gone into the wings. He'd stayed onstage prancing around the whole time. I said, 'Do that again and I'll punch your face in!' And for the next couple of gigs he was alright."

"Don't get me wrong. Joe's a great singer, but he's too smooth to sing rock 'n' roll. So anyway to get back to my original point, at the end I was kind of faced with a great dilemma with Rainbow: should we carry on doing ballads or get back to rock? I enjoyed the band's softer phase; 'Stone Cold,' 'Street of Dreams' and stuff like that I really liked. But it died a death, particularly in Britain, which hurt a lot, because it means a lot to me to be successful in my home country. So in the end I got very frustrated, and that's when the first really serious thoughts of a Purple reformation entered my head."

Years later, speaking with the author, Ritchie reflected back on the JLT years with a bit more fondness.

"Those were great times, because Joe was a very, very musical, melodic singer. So I could relate to that. His singing was more along the lines of something a violin could play. Ian was more gruff and rough, and Joe Lynn is more of a sweet, melodic singer. So that kind of appealed to me. And of course, I've always liked Paul Rodgers' way of singing. So he was along those lines, too, that bluesy kind of voice."

But with respect to his own guitar work at the end, Ritchie is less enthusiastic.

"To be honest, I don't think I was playing very well. Listening back to some of that stuff, I hear it now and again. I don't have it around the house, but sometimes it's played... I was very kind of staid in my playing. I wasn't letting go, I was suffering a lot from inertia and kind of analysis paralysis in the studio. I used to find that I would spend so much time arranging it, writing the riff or making sure that it was a good song to sing and a good idea. I used to back myself into a corner, when I came to, 'Okay, let's put a solo on it.' And I'd be thinking, wait a minute, this is not a good rhythm for a solo, nor a good idea for a solo. So I often found myself caught in a corner doing an average solo. Whereas some guitar solos, we'll write around that guitar solo—they will write the song. Really good guitar players will often go towards making sure the whole song revolves around their way of playing, which is comfortable for them. And I found myself at odds with some of the solos, which is a strange position to be in. I felt I was a little bit... there wasn't a lot of creativity in my solos. I think it's gotten a lot better since. But it was like an empty period for solos. If I hear some of them, they're okay, but nothing outstanding."

But that attention to the song, made, naturally, for good songs. "Yeah, I was more into... for instance, I was more proud of the fact that I could write something like 'Street of Dreams.' That's my favourite song. I was more pleased with that than getting into guitar solos, because I'd played so many guitar solos in my life. It was starting to wear off, the effect. So I was more into writing songs in those days, than what was a good idea for a solo."

Chapter 10

Finyl Vinyl

"We were just on top of the world."

In February of 1986, nestled between the release of Deep Purple's *Perfect Strangers* in November '84 and its under-rated follow-up *The House of Blue Light* in January of '87, Rainbow was still making records (sort of), with the issuance of a double gatefold compilation called *Finyl Vinyl* (tongue-in-cheek working title: *Are We Having Fun Yet?*). Somewhat ignored at the time, the album was nonetheless a treasure trove of gold at the end of the Rainbow, offering a sweeping array of live tracks representative of all eras, as well as a complete collection of the band's scant few B-sides. In fact, both Roger and Ritchie would rather have had a proper live album issued, consisting of selections from the band's momentous last dates in Japan. However, Polydor saw things differently. Ritchie had also plumped for a version of "Stargazer" to appear on whatever type of release was decided, even suggesting they monster it together in the studio, but this also was not to be.

"When the Deep Purple reunion came about, there was no way we could pursue two different bands, two separate careers," explained, speaking with Hank Borowitz in 1986 about the assembly of the album. "So Rainbow had to cease in order to make way for Deep Purple. Whether or not, at some future time, Ritchie may decide to form another incarnation of Rainbow, that's entirely up to him. But I wanted to come out with an album that spanned more of the time that Rainbow was in existence. Rainbow started in '75, I think, at least '76. The earliest recording I could come up with was '78 on our shelves. There may be some other recordings somewhere, but I couldn't search them out and neither could our office, which is a shame because I wanted to find some early vintage Rainbow."

Roger told Hank the work on *Finyl Vinyl* took him, "about a month. Actually, listening itself, I spent three or four days listening to tapes before I made any decisions. Then I compiled my notes. I tried to figure out if we had enough material for an album. There were some performances I didn't like very much. In fact, initially, I was very doubtful whether it was even worth bothering with this. First of all, Rainbow's been finished two years. I'm fully involved in Deep Purple now. It's very exciting; I love it."

"And doing a project for my old band was really tedious. But the more I got into it, the more I listened to it, the more memories it brought back, the more I thought that, for Rainbow fans—and I'm not sure this album is going to set the world alight— but for Rainbow fans it's a really interesting piece, because it does span six years of the band's history, and there are some older recordings, some classic recordings from Ronnie and Graham. I thought it was a valid album to put out. It's a live album, with a few odd studio pieces that never really saw the light of day. Rather than just watching them gather dust on the shelf, I saw no reason why they shouldn't be out for the people to listen to and maybe get some enjoyment out of."

Digging in, side one of *Finyl Vinyl* offered solid, punchy, boldly recorded live versions of "Spotlight Kid," "I Surrender" and "Miss Mistreated," from the band's very last shows (before reunion) at Budokan in Tokyo, mid-March of 1984. Of note, the two-CD reissue for the "Rainbow Remasters" series adds a somewhat wobbly live version "Street of Dreams" (this was also on the original cassette version of the album) from those same Budokan shows, sequencing it where it should be, right after "Miss Mistreated." The original CD issue of the album, however, had omitted both "Street of Dreams" and "Tearin' Out My Heart," to make the material fit on a single disc.

Side two kicks off with the previously discussed studio B-side "Jealous Lover," followed by a thrill-ride version of "Can't Happen Here" (Nassau Coliseum, Uniondale, NY, April 2nd, 1981;

Pat Travers as support) and a massive eight-minute "Tearin' Out My Heart" (Convention Center, San Antonio, Texas, August 18th, 1982; Saxon as support—that band's cozy relationship with San Antonio continues to this day), featuring bluesy Ritchie soloing at the beginning, yards and yards of more aggressive fret-fire throughout, and a sped-up break beginning at the halfway point, during which clearly can be heard the band's female back-up singers, Lin Robinson and Dee Beale. Next up was "Since You Been Gone" from the fateful Monsters of Rock festival, the side closing out with the aforementioned Bonnet-era studio rarity "Bad Girl."

Side three of the original vinyl opens with the 11-minute version of "Difficult to Cure," recorded at those final Budokan shows, with orchestra. Recalls Joe, "Yeah, it was monstrous; it was incredible. I mean, here we are in Japan, selling out, 25, 30,000 people a night, crazy stuff. We had the full orchestra behind us at that point. I mean, we were just on top of the world, just making great music with great presentations. What can be said about the magic of that? You had to be there. Dave Rosenthal wrote the score for that. David wasn't the keyboardist on that album, but when we went to Japan and did that, on the last tour, we had, what, a 26-piece orchestra behind Plexiglas, and Rosenthal scored that, for the live recording of that on that album. 'Difficult to Cure' is really just 'The Joy of Mankind,' Bach or Beethoven (Bach). I can't quite remember, because we did Bach and we did Beethoven and we did Brandenburg and we did so many of these guys. And I'm a big fan of classical too, so we got along on that level. But yeah, any of that Budokan live… come on."

Two more tracks, "Stone Cold" and "Power," from the aforementioned San Antonio stop, closed side two, "Stone Cold" opening with a fair bit of keyboard soloing from David Rosenthal. As with "Tearin' Out My Heart," Lin and Dee are fully represented, blending nicely with Joe's powerful, high register pipes, to positive effect on both these tracks.

Side four offers two BBC recordings from the Dio era, "Man on the Silver Mountain" and "Long Live Rock 'n' Roll," the band captured June 24th, 1978 at The Omni in Atlanta, REO Speedwagon being the headliner. "Man on the Silver Mountain" is eight minutes long, housing a manic and electric Blackmore solo (scurrilously dubbed in after the fact) as well as the band's sleep-inducing slow blues, Ronnie's blues improvisation of the "Silver Mountain" tale included. "Long Live Rock 'n' Roll" is offered at seven minutes, with cool new intro, a few extra notes, licks and altered melodies from Ritchie, and an insufferable crowd participation segment. Closing the record is "Weiss Heim," the rare instrumental studio track from 1980, drum credit erroneously given to Bobby Rondinelli, when in fact it features the late Cozy Powell.

Somewhat off to the side of official Rainbow releases was 1990's *Live in Germany*, issued on the UK's archivist Connoisseur label in both two-CD and double gatefold vinyl format. The album was reissued in 1996 through Mausoleum as *Live in Europe*, and still later by Spitfire in 2001 as *Live in Germany 1976*.

The included selections were recorded over four dates in Germany, late September of '76, on the *Rising* tour, with AC/DC as support. The band is positively on fire and the recording is acceptable, oddly blocky and sympathetic to the production tones of both *Rising* and *Long Live Rock 'n' Roll*. The track listing—in total, "Kill the King," "Mistreated," "Sixteenth Century Greensleeves," "Catch the Rainbow," "Man on the Silver Mountain," "Stargazer," "Still I'm Sad" and "Do You Close Your Eyes"—only offers two advantages over *On Stage*, namely "Stargazer" and "Do You Close Your Eyes."

Indeed, the material for *Live in Germany* was recorded on the same tour as the *On Stage* material, in very close temporal proximity in fact. "Stargazer," prefaced with a five-minute Tony Carey solo, stretches to 17 minutes, thanks to superlative, carnal soloing from Ritchie. The performance is blustery to say the least, and a fair bit faster and more percussive than the original as well. "Do You Close Your Eyes" is also (much) faster—and considerably heavier—than the relatively behaved version found on *Rising*, stretching to nearly ten minutes, thanks to both (buried) keyboard soloing from Tony and very noise-polluted axe work from Ritchie. All told, "Do You Close Your Eyes" is summarily transformed into a freight train of a rocker, steaming full-tilt for its entire duration, culminating in a wind-up that demonstrates the unstoppable intensity of Rainbow as it existed during the peerless Dio years.

As alluded to, Rainbow, in any form, would not exist for another ten years—1984 until 1994—following the long-discussed reunion of the Mark II lineup of Deep Purple. In that time, Ritchie would make four studio albums with the UK rock legends, one of them, *Slaves and Masters*, featuring a lineup that included Roger Glover and Joe Lynn Turner, causing massive fan derision at a legacy tarnished. Known by many of these disgruntled fans as a "Deep Rainbow" record, *Slaves and Masters* was indeed very much like the fourth Turner-era Rainbow rounder that never was. After all, Jon Lord and Ian Paice didn't write per se, so what you got was a trinity of Rainbow's thoroughly proven three writers giving it their all, coming out of the scrum with an album much more like a Rainbow record than a Purple one. And quite a nice album it is, although a few notches below the standard set by both *Perfect Strangers* and *The House of Blue Light*.

Joe Lynn Turner also spent some time with Yngwie Malmsteen, his pipes featured on the shredding Swede's *Odyssey* album, issued May of '88, as well as the live album *Trial by Fire: Live in Leningrad*, released October of 1989. His very poppy, major label solo album, *Rescue You* was issued in 1985. Joe also worked extensively as a studio/guest vocalist throughout these years, adding his sweet science touch to recordings by the likes of Cher, Michael Bolton, John Waite, Don Johnson, Mick Jones, Billy Joel, Paul Carrack, Bonnie Tyler and Lita Ford.

Graham Bonnet, post-Rainbow, fashioned together a band called Alcatrazz for three studio albums and one live one (the debut, *No Parole from Rock 'n' Roll*, and scrappy live set, *Live Sentence*, also featured one Yngwie Malmsteen!). But first he was to issue a solo album in 1981, the following year getting collared for the Michael Schenker Group's thrilling *Assault Attack*, released in October of 1982. As well, Bonnet would sing for (shredder Chris) Impellitteri, featuring on the competent *Stand in Line* record from August of 1988, then briefly leading a bit of a supergroup called Blackthorne, issuing an album called *Afterlife* in May of '93.

Ronnie, of course, soldiered on with Dio through the late '80s and the early '90s marking a decline from the heady heights achieved through '83's *Holy Diver*, '84's *The Last in Line* and '85's

Sacred Heart. In 1992, Ronnie led a reunion of Black Sabbath's *Mob Rules* lineup for the disappointing *Dehumanizer* album, after which it was straight back into Dio for 1993's *Strange Highways*.

Roger Glover's primary non-Deep Purple works would be a glossy yet world music-influenced solo album called *The Mask* (issued in May of 1984, a mere two months after Rainbow was put aside for the Purple reunion), and a collaboration with Blackmore nemesis Ian Gillan for 1988's quite charming *Accidentally on Purpose*.

Chapter 11

Stranger in Us All

"Everybody has a recording studio in their basement —I have a bar in my basement."

Despite the Deep Purple responsible for *The Battle Rages On…* crashing in flames hotter and harder than any of the previous crunch-ups, Ritchie Blackmore took it in stride, joking that he needed to find some new football mates, given that the rest of the Purps had aged, and alas, given up the game.

Joe Lynn Turner, who wouldn't figure in the lineup for the next and thus far final Rainbow record (but almost did), explains what went down, beginning with dissension over his presence in Deep Purple on *Slaves and Masters* and the subsequent re-delivery of Ian Gillan back to the ranks for *The Battle Rages On…* This of course would represent the third go 'round for Deep Purple Mark II, only to be supplanted by the Steve Morse era, which thrives to this day.

"As we progressed, obviously what happened was that the egos and the seniority… and there's now this new kid. People are starting to call it Deep Rainbow, it's the Ritchie and Joe show, all this kind of crap. Animosities really built. And there were wars over the publishing. Ritchie was really tired of giving away all the songs. He had told me some really inside stories about the old Purple, *Machine Head*, all that kind of stuff. I mean, he would write all this stuff and these guys would just take credit for it, and he was fed up with that. And he just said, 'Look, if you work, you get it; if you don't work, you don't get it.' And we tried bringing these guys in to write certain musical passages or whatever—this is pretty much Jon and Ian, because Roger was quite involved with lyrics and producing—so there was dissension. But we ended up turning around and giving them 15% for no reason at all. So we wanted to share the wealth but at the same time it was just throwing them a bone and saying okay. And I guess they wanted more and they felt put out."

"In the meantime, they felt threatened by me and Ritchie because we were pal-ing up again. Now there were three guys from Rainbow and four guys from Purple, so what the hell do you expect? It was crazy. Now I'll shoot right to the end when we were already doing a second album. Some of the tracks are coming out amazing and we really wanted this thing to be strong, so we called in great writers like Jim Peterik from Survivor, who wrote all these hits. And Jimmy was really, really great. He understood where we were going and the heaviness of it all, and we were really writing some great songs. And again, the other guys got very, very jealous. So you could cut the tension with a knife. It was *this* thick. So it finally got to a point where it just snapped and there was a whole big fight and an ostracization of each other and all this other crap and apparently somebody had to go down—the sacrificial lamb as Ritchie put it—and that was me."

"So what happened was they said, 'Look, we want Gillan back' and Ritchie said 'No way!' And they said, 'Well, we don't want Joe' and he said, 'Look, what do you want me to do?' He came to me and said, 'They're putting you on the block. They're hanging you.' I said, 'You know what? It's just as well because I just can't deal with all the fucking backstabbing anymore.' And these guys were really starting to… one minute it was 'Hi ya mate, nice to see you.' The next minute they're just tearing you up. So I couldn't deal with that emotionally, and I started to get more into drinking and drugs just to cover it, mask it up. My life… you know, I was on top of the world and I was in the shitter! I couldn't deal with this. So the best thing to do for me was to back off and leave. And we had all these great tracks, vocals to them and everything else, and it was really a crying shame."

"I was so disappointed that I actually quit the business for about four years and just watched my daughter grow up. I was just fed up with people, the whole business and everything. It really, really disappointed me. So I was the sacrificial lamb and they asked Ritchie to get Gillan back, and he hates Gillan. To make a long story short, six months later they were still looking for a singer. And BMG finally went up to Ritchie and said, 'Look, if you let fucking Gillan back in, we'll give you like $1 million for a solo deal.' So that's a lot of money. So Ritchie went, okay, fine. So Gillan came back in, Ritchie signed his contract for a million dollars, all by himself, which is a nice chunk of change. And they got Gillan in and they made that album, *The Battle Rages On…*, which I think only has one or two good songs on it. It's a fucking awful album, I think, sorry. We call it *The Cattle Grazes On…* So then the tensions obviously got so thick with that… you know the story, they were sending notes, they weren't talking on these live dates and Ritchie quit. And that's when they got Joe Satriani and finally Steve Morse."

Enter this so-called "solo deal." "Ritchie ended up making that other Rainbow album, *Strangers in Us All*," explains Joe. "He used that money with Doogie and those guys and made that album. And let me tell you, those guys, Greg Smith from Alice Cooper's band, John O'Reilly… those guys were all in *my* band. I mean, the only other guy was Doogie. Paul Morris, everybody else, they were in my band. And they were like the Joe Lynn Turner All-Stars and we were playing gigs in the Midwest, whatever we were doing. And they all came up to me and went, 'Um, is it okay if we join Rainbow?' And I said, 'You know what? Far be it for me to hold back anyone's career.'"

"I left and I really felt good that I was out," says Ritchie, a dozen years later, leaving Purple seemingly for good (never say never). "It really didn't have much to do with music. Although they're very good musicians, it was more of an armchair kind of band. With Deep Purple, we can make an excellent amount of money, go around just playing and we'll all have big cars and that's wonderful. That only lasts with me for a while. There has to be reason why I'm playing the guitar. It's not just for money. It's got to be an inner fulfillment. I had no fulfillment in that band whatsoever other than just money."

Ritchie confirms the opportunity to do a solo album was a kicker in the deal. "That's right. The basic bottom line was, they wanted to have Ian Gillan back in Deep Purple and I didn't want to have Ian back because he wasn't singing very well. I wanted a new singer. The rest of the band kind of went to the committee meeting as usual, and they all decided that it would be better to have Ian back. And I'm saying, 'Yes, but he can't sing.' And they're going, 'Ah, but it doesn't matter. The fact is we'll be all-original.' And I said, 'Well I can't work with those conditions.' This went on for a couple of months, and in the end, I remember the manager saying, 'Is there any way you would work with Ian Gillan?' And I said (laughs), 'Only if they would pay me a lot of money.' And the management immediately said, 'How much?' And I told him what I think I should have got, which was like ridiculous. Just doing it. I made up a figure, and I think that within the hour, they came back saying that the record company would pay it. So I was like, 'Okay, I'll make a record with him and I'll do some touring. For that money.' So I was becoming a mercenary. Working for money. And then they said, 'And also we'll throw in a solo deal, and you can record any music with whomever you like as well, afterwards.' That was part of the deal. So I went, okay."

Candice Night, by then Ritchie's life mate, soon to be a key figure in the writing of the *Stranger in Us All* album, and now the fairer half of Ritchie's Renaissance duo Blackmore's Night, chimes in with, "And they also offered for him to play with the German national team too; that was a nice little perk. Because Ritchie's such a fan of theirs."

"Yes," continues Ritchie, "I wanted to play soccer with the German national team. I wanted to go to their warm-up. So that's... I was doing the whole thing for money. But of course, when you're doing something for money, it doesn't usually last. And I think we were on the road for about a week before Ian and I fell out with each other. And it was more from the point of view of, I just... his singing was not right, you know? He was croaking away there. And I thought, music is too valuable for me. The singer is so important. If I'm backing a singer, the singer's got to be able to sing. I can't just close my ears and eyes and take money for playing. So that's when I fell out and said that's it, I'm leaving."

Ritchie explained the situation this way, back in 1996, to Guitar's HP Newquist. "With the last go around in Deep Purple, the guys were very, 'Well, another day, another dollar, just get the job done. We're doing good business.' And I thought, 'Good business, yeah, that's great, but we're not sounding good here, lads. We've got someone out front there who's making a mockery of things.' But nobody seemed to give a damn. Maybe I don't have much to say, but I decided I've got to say something other than being in this lot. So that's when I decided to pull out."

As all this was going on, Deep Purple's management decided to exile the increasingly unhappy guitarist. "They must have decided I didn't fit in any more, maybe because they don't play soccer. It's too vicious, too violent. They're always skiing, golfing, diving, going to St. Croix and Vermont, the whole thing. And I'm the opposite. I'll play soccer and be in the worst places. Roger Glover would love to do crosswords, be on the computer, very cerebral crap. I'd always be, 'Hey, let's play a practical joke on someone, and go look for some ghosts.' They'd say, 'What? Don't do that!' So there was always that disparity between myself and the rest of the band. They're more academic people by nature, but there was no passion there with them. It was too safe, much too safe."

"Then I put together a new band," continues Blackmore, "and I wasn't going to call it Rainbow. But the record company decided that's what they wanted—Blackmore's Rainbow. And I said I didn't really want to go back to that; it's not the same guys. I want to call it something else. No, they argued, there were marketing concerns, demographics, all those very important business concerns. So I went okay, I'll go along with it. Again, I would prefer to call it something else and take it from there. The drummer I had played with before, and the singer, Doogie, I found because I literally stumbled across his demo tape. I had thought about Joe Lynn Turner, because we're still friends, but he has more of what I call a ballad voice, and I wanted something more bluesy and raw. The others were guys I had jammed with or were brought in by various friends and recommendations."

"Everybody has a recording studio in their basement—I have a bar in my basement," said Ritchie, making a point about his disdain for recording. "I don't want a recording studio downstairs, because recording to me is like going to a hospital. Music is an extension of my life; recording is like root canal work, going to the dentist. It's all, 'Well, we better get this one right, lads, so we're going to get everything in tune.' I always feel like I'm in this torture chamber. But there's a professional side of me that's managed to kind of get by. I play better live, because I know it's one go at it. I have two strong drinks and I can just go, 'Yeah, I'm really getting into it, there's the audience, let's go.' If I'm in the studio, every time I go to run, jump and dive, suddenly it's, 'We've got to do it again.' That's my biggest fear, I think, hearing that line, 'Can we try that again?'"

But when asked at the time about touring with Rainbow all over again, Ritchie offered cryptically, "Yes, but I'm not necessarily pleased with the way we're sounding. I'm not pleased with anybody. It's just a thing I have. I think as soon as I've known anybody for more than three months, I get tired of them. Really, it's probably a psychological thing with myself. I'm basically kind of insecure with myself, and I take it out on other people."

And so a new "Ritchie Blackmore's Rainbow" record called *Stranger in Us All* was indeed constructed and offered for sale, featuring, on guitar, one Mr. Blackmore (resplendent in top hat, new hair, pencil-thin moustache and an array of scowls), Paul Morris (ex-Warlock) on keyboards, John O. Reilly (Mother's Army) on drums, Greg Smith (Americade, Wendy O. Williams, Red Dawn) on bass, and a Scotsman named Douglas "Doogie" White in the all-important vocal role.

I asked Doogie if he had ever caught wind that Joe Lynn Turner was supposed to be the guy for the job.

"No, but there was one guy in before me, and his name, I think, was Kevin. And he was the only guy that Ritchie auditioned. He was a local Long Island guy who sounded like Bryan Adams. Ritchie loved his voice, but the guy couldn't jam and couldn't write. And Ritchie was starting to panic a little bit, and my name came up through a tape that I had given to Colin Hart two years earlier. I had said, 'Look, if Ritchie ever needs a singer, here you go.' So Candy (Candice Night) had found that and had given it to Ritchie. Ritchie played it, liked it, called me up and flew me out. We sat in the restaurant and he said, 'Listen, I'm not trying anybody else out; you're the guy.' And I was like, fair enough."

Adding to the story, Doogie had said that in terms of getting the tape to Ritchie, Rainbow had come to town and he'd been broke but wanted to go. An industry insider obtained for him a ticket and an after-show party pass. It was at that point he handed off a four-song demo cassette he had fashioned for the occasion. Two years later, Doogie sees a sign on his door that Ritchie Blackmore's secretary had called. Doogie replies, but he's not there. Later the phone rings and a voice says, 'This is Ritchie Blackmore.' Doogie doesn't believe it and says, 'If this is Ritchie Blackmore, answer me one question: on 'Hold On' from *Stormbringer*, what's special about the guitar solo?' To which Ritchie replies: 'I played the whole thing with my thumb.' 'Right then, what can I do for you, Ritchie?'"

"I started out as a big Bowie fan," says Doogie, later of Cornerstone and Yngwie Malmsteen fame (and still later, Tank and Michael Schenker's band!), when asked about influences. "That was the first thing, David Bowie; I really liked that. And then I heard *Come Taste the Band* and I loved the blend of Glenn Hughes and David Coverdale. I thought, well, that's great. My brother's a singer as well. When we were kids, we used to sing along to that, and then *Burn* and I worked progressively back. So it's Glenn Hughes, David Coverdale, Lou Gramm, David Bowie, Ronnie Dio, Ian Gillan, a guy called Terence Trent D'Arby, Michael McDonald, James Taylor. You know, there are a lot of little wells to pull from, depending on what it is you're doing. These days I listen to musicals, sadly enough (laughs)."

Remarks Joe Lynn Turner, good-naturedly, on the man who would get the Rainbow gig. "Doogie thought I hated him because he slagged me off in one of the interviews, but he stuck his foot in his mouth. They asked him who is favourite singer was for Rainbow, who the best and worst was. Doogie said the best was Dio and the worst was me. Ritchie turned around and said, 'Oh no, the best by far was Joe Lynn Turner. He was the most colourful, had the most personality, he could do a ballad, he could do a rocker—this guy really had it all.'"

"When Doogie heard I had read that, obviously he got real worried that I was going to dislike him, but when I met him, I put my arms around him and said, 'Hey Doogie, come on, have a beer.' He was like, 'You're not going to hit me then?' And I said, 'I made mistakes too; it's water under the bridge.' Then I said, 'Besides, what you said doesn't matter to me, because right underneath it, Ritchie said I was the best singer, and that matters to me.' In the end we just laughed about it and I went, 'Because I've worked with Ritchie, I look up to him. But you, you're some guy from Scotland who wears a dress on stage—what's with the kilt?' And he said, 'I can't believe it; you're such a nice bloke and everything.' I said, 'Doogie, I have no resentment. I don't need that kind of shit anymore. I'm free of all that. I'm beyond that. I'm on a higher ground spiritually.'"

"I think he was trying to sound like me," continues Joe. "I think Ritchie kept saying, 'Do what Joe would do; Joe wouldn't sing it that way. He would sing it this way.' It was funny when I heard the album. I didn't go out of my way to get *Stranger in Us All*. I happened to be at Yngwie Malmsteen's house in Florida when I first heard it. Yngwie threw it on, and I said, 'This guy is trying to sound like me.' And Yngwie goes, 'I know.' I said, 'What's that all about? I heard he didn't like me. I heard he didn't like my style and yet he sounds like me.' It was crazy. So I never figured that out."

So Doogie White, who, incidentally, had tried out for Iron Maiden and Pink Cream 69 as well, arrived on these shores within a mere ten days of that fateful phone call, auditioning to the mellow croon of "Rainbow Eyes." Previous credits were scant, including bar band La Paz, a record with AORists Midnight Blue and a Japanese tour as erstwhile lead singer for NWOBHM stalwarts Praying Mantis. Following, White offers a thorough look under the hood of this dark horse Rainbow record he's on.

"The *Stranger in Us All* album, I think—and it's not just me that thinks this; a lot of people do—that it's an unknown classic from the band. We worked hard on the songs, and I actually found in my daughter's loft recently, when I was there about four or five months ago, a box with ten other songs that we never actually finished, just different things. And I thought there were only two. Now how I got this stuff back, I have no idea. It must have just been lying around and I gathered it up. I never even knew it existed. And it said Rainbow demos. So I put it on just to see what it was, and it was completely different songs from those sessions."

"But that's how we did it. We would work from one or two o'clock in the afternoon until dinnertime, which was generally seven o'clock at night. And it was my job to tape everything, because, you know, if it wasn't caught, if it wasn't taped, it would be lost forever. So my job was to sit there was a little tape recorder and just press the buttons and record. And then after we came back from dinner, I would sit until two or three in the morning and edit the tapes and say, 'This is good; this is the best version of this sort of idea we had' so we would have the best hits of the day tape. That was my job, which I loved doing. I'm getting to listen to Ritchie and me and the other guys in the band creating songs. You always wonder how the process goes with guys like that, and now I know. They were all mapped-out. I had sheets that had the number counted on them, and they would all be numbered off so I could find them when I needed to get them. It was a fascinating way of working. We're talking ten years ago. You wouldn't do it like that now. You'd be sitting there with your DAT machine or your ProTools system and record it directly into that, and it would be much easier to find things and move them around."

Continues Doogie, "Ritchie was great to work with and he was great to play with. I was a big fan for a very, very long time. So I had a bit of an idea of what to expect, only because I had heard the tales before. So when I first met him, he knew nothing about me, but I was under the impression I knew everything about him, if that makes any sense. So he was a little bit guarded. And when we went to upstate New York, we stayed in a big house there. And I can remember lying in my bed one night, just lying on my back, and you just feel the air moving, definitely. And I looked up, and there was Ritchie Blackmore with the top hat on, sunglasses and the big coat, a big sort of French frock coat, just staring at me, through these glasses. And I thought, just get out of here. And he floated—and I'm not kidding when I say this—he floated out the room. The door slammed, so I reckoned he must have been on some sort of skateboard or some sort of roller skates or something so that he could get that effect."

"The other thing he used to do... we had a guy called Paul Morris on the keyboards, and Paul was a bit freaked-out by... because there would be séances and stuff going on. I didn't partake of them because I didn't want Ritchie Blackmore running around in my head, and just fucking with me generally; I didn't want that to happen. So I stayed away. But Paul stayed away for different reasons. So Ritchie would take a tape recorder, a cassette recorder, and take an hour tape, and just before it was time to go to bed, he would put the tape recorder under Paul's bed, so it would be there for 60 minutes, 59 minutes and 20 seconds, and this almighty scream comes screaming out, and Paul would be absolutely terrified and he wouldn't be able to get back to sleep, because he wouldn't know where the scream had come from."

"So there were just things like that. Just funny stuff. I remember we were going out for dinner one night and it was sort of autumn time, fall time, and Ritchie said, 'I'm just going to go up and get my wallet; I forgot my wallet.' We came back, all the lights in my bedroom were on, the windows were open, the bug guards were off, and there were millions of beasts just all over the ceilings and crawling down the walls. And you know what that's like— these bugs the size of small dogs. It's funny stuff. There was never any malice in it; I never found any malice in what he did. If he didn't particularly like you, or if he didn't particularly care about you, he didn't do anything to you. He just sort of left you alone. But if he thought he could get away with it, he would play around with you and play tricks with you."

And true to Ritchie's quip on leaving Deep Purple, he did indeed inherit new soccer mates. "Oh, yes, we'd play every day! Every day," notes White. "When we were recording the album, almost every day. Because we were in North Brookfield. You know what it's like up there. It snows and it's icy and it's cold. But I mean, whenever we'd get the opportunity, and there was no chance of sort of breaking your neck, we were out there. Yeah, even on tour, we had games organized in lots of places—Germany, France, Japan, even in America. We were in Arizona and we just gathered a whole lot of people together, put them in taxis and took them out to a field and played football until it was dark."

"It was always going to be a Rainbow record," explains

Doogie, considering the "solo deal" origins of the *Stranger in Us All* situation. "There's a lot of sort of rumours that go around, whether it was going to be called Moon or Rainbow Moon (of note, Ritchie had suggested Moon, as it was his grandfather's surname), and that the record company said, 'No, it's got to be called Rainbow.'"

"That may or may not be true. I mean, the first tapes that I have of the rehearsals, when I rehearsed with him, the audition, were called Rainbow Moon. And I said, 'You can't call it Rainbow Moon! Why don't you just call it Ritchie Blackmore's Rainbow? I mean, that's what it is.' Because then you've got your established audience. You can go out there and play the old Rainbow stuff and you can play the new stuff that we'll write together. And then it became Ritchie Blackmore's Rainbow, or Rainbow, or whatever it was called."

To reiterate, *Stranger in Us All* is, in fact, credited to Ritchie Blackmore's Rainbow, which, perhaps unwittingly, ties a bow around the existence of Rainbow, given that previously, the debut—and only the debut—was thusly monikered.

And what are we to make of that enigmatic title for the record itself? Reflects Ritchie, "It was a kind of play on words with *Perfect Strangers*, and then I came up with *Stranger in Us All*, just following that road. The stranger in us all is obviously that part of us that we don't really know, or associate with. We all have dual personalities, I think. There's always another side to someone, back and front. And if you believe that, you'll believe anything (laughs, followed by a pause). Okay, I've just been corrected. I forget this stuff. How did it happen?"

"No, that's all right," interjects Candice. "You can steal the credit; I don't care (laughs). I know that they were having a hard time at one point coming up with lyrics, for the songs, because the guys were all stuck in this farmhouse in Massachusetts, and there was about six feet of snow. They stayed there for like three months and they were going a little stir crazy after awhile. There wasn't a lot to do out there in the farmlands of Massachusetts. So every once in awhile I would come back home, and if the singer wasn't coming up with lyrics that they felt were strong enough, or they didn't feel represented the song, they would call me up and play the backing track over the phone and see if I could come up with anything."

"I would take the ferry over from Long Island to Connecticut and travel up to Massachusetts. So on the ferry ride, I would just sit there for the hour-and-15-minutes and write as many verses as I could come up with. And that was one of them, which was actually 'Wolf to the Moon,' and the line was, 'The full moon unmasks the stranger in us all.' And Ritchie had a tendency to read all the words or all the verses I came up with, and they would circle the ones... like, on that one, I came up with 14 verses and they had chosen four or five of them out of that 14 that they wanted to use. And that was one of the quotes in that song. And it ends up becoming the title of the album. Ten years later it takes on different meanings, depending on how you feel at the time and then you start to remember it as that. So what Ritchie said is fine (laughs)."

"I forget these things," sighs Ritchie. "On this subject of remembering things, you go way back, and I've heard... there was a time when I heard somebody interviewing Roger Glover and I was there. He's telling a story about what happened, and I'm sitting there going, 'That never happened and this never happened and that's not how it went!' And I'm thinking, how odd, how we all change our stories, not meaning to. We all have lapses of memory and remember different things. And in actual fact, many a' story I've heard from the old days is not what happened. And obviously I'm probably guilty of this too. I've probably told stories and somebody's actually said, 'Well, that's not really what happened.' It's amazing how you distort a story, when you're talking about something over 20 years old, how you remember things. You tend to change the story to your convenience, and to how it sounds interesting. And I remember hearing Roger Glover speaking, and I'm going, 'That's absolutely nothing like what happened.'"

In this case what happened is that the rock world was surprised by the low-key appearance of a new Rainbow album, *Stranger in Us All*, issued August 21st, 1995, on RCA/BMG, same label, of course, as the stodgy last Deep Purple record.

Rainbow's eighth album opens with the aforementioned "Wolf to the Moon," which, in its final state, does not include the "stranger in us all" reference. The song is a fitting microcosm of the record as a whole in that, like the sum total of the *Stranger in Us All* experience, it strikes an alchemical alloy between *Down to Earth* and the Joe Lynn Turner years. It is heavy yet very melodic and precise like those later behaved Roger Glover productions. In fact, the production is unfortunately all too polite, much of the life sucked from the thing, especially with respect to the rhythm section. Still, all sorts of post-Dio Rainbow trademarks are there, and it is a gorgeous construct, thoroughly capable as an introductory track #1.

"'Wolf to the Moon,' yes, those lyrics are Candy's," explains Doogie. "We had already had that done, and it was a song called 'Temptation,' and it was a story of a gold-digging young woman who was running around putting sexual favours out to all the richer men, and that was axed. Ritchie didn't like the idea of... he didn't like religious things in there either. As well, I had written a song called 'Life's a Bitch,' which was really good, but he didn't like the idea of the word bitch, and he didn't like the idea of this gold-digging woman, who was a girl that I had met. Once she found out I was in Rainbow, all of a sudden I became very important to her. It was a story about her really. But he didn't like that. So Candy wrote the lyrics for 'Wolf to the Moon.'"

Next up was "Cold Hearted Woman," a song more squarely in a JLT-era mindspace, both lyrically and musically. Laughs Doogie, "'Cold Hearted Woman' was about the same woman in 'Temptation.' Because I couldn't get my frustrations out in 'Temptation,' which subsequently became 'Wolf to the Moon,' I needed to get this out of my system. So it was about a German woman I had known who had hunted and chased me around, and then whatever. So that's what that was about: she was a cold-hearted woman."

Track #3, "Hunting Humans (Insatiable)," marks a further gradation along the path from Bonnet through to JLT, this one being mellower, moodier, more atmospheric along the lines of "Can't Let You Go" or "Street of Dreams."

Explains Doogie, "'Hunting Humans' is about a serial killer called Dennis Nilsen. And he worked for the Social Security Services over here in London. He's a Scotsman, but he worked in London, and he murdered 17 young boys. He cut them up and flushed them down the toilet, and he was caught... he used to sleep with the dead bodies. You know the 'Touch my skin, let the fun begin'… so he was just going around hunting humans. And he could never satisfy sexual lust unless it was with a dead person, preferably a dead boy. And he would dress them up and paint them and stuff. On the first tour, a guy came over and said, 'I love that "Hunting Humans;" we played it at our wedding!' (laughs). 'Nice one!.'"

Further with respect to the title, there is a book by David Lester called *Serial Killers: The Insatiable Passion*, which has as its cover, a shot of the staircase leading to Nilsen's apartment. The staircase figures prominently in the killer's downfall, in that Nilsen chopped up the bodies (eventually plugging the building's pipes, hence his capture) because he didn't figure he could carry the bodies down these particular stairs. Doogie has also said that he wrote the lyric in the barn at Long View Farms, in 45 minutes, on a cold day the day after another British serial killer, Fred West, had hung himself.

"Stand and Fight" was a solid and infectious party-time rocker with a relaxed verse reminiscent of "All Night Long" or even more so, "Can't Happen Here." Doogie's vocal is bluesy in that JLT/Paul Rodgers style Ritchie is known to love.

Says Doogie, "'Stand and Fight' was one of the first songs we wrote in Cold Spring, on the Hudson, where the bugs came in. That was one of the ones that we remembered to tape. Because what you have to remember is that we did six weeks in upstate New York. Like I said, I recorded all this stuff and Ritchie took all the tapes away, and he never brought the tapes with him, to Long View Farms in North Brookfield, in Massachusetts. He never brought them. So all the stuff was missing. But Paul Morris remembered 'Stand and Fight' and 'Silence.' And we had demoed 'Black Masquerade' and something else; maybe it was 'Stand and Fight,' actually. And that's why they were remembered. But the other stuff, which subsequently turned up in my loft, had been lost, in the mix, sort of thing. But, 'Stand and Fight' was just a rock 'n' roll tune. I think it sounded better with the Hammond organ on it. On the demos, we used Hammond organ, as opposed to the harmonica, and I liked it better with that."

"Ariel" (with lyrics that are all Candy's), provides relief from the rocking, being halfway towards what this record led to, namely Ritchie and Candice's band, Blackmore's Night. It is a dark ballad, but played with full loud band—there's even a doomy heavy metal bit to it. There's also a ghostly, angelic cameo from Candy herself. The stark musical contrast between parts comes from the fact that Doogie, in his role as manipulator of the tapes, simply married two of Ritchie's riffs together to get the effect. "Ariel" was actually edited down and issued as a single in Europe, backed with a live rendition of debut record obscurity "Temple of the King."

On becoming inspired for "Too Late for Tears," Doogie explains that, "Van Halen had just come out with a great video. I can't remember what the song was called, but the video is all these early gang kids getting stabbed, and they were showing the gun wounds and stab wounds and stuff, and I thought that was a great idea. It was originally going to be about someone who killed someone and was on death row, but of course, you couldn't have that either, because the lyrics had to be things that girls would like. So it sort of morphed into whatever it became after that."

Musically, Ritchie, along with erstwhile songwriting partner Pat Regan, turns in another groovy rocker somewhat akin to "Stand and Fight," although the central riff sounds suspiciously like that of "Lost in Hollywood."

Which brings up an interesting point. Doogie had said that Ritchie had asked him to tell him if he was repeating himself, Ritchie explaining that he simply didn't know if and when that was the case. And indeed, through interviews with Ritchie, it becomes apparent that he doesn't play his back catalogue much at all and doesn't remember much about it (Ritchie once told me he doesn't even own a copy of *Fireball!*). On top of that, he does rely on certain recurring patterns. Doogie relates an amusing anecdote in that he did, as requested, call Ritchie on it once, saying that they couldn't use something he had come up with, because it was essentially "Can't Happen Here," to which Ritchie replied, "Yes, but that's one of mine, isn't it?"

"Candy wrote a lot of the lyrics on the album actually, but 'Black Masquerade' is a kind of combination," says Doogie of the bracing, malevolent, subtly melodic and thoroughly sly speed rocker that came next. "Most of that is Candy's to be honest with you, but the melody and the title and some of the stuff in there is mine."

"Silence" slows things down with a bit of a black and bluesy stripper beat, vocal melody nicked from *Burn*'s "You Fool No One." Marring the track is the presence of braying, dated keyboard tones meant to sound like horns.

Second to last track on the record was a brisk heavy metal adaptation of classic classical piece "Hall of the Mountain King." "That, again, is a mixture between Candy and I, although I don't get credited in that; Candy and Ritchie get the credit for that. But again, the melody is mine. Although it's a reworking of a classical piece. 'Hall of the Mountain King' was something that Ritchie had always played, from his days back in The Crusaders in the early '60s, and he always included it in little bits of Purple and Rainbow, and he just decided he wanted to jam it one night. And we just jammed it, and it just sort of became, you know… that." Candice again cameos on cool, understated vocals, even if all told, the song is a bit of a lark, a bit silly.

Doogie relates the humourous story of struggling valiantly to render his vocal in a bluesy style, as requested by producer Pat Regan, who Doogie most definitely had the daggers out for during this excruciating exercise. Knowing that it wasn't in a blues key, and that classical was as far away from the blues as could be, his torture was finally ended by Ritchie firing water pistols at him from the balcony. It turns out that Blackmore had told Regan to tell him to sing it as a blues because he knew it couldn't be done!

We discussed how the band was called Ritchie Blackmore's Rainbow as a bit of a "coming around," the right-side bookend to the left from exactly 20 years earlier. Well, closing the album was another pairing to a similar set of shelving solutions, the band, once again, covering the Yardbirds' "Still I'm Sad," just as they had on *Ritchie Blackmore's Rainbow*. This version chugged a bit more, and was an exercise in bubbly precision, but still, as Doogie explains, it was a bit pointless.

"I thought 'Still I'm Sad' was a lazy choice for the record, really," points out White. "I mean, that should have been the Japanese bonus track, and we should have kept 'Emotional Crime' (note: the actual Japanese bonus track), or we should have worked a bit harder on a couple of the other ideas we had kicking around. But 'Still I'm Sad,' actually, that was my fault, because there was something going on and I just started singing it. The band joined in. I think there was a pulse going (digga digga digga) and I just started singing it. 'See the stars, falling down from the sky.' And the band just joined in and the next thing you know, it was there, and it was down on the album. It was a weird sort of tie-in, the first era and the last era together, I suppose. But I thought it was a lazy choice to put on the record."

And it's not like there wasn't a surfeit of material. Other compositions that the band had on deck included "Ask God for That," "Pagan Love Song," "Judgement Day," "There Was a Time When I Called You My Brother," "Treason and Pain" and finally "Wrong Side of Morning," an old song by Doogie's band Midnight Blue refashioned.

On stage, the somewhat starchy *Stranger in Us All* really came to life. The latent potency of the songs, smothered on record by clinical production values and stiff drumming from John O'Reilly, was unleashed once these bunch of longhairs got to leaping about.

"We had a massive European and Japanese tour in '95 (note: the album sold briskly in both territories, eventually hitting 350,000 in worldwide sales) that started in September and went on to the end of November," recounts White. "Then we had a nine-show South American tour and another European tour, including festivals, in '96. And then we had an extensive US tour, including Toronto, early '97 (it is of note that it took two years for the album to get issued stateside, and by this point, Blue Öyster Cult and Meat Loaf drummer John Micelli was in the band). Which took us sort of through February, March and April, in '97. In terms of back-ups, we had Great White at one point; I think they played a couple of shows with us; I think they played with us in Boston. But generally, in Japan it was an up-and-coming Japanese band, and in

Europe it was a band that was on the same label, a BMG band that was Danish or Swedish or something."

"He never smashed a guitar, which was a great disappointment for me," laughs Doogie. "You know, he didn't do that. There were only two nights that we didn't do encores, and they were more for technical reasons. In fact, whatever he may say, Ritchie was very happy during that period; he was enjoying it. He had total control by then. He had musicians round about him… he had Chuck Burgi who had played with him ten years previously. He had the professional ability and know-how of Greg Smith, who had been Alice Cooper's bass player and Blue Öyster Cult's bass player for ages, and he had me running around the front of the stage who could sing and do anything he wanted. And that's what he liked with me, the fact that I could sing anything; anything he gave me, I could just sing it. Whether it be a lullaby or folk song or blues or a rock song or improvisation on the spot. He liked that, because it gave him the freedom to work with his guitar."

"And I mean, he was playing better guitar then than he probably had done in the past decade. You know, especially since… and I'm only saying Joe Lynn Turner because of the era that Joe was in. But I felt Ritchie was very lazy during that period, guitar-wise. But he really got fired up on the *Battle Rages On…* tour, which subsequently led itself into the *Stranger in Us All* tour. And I never had any problems with him at all. It's his gig, you know? So I just kept in line. And if he came at me, I'd just take a little sidestep, bob and weave, and step back in again."

As for the set list, Doogie says, "We would start with 'Spotlight Kid,' then we would do 'Wolf to the Moon,' 'Too Late for Tears,' 'Long Live Rock 'n' Roll,' 'Mistreated,' 'Still I'm Sad,' 'Man on the Silver Mountain,' 'Black Masquerade,' 'Hunting Humans,' 'Hall of the Mountain King,' 'Burn,' 'Perfect Strangers,' 'Smoke on the Water,' a bit of 'Black Night.' And then of course, we went to Japan and because the Joe Lynn Turner era of Rainbow was very popular there, we had to do 'Street of Dreams' and 'Stone Cold' and stuff like that. Rather than the good stuff, you know (laughs). Rather than 'Fire Dance' or the other heavy ones."

"It was a varied set, but then we interspersed it with a lot of improvisations, and with lots of little songs, old folk songs. You know, we would do 'Waltzing Matilda,' which is the other Australian national anthem. But I would have it as 'Waltzing with Ritchie, waltzing with Ritchie, we go waltzing with Ritchie and me.' You know, or just make up something about the town we were in wherever we were. And if he felt that I was getting too cocky for myself, he would make me do another verse of it and then another verse, so we could be doing that for nine minutes. I mean, we did some shows that were two-and-three-quarters hours long, just because we were assing around."

Interestingly, Doogie found it impossible to handle any of the Graham Bonnet material (citing his range and his use of multi-tracking), often telling the story of attempting 'All Night Long' in rehearsals and having the band crack up with laughter.

In terms of live show extras, Doogie explains that, "There were backdrops of the fist coming out of the sea, and the guitar castle and stuff like that, but it was more of a light show, and more really about the dexterity of the band and Ritchie getting out front and playing. That was just how it worked. At the start of the set, where it's going, 'We must be over the rainbow, rainbow,' we had the *Stranger in Us All* album sleeve, and then we had got a little prism projector, to project a rainbow between the arms, which was quite cool—that looked good."

As Doogie has mentioned, Chuck Burgi (last seen on the *Bent Out of Shape* album), was back behind the drum kit for the band. "He's one of the nicest men in rock 'n' roll, old Chuck. No, he was very good. He was a very calming influence, when things, you know... once you've been on the road for four or five weeks, things would get a bit hairy and Chuck would just put an arm around me, walk me down and buy me a coffee."

And why not use John O'Reilly, drummer for the album? "Well, that is something you'd really have to ask Ritchie. The story being told is that John injured himself playing soccer, which was a story that was true. But he decided to debunk that and say that there were other reasons. So maybe John is the guy you should ask."

Doogie adds a closing tale from the road. "There was a great moment in Japan, where we had just played in Osaka, in the Festival Hall, and we had been invited down to the Hard Rock Cafe, and they had set aside a little area for us. And Paul Morris came walking in and Greg Smith, the bass player and I were talking. Paul walks in and everybody just ignored him. So he left and went back to the hotel, and he changed, and he came back in again—and everybody ignored him. And he went back, and he put on his gig clothes, and finally somebody went over and spoke to him. So he had three goes at trying to get any attention, or any food (laughs)."

"But on the road, it was very professional, because you know, for me, it was my first time doing a really big tour, really major stuff. And playing with my favourite guitarist and favourite composer in the whole world. So I treated my time in Rainbow the way Muhammad Ali would treat the heavyweight crown. You know, I wasn't going to do a Buster Douglas and go out there and just blow it out after one blast. I wanted to be there and I wanted it to be important and I wanted it to last longer. I mean, that's what I wanted it to do. I wanted to be there longer than Graham Bonnet. I wanted to do more albums than Joe Lynn Turner. But it just wasn't to be."

And the reason being…

"There's something you may have heard of called Blackmore's Night," says Doogie, with a wink. "So that was kind of what happened. I mean, that just seemed to take off. That was something he had actually been working on before we did the *Stranger in Us All* album. Him and Candy had been working on stuff, and he had said to me, 'Well, let me go and do Candy's album.' Which is what it was called at the time: Candy's album, Candy's album. 'And we'll regroup later on.' In 1997 we were going to get together and start doing a new album together, but I think the success of Blackmore's Night, and the fact that he actually enjoys it… and he doesn't have the pressure of having to deal with a band situation, because Blackmore's Night is just him and Candy, and whoever happens to be available at any particular time. It's a revolving door of musicians, as you'll see. Someone will be in one day and then he'll be out. Because it's just who's available at the time."

Ritchie himself affirms this chain of events. "In 1995, when I reformed Rainbow and recorded *Stranger in Us All*, Candice and I had been together since 1989 and I knew that she could sing. When we were in the studio with Rainbow she helped out a lot by coming up with lyrics for songs and singing background vocals. But even while we were recording *Stranger in Us All*, we were writing songs for our own pleasure. We never thought that we would record them, but they were later the songs that we put on *Shadow of the Moon*. Actually, 'Ariel' from *Stranger in Us All* was a song that Candice and I had originally written together as a ballad. We may even re-record that the original way it was written at some point. When we started playing the songs we wrote together at one of our parties for our friends, a neighbour came up to me and said, 'I don't know much about the music that you recorded with Deep Purple or Rainbow, but if you two recorded this, I would buy it.' That's when I started seriously thinking about recording the songs."

But of course, the roots of Blackmore's Night go back much further. After confessing a love for Jethro Tull, Ritchie explains that, "I've been listening to this music ever since I heard David Munrow; he recorded with The Early Music Consort of London. He recorded some music for Henry VIII. It was a TV program on BBC, which I saw in 1972, and I loved the music and it was David Munrow's music, playing Tielman Susato. Ever since I heard it, I've been hooked on it, but more from the point of view of listening for pleasure. I very seldom listened to rock at all. I would only listen to this other stuff, and then I would play it around the house. Then Candy started singing it around the house. And I suddenly noticed and realized that it was working in the context of the melodies being so good from those days, the 1500s. She would interpret those melodies and put lyrics to them, and that was the way we put the songs together."

And quite obviously, Ritchie was already putting Blackmore's Night-styled melodies and modes into various Deep Purple songs along the way anyway. "I suppose I was, in a way. There was another band out at the time called The Nice, Keith Emerson's band, and they were doing similar stuff to what we were doing—they were doing classical music rocked-up. So I suppose the music I'm doing now is not so different from the music I was doing then. It's just that we're not doing it with such a loud guitar, but mostly acoustic. But the progressions are very similar and the arrangements are similar to what we would have done back in those days. But I've always been impressed with the classics. They have a sense of drama, a sense of depth that rock 'n' roll doesn't have for me so much."

"I can't believe you know Gordon Giltrap!" exclaims Ritchie, when I asked if that pioneer of the British folk explosion was any influence as well, as Ritchie's predilection for this sort of music slowly took shape through the '70s. "He's helped me a lot, put this whole thing together from the perspective of... I think he's a brilliant guitar player. When I started playing the acoustic guitar, probably about eight years ago when I was really getting into it, he was kind of my model that I was listening to. He seemed to be the guy who could play, in my mind, better than most, so I was getting a lot of tips from Gordon. In fact, I used a lot of the same guitar strings that he used. I spoke to him. I get the same guitar strings from England that he manufactures, along with his friend. So Gordon was a big influence on me and I wish he had more acclaim than he does. John Renbourn, I saw down the road the other day. He's another favourite. But I never listened to John Renbourn in the old days. I listened to Gordon, but I didn't hear much about John, or Bert Jansch, but now of course I do. But Gordon is my favourite, along with Leo Kottke."

"So yes, I have been listening to Renaissance music since 1973," continues Ritchie. "It was just a natural progression and continuation after 20 years of listening to it to start playing it. After playing rock music for such a long time, and seeing the way that the music industry has changed from when I first started playing music to the music they play now... Renaissance music excites me much more these days. It may sound simple, but there is a lot of complexity and rigidity to it which is something that I have never dealt with in music before. So it presents a whole new challenge to me musically. By playing this music, you feel much more vulnerable. You can't hide behind volume and distortion effects. Emotionally this music is much more challenging to play and I feel like I am learning something more every day. And I've always been into the lifestyle of the Renaissance people. I read a lot of history circa 1500 and attend Renaissance fairs regularly. Many of my friends are involved in various re-enactment groups of the Renaissance times. Whether they are minstrels or arrow makers. But yes, this music is technically challenging. I mean a Fender cranked through a Marshall is a wonderful thing but what we are doing now requires a delicate touch and leaves no room for error. You can't hide behind volume."

Ritchie cites one other Blackmore's Night-related light bulb moment. "I first got into minstrel music when I was in Germany in 1985 and ended up being in this castle with a group of friends on holiday. There was this big thunderstorm going on, typical gothic horror set. We were having a few German beers, which in itself is fantastic, and all of a sudden there was this minstrel group singing and playing in the castle with a hurdy gurdy, horns and a lute. They're playing away, and I'm going, 'This is unbelievable; this is what I want to do.' I asked them at the time, would you want a guitar player in your band? They said, 'No, we don't need a guitar.' That was the first time I'd ever been turned down (laughs). But when they played, it was magnificent. I just remember how they moved me, and I would love to be able to move people like that. To me, that was so innocent, and it was 100% music."

Back over the waning vestiges of Rainbow, Ritchie struggles to find words to describe the (relatively loud, then) *Stranger in Us All* experience.

"Yes, well, I felt that the... every now and again, I hear the CD. Not that I play it, but I hear bits and pieces of it. And it turned out really well, I thought. It was a good record, considering. I don't think it did particularly well. I don't even know. But it was good fun doing the record, good musicians, Greg Smith, very good bass player. And we had a few other guys in. Of course, whenever you put a band together for the first time, there's always a lot of good camaraderie. And usually you're sharing the same residence, so you have a big house and everybody's having fun. So for me, I was having fun making that record. Candy was there; she was the only girl around. That's the way it is when Candy's around."

Doogie is a bit more forthright on the album. "Well, I like a lot of the songs on the record; 80% of the album I really like and there's 20% that I think we could have done better. I'm not going to tell you which ones, because people have their own favourites and the ones they don't like. I think we were too slick—I think *it's* too slick. We spent too long on the vocals and we spent too long on the overall production and we lost the vital edge in the performances. Not in the songs, but in the performances that are actually on the record."

"Because the songs are strong. And if you saw the band live, you would realize just how good the songs were, and how good they could have been on the record, had we not... had whoever was in charge of making the decisions about the production, or making the decisions about how it should sound... they overdid it, and over-saturated it for the American market. And that's what my problem with it is. It's too polished, and I mean sound-wise and performance-wise. You know, it took me 23 days to do ten vocals; now that's ridiculous, you know? That's ridiculous. What happens is you eventually beat the flavour out of the performance you're trying to put in. Now the argument on the other side would be, 'Listen, if you got it right the first time, man, you wouldn't have to do it for 23 days.'"

"But there was just something about the slick American producer way of working. We weren't making a Def Leppard album. We were making a Ritchie Blackmore record that should have had more of that urgency that comes from Led Zeppelin, Deep Purple, Black Sabbath, and doesn't come from, you know, Bon Jovi and Def Leppard. It's got to have more of that British, Maiden-y kind of feel. You know, Aerosmith have got a very British approach to the way that they do the music, whereas Def Leppard have a very American approach to the way they produce the music. Do you see what I'm getting at here? So that's my disappointment. I don't listen to the album, and haven't listened to it for a long time. Because we spent too long writing and recording it."

That analysis from Doogie confirms the great taste in music I knew he had, for the man has hit it smack on the head: *Stranger in Us All* might have been a very, very good record, simply through two things, a bit more of the stiff drink applied to the performances and then beefier, rougher production dialling them in. Also, incredibly, he's right about his percentages: re-perform it, re-record it, but first switch out the worst 20%, and we'd absolutely have on our hands a perfectly competitive Rainbow record. And the final icing on the cake in this fantasy baseball game: rechristen the band simply Rainbow. And one other thing, make no changes to the album graphics—front, back and insides all look on message and classy. Even the album title is awesome.

Chapter 12

"Since You Been Gone"

"The 21st century was not a place for him to be."

On April 5th, 1998, less than a year after the concluding dates of the *Stranger in Us All* tour, Cozy Powell was killed in a high speed car crash. He had been traveling at over 100 mph on the M4 in his Saab, talking to his girlfriend on a cellphone, his blood alcohol limit just slightly above the legal limit. He died en route to the hospital.

So yes... Cozy, rest in peace and Rainbow rest in peace (for all intents and purposes—more on that later), with the flame of at least the latter kept alive through the enduring presence of Blackmore's Night, who now, ten studio albums and three live albums in, are still enthusiastically active, taking their lush, full band Renaissance revival show to castles and concert halls the world over.

In the meantime, Deep Purple was inducted into the Rock and Roll Hall of Fame in 2016. Ian Gillan, Ian Paice and Roger Glover were incensed that Steve Morse and Don Airey weren't inducted (those three were, along with Jon Lord, Ritchie Blackmore, Glenn Hughes and David Coverdale), and specified that they preferred to play with the current lineup. Ritchie took that as being "banned," and did not attend.

"About four months after he left the band, I was in New York," says Roger, concerning a brief spot of modern-day contact with the Man in Black. "I was taking my wife to see Frank Sinatra at Radio City, and we got there early and we had half an hour or so to kill, so we decided to have a quick drink at the bar at the Warwick Hotel, which is a place we always used to stay at. And as I walked in, Ritchie was walking out, and we literally bumped into each other. Anyway, he came back in, and we sat and had a drink and he was fine. I have no axe to grind with Ritchie, really. He may have with us, and with me—apparently, he's never going to talk to me again. Because he thinks I messed up his solos, without his permission, on the *Machine Head* remix. I didn't need his permission because it's actually owned by EMI. I didn't get permission from anyone else in the band either. But he's decided he doesn't like me for that. So, I'm sorry about that."

"I admire him greatly, and he's happy with what he's doing," continues Glover. "I'm happy for him. For Ritchie, he's absolutely right. He's drawn a line. He wants to move on; he wants to do music that is closer to his soul, and I think that's fantastic; that's absolutely fantastic. As a fan, I've heard bits and pieces and I'm not really going to comment much. But as a fan, I was always frustrated because I could hear Ritchie doing an album that he would never do. I could always hear him doing a solo album surrounded by just great musicians and you know, just killing it, just flooring it. As a producer and as a friend, that's what I want for him. And I sometimes am frustrated that he's hampered by his own decisions and his own view."

Going back to 1997, Ronnie James Dio addressed the rumours of a Rainbow reunion, a hot topic that regularly surfaced in the heavy metal music press of the day. "No, we haven't spoken at all. I only mention it because the rumours are just everywhere. In fact I've seen a few magazines in Germany that actually announced that, 'Yes! Ronnie James Dio and Ritchie Blackmore are together again.' And I thought wow, when's this going to happen? No one told me about it. But the good thing about it is that over the years, and especially now, it's really getting strong again. There are so many people that want to see this happen, that are kind of almost forcing us to do it again."

"But again, I have not spoken to Ritchie, and it's Ritchie's decision to make," continued Dio. "After all, Rainbow was his band, and if he wants to do something about it, then he has to contact myself or Cozy or Bob Daisley or whoever else he wants to contact. And then it's up to us what we want to do with it. Just because there are rumours and the opportunity to do it, doesn't mean that I want to do it, or that Cozy wants to do, or that Ritchie wants to do it. It's still a rumour and I'm treating it as exactly that. I don't think about it at all, and I just carry on with what I have to do. The most important thing to me is the Dio band. Rainbow was a part of my past, and if it could ever come together again, it might be interesting."

Later, into the early 2000s, Ronnie explained the situation to me the following way, which, amusingly, contains many of the same sentiments voiced years earlier.

"It came pretty close at one point but that went away. There were just a lot of problems involved in it. There has been contact made between Ritchie's faction and my faction and Ritchie and I, but not for those purposes. I mean, I haven't initiated that contact because I just left that up to Ritchie. It was his band in the first place, so it was up to him to make a move and obviously it wouldn't be that way anymore—it's a different world out there now."

"I think the crux of that band was always, aside from Cozy who is not with us anymore, myself and Ritchie, from the way we wrote and played together. But there is still an outside chance. As far as ever touring or doing anything like that, I would think that that would be an absolute impossibility. It's really hard; it's like doing the Sabbath reunion, and you think that everything is going to change, but nothing ever does—nothing ever changes."

"I don't know if at this point in my life if I want to put myself through that," laughed Ronnie. "I'm so happy doing what I'm doing now. I'd have to really think about it. Let's face it, money is a big enticer and I'm sure they are going to chuck some big bucks at us because they already did once. But you've got to be a bit more true to yourself than that. I would do it if I wanted to do it, if it was important. Because I think it is important to a lot of people out there. That band has become… I don't know what happened with it, but it became this template for music for a while and it just seems like such an important thing to so many musicians that I think it would be a shame for them, for the ones who have never seen it, not to see it one more time. I think it would be great. But who knows? There is always a chance."

"Actually, Glenn and I wanted Ritchie to do a track on our HTP record," explains Joe Lynn Turner, who gets around to a pure, almost innocent excitement over his own Rainbow reunion dreams. "I might just have to call Carole (Stevens, Blackmore's Night manager, and actually Candice's mother) but she's not going to get the message through and I know it. We're a threat! He might like it! He might see the light."

Just imagine Rainbow with Glenn Hughes on bass.

"That's what I mean! Rainbow with Glenn Hughes. And Glenn's willing to do it! He's like, 'Fuck, the three of us together, it would be like a fucking... forget it! Come on! We'd do 'Burn' 2002! So what I'm going to do is actually put a call in to her. But I know she's going to nix it. He'll never get the message. The only thing he might see is this CD that we send him, because he tends to like to get CDs to see what we're doing."

Joe then reveals plans of an earlier attempt to get the Rainbow rising… "It was last year. We were all on the conference call (laughs), all of us, Rosenthal, Burgi, me, Greg Smith, the bass player at that point—because Roger, forget it—but all these guys had been in Rainbow… Paul Morris, whatever, on the keys. But a lot of different incarnations of Rainbow members coming together. We had put a perfect Rainbow package together, on the line to Carole, and she just never put it through. We wanted to speak to Ritchie directly and it was just like, 'Sorry.' We called twice. It's a shame, and I hope he comes to his senses because we could use him out there again."

"Oh, those are always going around!" says Joe on the reunion rumours that revolved around Ronnie. "I heard that about two-and-a-half years ago, and that that was Ritchie's choice, but that wasn't entirely true. Because I think we had a very popular band. Our incarnation of Rainbow was probably one of the most popular ones. I mean, there are a lot of Dio freaks out there but it wasn't across the board like this was. Our audiences definitely had a different demographic."

"There was somebody at a radio station that sent me a chart, funnily enough, that the demographics of Dio are these guys that work at Wendy's, leather jackets, toothless. And my demographic was college-educated, white-collar, six figures a year type people, more intelligent. Not that that's better, but there's a real contrast. But you know what? Whatever. Go ahead guys, do what you gotta do. But Dio is doing well enough on his own and I don't think he really needs to get involved with this again. Plus I think he has too many memories. On the other hand, I would welcome it. You never know, man, we might be able to change the world."

"I don't think I made anybody commercial," continues Joe, back on the subject of the nature and legacy of the band with him at the mic. "I think it had to be there to begin with. I think that what I did was probably put a face and a voice to the situation that made it more accessible—the girls, for example, liked my voice and my look. That was great; thank God for that, because there were never any girls at a Rainbow concert before. The roadies loved me because of that. Even the band did, because they never had any girls."

"All they had was these geezers that were into some kind of wizardry, but they weren't really into wizardry. They're not into black magic; they're not into Aleister Crowley. They think they're into it. Drawing a pentagram on your forehead doesn't make you a witch. It was all demons and dragons and all that crap. And I just put a reality to it. I mean 'Street of Dreams' is a very supernatural song, but at the same time it has an earthy feel. People can relate to it. I think I touched more common people. Musically, Ronnie James Dio always sounded a certain way. I respect Ronnie, and I like his stuff too, but Ritchie always said I had more colour, more shapes to my voice and my personality. So I guess I made it more commercial because we were successful. In the States, we were in the Top 20. Who the hell doesn't want that? I mean, unless you're some grunge artist with millions of dollars in the bank."

"But Ritchie is now doing what, in my opinion, he's always wanted to do. He always told me he was a sixteenth century Renaissance man that was born out of time. He was reincarnated out of time (laughs). The twenty-first century was not a place for him to be. He felt miserable here, and so, he always loved that music and I know that he's happy doing that music."

Still, three years after Joe spoke those words, the enthusiasm of the guys to revive the esteemed Rainbow institution was palpable and unwavering.

Explains Joe, "I was doing an interview on an internet station that Ritchie was supposedly listening to because it was his birthday this weekend; the 14th was his birthday, today actually. So 'Happy Birthday,' I said, 'and we'd love you to play on the new HTP' (laughs), so he might have heard it on the airwaves. But everyone in the studio… it was like everyone was there except Ritchie! Chuck Burgi was there, John O. Reilly was there, Greg Smith, Paul Morris came in, Doogie sent me an email saying, 'Sorry, I thought I was going to be in New York, but I'm out with Malmsteen.'"

"So it was Rainbow all over the place! This is all people gathering for my record. And we said, 'Look, we've got to get Rich and we've got Rainbow.' We've got two configurations going. Everybody still wants to do it; everybody thinks it would be a tremendous idea. We really don't want to take Ritchie away from his Renaissance music or anything. I don't understand why people can't do several projects, really. It's just multitasking. I mean, I certainly can."

In fact, Joe's one of the best at it. Maybe his example—if Ritchie would ponder upon it for a few serious minutes—could potentially rub off on our favourite enigmatic minstrel. Here's one fan (among what… hundreds of thousands at least?), hoping that he might find it in his heart to plug in once again with Joe Lynn Turner at the microphone. After all, it need not be seen as a threat to Blackmore's Night. In fact, I wouldn't be surprised if a potent synergy comes into play, and Ritchie and Candice see business for their duo-plus double in scope in the light of the exposure one could logically expect given a legitimately reformed Rainbow. And the troops are ready. As Joe just told you, "Look, we've got to get Rich and we've got Rainbow."

Flash forward to 2015 and, with Ritchie characteristically contrarian in the making and baking, indeed "we got Rainbow." But did we really? Most fans say no. Playing under the banner of Ritchie Blackmore's Rainbow (this is now the third specified thusly) was lead singer Ronnie Romero and bassist Bob Curiano (both unknowns), along with keyboardist Jens Johansson of Yngwie Malmsteen and Stratovarius fame, Blackmore's Night drummer David Keith, and the Man in Black, looking on bemused. The band played three pretty darned big shows in 2016, two in Germany and one in the UK, and then performed similarly very sporadically through 2019, each year characterized by a small clutch of summer dates.

More impressive, a 2018 live DVD and double CD set called *Memories in Rock (Live)* was generated from the band's very first two shows together back in 2016. Seems a little crazy in retrospect. Ronnie Romero was still pretty rough on vocals, a little off-key, and he got some stick for it, not to mention his English-as-second-language accent—the guy's from Chile! Fact is, he's worlds better now.

And there was even new music recorded, first an all-new original track called "Waiting for a Sign," which was serviceable enough, with Ronnie proving himself intriguingly bluesy across a strong song with tendencies toward "Jealous Lover." Then there was the biting, rhythmic re-do of "Black Sheep of the Family," which proves that there's both creativity and aggression in the new unit, even when essentially covering what was already a cover. Finally there was a tight heavy metal remake of a Blackmore's Night track called "The Storm." And just like that, the new version of the band, despite the disconcerting tendency toward covers, was demonstrating identity, an identity that in fact was approximately the idealized version of the *Stranger in Us All* project that Doogie had described and wished was his purview and domain.

But really, consensus among the fans is that the Romero-fronted version of Rainbow isn't quite there yet, even if it's somewhat a salve on past wounds, even spirited at times, Romero always improving (and now in fact quite authoritative). But it's not nearly as substantial as we would wish… yet? I mean, the staff is just too new. A full studio album would certainly help, but, as we shall see, that's not where Ritchie's head is at.

There's a huge sadness across the Deep Purple and Rainbow communities (they are one and the same, really), that

Ritchie and Ronnie could never get it together for a reunion during all those years that they were more than capable of doing so. And for those not on board with the new band, well, those fans can always wish for Ritchie and Joe to half right that perceived wrong. Add in a few other pedigreed Rainbow alumni on keys, bass and drums and there's a story that can still make headlines.

Explained Ritchie concerning the current situation, doing German press in the spring of 2019, "'Black Sheep of the Family,' 'Waiting for a Sign' and 'The Storm'… the latter is an old song from Blackmore's Night, which I re-recorded with my Strat and loud amps. The result is a completely new piece of music—very fast heavy rock. 'Black Sheep of the Family' was the first title I recorded after my departure from Deep Purple with Ronnie James Dio. Ronnie Romero sings it brilliantly now, changing some parts."

"Nowadays you do not go to the studio anymore to make long records," replied Ritchie, asked if we'll ever see a new Rainbow album—in later interviews, Blackmore said that he would not be writing any more heavy rock music! "We're going to get these three titles out for now. I think there is far too much music published. But around Christmas, there might be a whole album of new Rainbow songs. However, the shows we're playing this year are pure nostalgia events. Sometimes I just enjoy looking back. But I do not want to warm up permanently, but rather stay flexible and only occasionally appear with Rainbow."

And as is to be expected with any of our aging heroes— Ritchie is 74 years old as I write this—the fans have to understand that the advancing years are going to have an effect on things like this—it's not all about us.

Explains a candid Blackmore, "My arthritis is mostly in the back, and one of my left hand fingers is not working the way it should. But I just keep playing. Django Reinhardt played terrific guitar with only two fingers. I should be able to play with three. This is one of the big topics of my tour with Rainbow this year. I regularly get painkilling injections in my back. I can only perform with Rainbow if I'm painless. I do not exactly make it easy for my concert agencies. That's one of the reasons why I rarely play with Rainbow. To stand on a stage all night long with a heavy

Stratocaster guitar is very exhausting. Last year in Prague I could not play an encore because I was in so much pain. But we all have our problems."

This state of affairs is even in evidence before shows. As he remarks about his pre-game warm-up, "I improvise a bit on the guitar and play some scales in the wardrobe. When I'm in pain, I take a sip of whiskey. And I meditate. That makes me hover."

On the brighter side of life, Ritchie is happy with his Chilean singer, Ronnie Romero. "He has an exciting voice. And he has the ability to imitate other singers like Freddie Mercury or Ronnie James Dio. When I first heard his voice, he reminded me of the early Rainbow. It was nostalgic feelings that brought Rainbow back to life. So I put together a set list of songs that Ronnie Dio once sang. I know that many Rainbow fans in Europe like this phase the most."

"About Ritchie, like I said, he's always been pretty much a stand-up guy to me," reflects Turner, who we'll give the final word, perhaps shedding just a wee bit more light on the Man in Black before we go. "I never had any problems with him, even after the split and all that, because obviously I told you that it wasn't he that was starting all this shit. It was really all these other guys in this quest for Gillan. You know, I guess they felt threatened because it was the Ritchie and Joe show, it was Deep Rainbow, it was this, that and the other thing, and they felt that they were being overshadowed by the two of us. Which is strange."

"As you can tell, jealousy and ego, they prevail no matter how long or how great your career is," sighs Joe, perhaps resigned to Ritchie not doing the obvious and giving him a call. "And if you don't evolve past that, then you're just going to carry that forward. And that's what happened with these other guys. And Purple is still going. I don't know if you can still call it Purple, but I think that maybe they just put out one of their better albums in years. But Ritchie, again, yeah, he can be strange and he can be moody. Oh, I'm sorry, moody if you're poor, eccentric if you rich. So he's eccentric. But not in a terrible way. There's a lot of misconceptions about Blackmore. And I really don't really want to pull the veil back and expose those things, simply because I think he wants to keep it that way."

That's indeed the spirit in which the new Rainbow, one that has softly persisted now for a surprising four years, operates, representing this sense of Ritchie sneering in the face of expectation, doing what he's advised against, and then true to the part of his character that he's glad to flaunt, replacing old blood with new. Whether he sticks with this particular cast of Rainbow demons is anyone's guess, but at least he's keeping his large and yet besieged fan base on their toes, attuned to his every move, possibly pranked but loving Blackmore's mischief all the same.

Discography

Rainbow's recording history is actually pretty straightforward. Having said that, what constitutes the sacrosanct, "true" Rainbow catalogue gets muddled when it comes to compilations and live albums, with most of those coming posthumously, a discography-polluter in my books. Which is why I've only gone for records released while they were still a band making studio albums (hence I've not included the Ronnie Romero live album. Also, *Live in Germany* from 1990 doesn't count because technically, there was no Rainbow between *Bent Out of Shape* and *Stranger in Us All*).

So, with respect to live albums, I've decided to include only *On Stage*. With respect to compilations, same sort of thing: I've recognized only *Finyl Vinyl* to be included as part of the sacrosanct discography (1981's *The Best of* was not issued in the US). I've moved both of these to a separate category so that the studio catalogue can read clean on its own.

In essence, then, this type of discography is designed less to be of the complete type (there are no discussions around crazy permutations, issues in different countries, singles, EPs, contribution to multi-band compilations and/or soundtracks etc., radio shows, VHS videos or DVDs). It's a discography constructed more to provide a roadmap as to where, crucially, the songs come from. It's also an index of sorts to the book, a plot map, hopefully a reference tool useful in a number of ways.

As well, I've stayed right the hell away from solo discographies because given the mass of humanity that has rolled through Rainbow's ranks, and the huge number of records most of these guys have been part of over the years, it would be a widening mess that doesn't mean much to the story at hand.

I've allowed myself a "Notes" section to mention in footnote form any fruity li'l foibles I found important or odd enough to mention (this section is not an exact science). I've not bothered with quote marks around songs—too messy: this section's virtually all songs. Catalogue numbers are from the

American issues, given that despite the many Englishmen in the band, and the Englishman-ness of its dear leader, there have also been many Americans, and Ritchie and Roger both lived in America. As well, America is generally the land of the highest quantity of record sales.

I've maintained the Side 1/Side 2 demarcation for every release from the vinyl years, i.e. everything except *Stranger in Us All*, mainly because doing so provides extra information as to how the band (and its extended family in management and perhaps the business office and over at the label) viewed and then sequenced these records. I've also made known the various lineups for the band, namely because I thought it might be a useful place to get an "at a glance" experience of something as important as the band's personnel changes.

Part 1 – The Studio Albums

Ritchie Blackmore's Rainbow

(Oyster/Polydor PD-6049, August 4, 1975)

Produced by: Ritchie Blackmore, Martin Birch and Ronnie James Dio

Side 1: 1. Man on the Silver Mountain (4:38) 2. Self Portrait (3:18) 3. Black Sheep of the Family (3:20) 4. Catch the Rainbow (6:40)

Side 2: 1. Snake Charmer (4:30) 2. The Temple of the King (4:46) 3. If You Don't Like Rock 'n' Roll (2:36) 4. Sixteenth Century Greensleeves (3:35) 5. Still I'm Sad (3:53)

Notes: Initial lineup: Ritchie Blackmore – guitars, Ronnie James Dio – vocals, Craig Gruber – bass, Mickey Lee Soule – keyboards, Gary Driscoll – drums. Gatefold; later reissued without gatefold. Paired in 1978 gatefold reissue, with *Rising*. Japanese limited edition with poster issue in 1975.

Rising

(Oyster/Polydor OY-1-1601, May 17, 1976)

Produced by: Martin Birch

Side 1: 1. Tarot Woman (6:11) 2. Run with the Wolf (3:48) 3. Starstruck (4:06) 4. Do You Close Your Eyes (2:58)

Side 2: 1. Stargazer (8:28) 2. A Light in the Black (8:12)

Notes: Lineup: Ritchie Blackmore – guitars, Ronnie James Dio – vocals, Jimmy Bain – bass, Tony Carey – keyboards, Cozy Powell – drums. Gatefold; later reissued without gatefold. Paired in 1978 gatefold reissue with Ritchie Blackmore's Rainbow.

Long Live Rock 'n' Roll

(Polydor PD-1-6143, April 9, 1978)

Produced by: Martin Birch

Side 1: 1. Long Live Rock 'n' Roll (4:25) 2. Lady of the Lake (3:38) 3. L.A. Connection (3:35) 4. Gates of Babylon (6:47)

Side 2: 1. Kill the King (4:28) 2. The Shed (Subtle) (4:46) 3. Sensitive to Light (3:08) 4. Rainbow Eyes (7:31)

Notes: Lineup: Ritchie Blackmore – guitars, Ronnie James Dio – vocals, Bob Daisley – bass, David Stone – keyboards, Cozy Powell – drums. Of note, Jimmy Bain and Ritchie Blackmore also supply bass to the album, with Tony Carey supplying some of the keyboards. Gatefold, with lyric sleeve; later reissued without gatefold. Some copies with black printed circle: "Featuring Ritchie Blackmore, Ronnie James Dio, Cozy Powell."

Down to Earth

(Polydor PD-1-6221, July 28, 1979)

Produced by: Roger Glover

Side 1: 1. All Night Long (3:49) 2. Eyes of the World (6:36) 3. No Time to Lose (3:41) 4. Makin' Love (4:36)

Side 2: 1. Since You Been Gone (3:10) 2. Love's No Friend (4:52) 3. Danger Zone (4:30) 4. Lost in Hollywood (4:51)

Notes: Lineup: Ritchie Blackmore – guitars, Graham Bonnet – vocals, Roger Glover – bass, Don Airey – keyboards, Cozy Powell – drums. Full colour, cardboard inner sleeve. Also issue in the UK on clear vinyl. Two singles released with non-LP b-sides: Since You Been Gone/Bad Girl and All Night Long/Weiss Heim.

Difficult to Cure

(Polydor PD-1-6316, February 3, 1981)

Produced by: Roger Glover

Side 1: 1. I Surrender (4:010 2. Spotlight Kid (4:52) 3. No Release (5:20) 4. Magic (4:05) 5. Vielleicht Das Nachster (Maybe Next Time) (3:20)

Side 2: 1. Can't Happen Here (4:55) 2. Freedom Fighter (4:20) 3. Midtown Tunnel Vision (4:31) 4. Difficult to Cure (Beethoven's Ninth) (5:55)

Notes: Lineup: Ritchie Blackmore – guitars, Joe Lynn Turner – vocals, Roger Glover – bass, Don Airey – keyboards, Bobby Rondinelli – drums. Black-and-white lyric sleeve. Non-LP Jealous Lover first issued as a B-side to Can't Happen Here, and then as feature title on a four-track EP.

Straight Between the Eyes

(Mercury SRM-1-4041, June 10, 1982)

Produced by: Roger Glover

Side 1: 1. Death Alley Driver (4:36) 2. Stone Cold (5:15) 3. Bring on the Night (Dream Chaser) (4:02) 4. Tite Squeeze (3:15) 5. Tearin' Out My Heart (4:00)

Side 2: 1. Power (4:23) 2. Miss Mistreated (4:25) 3. Rock Fever (3:40) 4. Eyes of Fire (6:41)

Notes: Lineup: Ritchie Blackmore – guitars, Joe Lynn Turner – vocals, Roger Glover – bass, David Rosenthal – keyboards, Bobby Rondinelli – drums. Black-and-white lyric sleeve.

Bent Out of Shape

(Mercury 422-815 305-1 M-1, August 24, 1983)

Produced by: Roger Glover

Side 1: 1. Stranded (4:30) 2. Can't Let You Go (4:22) 3. Fool for the Night (4:05) 4. Fire Dance (4:31) 5. Anybody There (2:41)

Side 2: 1. Desperate Heart (4:37) 2. Street of Dreams (4:27) 3. Drinking with the Devil (3:45) 4. Snowman (4:33) 5. Make Your Move (5:25)

Notes: Lineup: Ritchie Blackmore – guitars, Joe Lynn Turner – vocals, Roger Glover – bass, David Rosenthal – keyboards, Chuck Burgi – drums. Black-and-white lyric sleeve. Colour variations on the cover art across territories.

Stranger in Us All

(RCA/BMG 74321303372, August 21, 1995)

Produced by Ritchie Blackmore and Pat Regan

1. Wolf to the Moon (4:17) 2. Cold Hearted Woman (4:30) 3. Hunting Humans (Insatiable) (5:45) 4. Stand and Fight (5:21) 5. Ariel (5:40) 6. Too Late for Tears (4:54) 7. Black Masquerade (5:36) 8. Silence (4:04) 9. Hall of the Mountain King (5:32) 10. Still I'm Sad (5:24)

Notes: Lineup: Ritchie Blackmore – guitars, Doogie White – vocals, Greg Smith – bass, Paul Morris – keyboards, John O. Reilly – drums. Japanese Victor issue includes bonus track Emotional Crime.

Part 2 – Live Album and Compilation

On Stage

(Oyster/Polydor OY-2-1801, July 7, 1977)

Produced by: Martin Birch

Side 1: Intro: Over the Rainbow (0:31) 1. Kill the King (4:59) 2. Medley (Man on the Silver Mountain, Blues, Starstruck) (11:20)

Side 2: 1. Catch the Rainbow (15:40)

Side 3: 1. Mistreated (13:04)

Side 4: 1. Sixteenth Century Greensleeves (7:35) 2. Still I'm Sad (11:05)

Notes: Lineup: Ritchie Blackmore – guitars, Ronnie James Dio – vocals, Jimmy Bain – bass, Tony Carey – keyboards, Cozy Powell – drums. Double live album, gatefold, colour inner sleeves. Cover of Deep Purple's Mistreated, preview of *Long Live Rock 'n' Roll*'s Kill the King.

Finyl Vinyl

(Mercury 422-827 987-1 M-2, March 1986)

Produced by Roger Glover and Ritchie Blackmore

Side 1: 1. Spotlight Kid (5:00) 2. I Surrender (5:45) 3. Miss Mistreated (3:21)

Side 2: 1. Jealous Lover (3:10) 2. Can't Happen Here (4:15) 3. Tearin' Out My Heart (8:04) 4. Since You Been Gone (3:40) 5. Bad Girl (4:48)

Side 3: 1. Difficult to Cure (11:15) 2. Stone Cold (4:30) 3. Power (4:22)

Side 4: 1. Man on the Silver Mountain (8:20) 2. Long Live Rock 'n' Roll (7:12) 3. Weiss Heim (5:10)

Notes: Lineup: Various (this is a compilation of both love and studio material). Gatefold double vinyl. Original cassette issue adds Street of Dreams. Original single CD issue deletes Tearin' Out My Heart. Two CD remastered reissue includes both tracks.

Interviews with the Author

All uncredited quotes are from the author's own interviews with Don Airey, Jimmy Bain, Ritchie Blackmore, Graham Bonnet, Tony Carey, Neil Carter, Bob Daisley, Ronnie James Dio, Roger Glover, Candice Night, Bobby Rondinelli, Joe Lynn Turner and Doogie White. Thanks to all these goodly music makers for putting up patiently with my questions on the old days.

Additional Citations

Asbury Park Press. Ritchie Blackmore: Blackmore says he isn't domineering by Andy Seeker. April 18, 1982.

Bordowitz, Hank. Interview with Roger Glover. March 1986.

Circus. Interview with Ritchie Blackmore by Jon Tiven. September 1975.

Circus. Nearer My Dio to Thee: The Blackmore & Dio Interviews by Scott Cohen. August 10, 1976.

Circus. Ritchie Blackmore Gets It Up by Jon Tiven. June 1, 1976

Circus. Rainbow Ready: Blackmore Calm in Face of First Tour Since *Rising*'s Success by Jim Farber. 1977.

Circus. Ritchie Blackmore battles his brazen image by Richard Hogan. April 30, 1981.

Circus. Blackmore socks America between the eyes by Richard Hogan. May 31, 1982.

Classic Rock Revisited. Interviews with Bob Daisley, Don Airey and Joe Lynn Turner by Jeb Wright.

Guitar. In Deep with Purple: Back in Blackmore by HP Newquist. December 1996.

Guitar International. Interview with Ritchie Blackmore by Steve Rosen. 1975.

Hard Roxx. Joe Lynn Turner Speaks Out: Part 1 Fandango/ Rainbow by Stig Myhre. Issue No. 38, December 1998.

Hit Parader. Rainbow: Full Speed Ahead by Andy Secher. December 1983.

Julie, Kevin. Interview with Ronnie James Dio.

Kerrang!. Ritchie Blackmore interview by Geoff Barton. November 1984.

Let It Rock/Dmme.net. Interview with Ronnie James Dio by Dmitry Epstein. September 2005.

MetalRules.com. Interview with Ronnie James Dio by Evil G.

MetalRules.com. Interview with Graham Bonnet by Marko Syrjala. November 6, 2007.

Oyster Records. Special Edited Versions from the Live Double Album with "Conversations from Australia." 1977.

Rainbow Official UK Fanclub Magazine. Interview with Ritchie Blackmore by Steve Gett. Second Edition. 1981.

Ram. Ritchie Blackmore Goes to Confession by Chris Welch. November 1976.

Sounds. Ritchie Blackmore: There'll always be a Rainbow as long as Ritchie's here by Pete Makowski. June 25, 1977.

Sounds. Clouds Over the Rainbow by Sylvia Simmons. August 5, 1978.

Sounds. A Light in the Black by Geoff Barton. June 23, 1979.

Sounds. The Ritchie Blackmore Interview by Armando Gallo. July 28, 1979.

Sounds. The Shape of Things to Come by Garry Bushell. September 17, 1983.

Uncredited German newspaper: Ritchie Blackmore: There might be a new Rainbow Album at Christmas. May 2019.

Personal Credits

The graphic design and layout of this book is by Eduardo
Rodriguez, who can be reached at eduardobwbk@gmail.com.
Pleasure working with the guy—he's done about 35 for me now.

About the Author

At approximately 7900 (with over 7000 appearing in his books), Martin has unofficially written more record reviews than anybody in the history of music writing across all genres. Additionally, Martin has penned approximately 85 books on hard rock, heavy metal, classic rock and record collecting. He was Editor-In-Chief of the now retired Brave Words & Bloody Knuckles, Canada's foremost metal publication for 14 years, and has also contributed to Revolver, Guitar World, Goldmine, Record Collector, bravewords.com, lollipop.com and hardradio.com, with many record label band bios and liner notes to his credit as well. Additionally, Martin has been a regular contractor to Banger Films, having worked for two years as researcher on the award-winning documentary *Rush: Beyond the Lighted Stage*, on the writing and research team for the 11-episode Metal Evolution and on the ten-episode Rock Icons, both for VH1 Classic. Additionally, Martin is the writer of the original metal genre chart used in *Metal: A Headbanger's Journey* and throughout the Metal Evolution episodes. Martin currently resides in Toronto and can be reached through martinp@inforamp.net or www.martinpopoff.com.

Martin Popoff – A Complete Bibliography

Sensitive to Light: The Rainbow Story (2019)

Where Eagles Dare: Iron Maiden in the '80s (2019)

Aces High: The Top 250 Heavy Metal Songs of the '80s (2019)

Judas Priest: Turbo 'til Now (2019)

Born Again! Black Sabbath in the Eighties and Nineties (2019)

Riff Raff: The Top 250 Heavy Metal Songs of the '70s (2018)

Lettin' Go: UFO in the '80s and '90s (2018)

Queen: Album by Album (2018)

Unchained: A Van Halen User Manual (2018)

Iron Maiden: Album by Album (2018)

Sabotage! Black Sabbath in the Seventies (2018)

Welcome to My Nightmare: 50 Years of Alice Cooper (2018)

Judas Priest: Decade of Domination (2018)

Popoff Archive – 6: American Power Metal (2018)

Popoff Archive – 5: European Power Metal (2018)

The Clash: All the Albums, All the Songs (2018)

Led Zeppelin: All the Albums, All the Songs (2017)

AC/DC: Album by Album (2017)

Lights Out: Surviving the '70s with UFO (2017)

Tornado of Souls: Thrash's Titanic Clash (2017)

Caught in a Mosh: The Golden Era of Thrash (2017)

Rush: Album by Album (2017)

Beer Drinkers and Hell Raisers: The Rise of Motörhead (2017)

Metal Collector: Gathered Tales from Headbangers (2017)

Hit the Lights: The Birth of Thrash (2017)

Popoff Archive – 4: Classic Rock (2017)

Popoff Archive – 3: Hair Metal (2017)

Popoff Archive – 2: Progressive Rock (2016)

Popoff Archive – 1: Doom Metal (2016)

Rock the Nation: Montrose, Gamma and Ronnie Redefined (2016)

Punk Tees: The Punk Revolution in 125 T-Shirts (2016)

Metal Heart: Aiming High with Accept (2016)

Ramones at 40 (2016)

Time and a Word: The Yes Story (2016)

Kickstart My Heart: A Mötley Crüe Day-by-Day (2015)

This Means War: The Sunset Years of the NWOBHM (2015)

Wheels of Steel: The Explosive Early Years of the NWOBHM (2015)

Swords and Tequila: Riot's Classic First Decade (2015)

Who Invented Heavy Metal? (2015)

Sail Away: Whitesnake's Fantastic Voyage (2015)

Live Magnetic Air: The Unlikely Saga of the Superlative Max Webster (2014)

Steal Away the Night: An Ozzy Osbourne Day-by-Day (2014)

The Big Book of Hair Metal (2014)

Sweating Bullets: The Deth and Rebirth of Megadeth (2014)

Smokin' Valves: A Headbanger's Guide to 900 NWOBHM Records (2014)

The Art of Metal (co-edit with Malcolm Dome; 2013)

2 Minutes to Midnight: An Iron Maiden Day-by-Day (2013)

Metallica: The Complete Illustrated History (2013); update and reissue (2016)

Rush: The Illustrated History (2013); update and reissue (2016)

Ye Olde Metal: 1979 (2013)

Scorpions: Top of the Bill (2013); updated and reissued as Wind of Change: The Scorpions Story (2016)

Epic Ted Nugent (2012)

Fade To Black: Hard Rock Cover Art of the Vinyl Age (2012)

It's Getting Dangerous: Thin Lizzy 81-12 (2012)

We Will Be Strong: Thin Lizzy 76-81 (2012)

Fighting My Way Back: Thin Lizzy 69-76 (2011)

The Deep Purple Royal Family: Chain of Events '80 – '11 (2011)

The Deep Purple Royal Family: Chain of Events Through '79 (2011); reissued as The Deep Purple Family Year by Year (to 1979) (2016)

Black Sabbath FAQ (2011)

The Collector's Guide to Heavy Metal: Volume 4: The '00s (2011; co-authored with David Perri)

Goldmine Standard Catalog of American Records 1948 – 1991, 7th Edition (2010)

Goldmine Record Album Price Guide, 6th Edition (2009)

Goldmine 45 RPM Price Guide, 7th Edition (2009)

A Castle Full of Rascals: Deep Purple '83 – '09 (2009)

Worlds Away: Voivod and the Art of Michel Langevin (2009)

Ye Olde Metal: 1978 (2009)

Gettin' Tighter: Deep Purple '68 – '76 (2008)

All Access: The Art of the Backstage Pass (2008)

Ye Olde Metal: 1977 (2008)

Ye Olde Metal: 1976 (2008)

Judas Priest: Heavy Metal Painkillers (2007)

Ye Olde Metal: 1973 to 1975 (2007)

The Collector's Guide to Heavy Metal: Volume 3: The Nineties (2007)

Ye Olde Metal: 1968 to 1972 (2007)

Run For Cover: The Art of Derek Riggs (2006)

Black Sabbath: Doom Let Loose (2006)

Dio: Light Beyond the Black (2006)

The Collector's Guide to Heavy Metal: Volume 2: The Eighties (2005)

Rainbow: English Castle Magic (2005)

UFO: Shoot Out the Lights (2005)

The New Wave of British Heavy Metal Singles (2005)

Blue Öyster Cult: Secrets Revealed! (2004); update and reissue (2009); updated and reissued as Agents of Fortune: The Blue Öyster Cult Story (2016)

Contents Under Pressure: 30 Years of Rush at Home & Away (2004)

The Top 500 Heavy Metal Albums of All Time (2004)

The Collector's Guide to Heavy Metal: Volume 1: The Seventies (2003)

The Top 500 Heavy Metal Songs of All Time (2003)

Southern Rock Review (2001)

Heavy Metal: 20th Century Rock and Roll (2000)

The Goldmine Price Guide to Heavy Metal Records (2000)

The Collector's Guide to Heavy Metal (1997)

Riff Kills Man! 25 Years of Recorded Hard Rock & Heavy Metal (1993)

See martinpopoff.com for complete details and ordering information.